Zero Trust Security

An Enterprise Guide

Jason Garbis
Jerry W. Chapman

Apress®

Zero Trust Security: An Enterprise Guide

Jason Garbis
Boston, MA, USA

Jerry W. Chapman
Atlanta, GA, USA

ISBN-13 (pbk): 978-1-4842-6701-1
https://doi.org/10.1007/978-1-4842-6702-8

ISBN-13 (electronic): 978-1-4842-6702-8

Managing Director, Apress Media LLC: Welmoed Spahr
Acquisitions Editor: Susan McDermott
Development Editor: Laura Berendson
Coordinating Editor: Rita Fernando

Cover designed by eStudioCalamar

Cover image designed by Pixabay

Distributed to the book trade worldwide by Springer Science+Business Media New York, 1 New York Plaza, New York, NY 10004. Phone 1-800-SPRINGER, fax (201) 348-4505, e-mail orders-ny@springer-sbm.com, or visit www.springeronline.com. Apress Media, LLC is a California LLC and the sole member (owner) is Springer Science + Business Media Finance Inc (SSBM Finance Inc). SSBM Finance Inc is a **Delaware** corporation.

For information on translations, please e-mail booktranslations@springernature.com; for reprint, paperback, or audio rights, please e-mail bookpermissions@springernature.com.

Apress titles may be purchased in bulk for academic, corporate, or promotional use. eBook versions and licenses are also available for most titles. For more information, reference our Print and eBook Bulk Sales web page at http://www.apress.com/bulk-sales.

Any source code or other supplementary material referenced by the author in this book is available to readers on GitHub via the book's product page, located at www.apress.com/9781484267011. For more detailed information, please visit http://www.apress.com/source-code.

Printed on acid-free paper

For Amy, Shira, and Shelly
—J.G.

For my beautiful and loving wife, Suzette—Thank you!
To our cherished daughters, Nena and Alex—You are loved!
—J.W.C.

Table of Contents

About the Authors

Jason Garbis is Senior Vice President of Products at Appgate, a leading provider of Zero Trust secure access solutions. At Appgate, he's responsible for the company's security product strategy and product management. He has over 30 years of product management, engineering, and consulting experience at security and technology firms. He's also Co-chair of the SDP Zero Trust Working Group at the Cloud Security Alliance, leading research and publication initiatives. Jason holds a CISSP certification, a BS in computer science from Cornell University, and an MBA from Northeastern University.

Jerry W. Chapman is Engineering Fellow, Identity Management, at Optiv Security. With over 25 years of industry experience, Jerry has successfully guided numerous clients in the design and implementation of their enterprise IAM strategies, in ways that align with both security and business objectives. His job roles have spanned enterprise architecture, solution engineering, and software architecture and development. As an IAM industry expert, Jerry provides guidance, support, and thought leadership across Optiv cybersecurity practice areas, with a focus on positioning Identity and Data as a core component within enterprise security architectures. He is a key spokesperson for Optiv's Zero Trust strategy and frequently speaks at conferences and other industry events. Jerry is active in the technical working group at the Identity Defined Security Alliance (IDSA), where he was the group's original Technical Architect. Jerry is a certified Forrester Zero Trust Strategist, has a BS in computer information systems from DeVry University, and is currently pursuing a degree in applied mathematics from Southern New Hampshire University.

About the Technical Reviewer

Christopher Steffen brings over 20 years of industry experience as a noted information security executive, researcher, and presenter, focusing on IT management/leadership, cloud security, and regulatory compliance.

Chris has had a variety of roles as a professional and/or executive, from Camping Director for the Boy Scouts to Press Secretary for the Colorado Speaker of the House. His technical career started in the financial services vertical in systems administration for a credit reporting company, eventually building the Network Operations group, as well as the Information Security practice and Technical Compliance practice for the company before leaving as the Principal Technical Architect. He has been the Director of Information for a manufacturing company and the Chief Evangelist for several technical companies, focusing on cloud security and cloud application transformation, and has also held the position of CIO of a financial services company, overseeing the technology-related functions of the enterprise.

Chris is currently the lead information security, risk, and compliance management researcher for Enterprise Management Associates (EMA), a leading industry analyst firm that provides deep insight across the full spectrum of IT and data management technologies.

Chris holds several technical certifications, including Certified Information Systems Security Professional (CISSP) and Certified Information Systems Auditor (CISA), and was awarded the Microsoft Most Valuable Professional Award five times for virtualization and Cloud and Data Center Management (CDM). He holds a Bachelor of Arts (Summa Cum Laude) from the Metropolitan State College of Denver.

Acknowledgments

Zero Trust security covers a very broad area, and the process we went through to explore, learn, and weave together technical, nontechnical, and architectural concepts was often challenging. We were fortunate to have many people willing to spend time speaking with us, educating us, answering our questions, and providing feedback and guidance. Some folks helped us by reading and commenting on our planned outline or work-in-progress, some contributed by brainstorming with us in videoconferences (a hallmark of 2020, we suppose), while others helped (whether they know it or not) by being part of the information security industry, and as part of their regular professional interactions with us.

Many thanks to Dr. Chase Cunningham for your broad industry influence, and Brigadier General (Ret.) Greg Touhill for your endorsement in the Foreword. And thanks to both of you for your careers in service to our country in military and information security roles. We'd also like to thank Evan Gilman, Doug Barth, Mario Santana, Adam Rose, George Boitano, Bridget Bratt, Leo Taddeo, Rob Black, Deryck Motielall, and Kurt Glazemakers. Also, a shout-out to the team from the Cloud Security Alliance and its SDP Zero Trust Working Group, including Shamun Mahmud, Junaid Islam, Juanita Koilpillai, Bob Flores, Michael Roza, Nya Alison Murray, John Yeoh, and Jim Reavis. And another shout-out to Julie Smith and the Identity Defined Security Alliance (IDSA) team, especially the technical working group for keeping identity in the middle of security. We would also like to thank our too-many-to-name colleagues for their many conversations and support, and our Apress editors Rita Fernando and Susan McDermott for their support, encouragement, and help throughout this process. And of course, a huge thanks to our technical reviewer, sounding board, and friend Chris Steffen.

Finally, we'd like to thank you—as a practitioner or leader in the information security industry, working every day to better secure your organization. We hope that this book makes your job easier. Please visit us at `https://ZeroTrustSecurity.guide` with any comments or suggestions, and to view this book's companion video series.

Foreword

Zero Trust wasn't born out of a need to sell another security control or solution. It was born from a desire to solve a real enterprise issue...Zero Trust is focused on simplicity and the reality of how things are now.

—Dr. Chase Cunningham, aka "Dr. Zero Trust"

I have been waiting for this book for over two decades and am delighted to introduce its arrival.

Well before the Jericho Forum's bold 2004 declaration of a new security strategy featuring "de-perimeterization," many of us in the national security community had come to the realization that the perimeter security model was no longer a viable security strategy for Internet-connected systems and enterprises. The unsatiable thirst to connect everything to the Internet, the rising cost and complexity of the layers of security tools, and the rapid pace of technological change were fracturing the perimeter security model around us. Our defense-in-depth security perimeter was a dike springing too many leaks for us to keep up with in any meaningful or fiscally responsible manner. The Jericho Forum's work pointed in a different direction, giving many of us a new hope.

Sadly, like Grand Moff Tarkin on the Death Star, many security professionals and pundits had grown comfortable with the status quo and scoffed at the notion that a new approach to securing modern enterprises was needed. One security commentator went so far as to say the Jericho Forum "missed the mark" and derisively forecast that its work would likely "end up on the scrap heap of unrealized ideas and wasted effort." I hope that he reads this book with a tinge of guilt and regret.

The work of the Jericho Forum did not go for naught, but it did not yield fruit right away either. After a little more than 5 years from the introduction of the "de-perimeterization" concept, John Kindervag, then an analyst at Forrester Research, in 2010 coined the phrase "Zero Trust" to describe the security model that organizations should not automatically trust anything outside *or* inside their perimeters, and instead must verify everything and anything before connecting them to their systems and granting access to their data.

For those of us in the military, Zero Trust was not a revolutionary security model. We had been practicing it with physical security throughout our careers. For example, every person was greeted by security personnel at the gates and had to produce proper identity credentials before being given access to the base. We practiced segmentation with protection zones around what were called priority A, B, and C resources. The flight line areas were the home of priority A assets and had tightly controlled access with armed guards. Role-based entry was tightly controlled and use of deadly force authorized against those who "broke the red line." As a lieutenant, I had to go through four levels of security before I could even get into my office. Security was ingrained in our culture, our processes, and our expectations.

Sadly, as my generation incrementally built out the Department of Defense Information Networks, while we followed a "Zero Trust" physical security model to protect our most valued facilities and weapons systems, the technology to implement a "Zero Trust" security model to protect our increasingly valuable and Internet-connected digital assets was lacking. Commercially available tools were exquisitely complex and expensive. For example, we had to contract with one noted vendor to create an "academy" just to train our already highly skilled workforce to properly use their complex networking products. Costs continued to soar as we continued our march to digitize every function we could, yet the security perimeter dike around us continued springing leaks. By the time I retired from federal service as the Chief Information Security Officer of the US government, I had come to the conclusion that the Zero Trust security strategy was our only hope to secure our digital ecosystem.

The COVID-19 pandemic spurred a massive pivot from traditional office environments to a work-from-home model that has accelerated the long-anticipated move to the Zero Trust security strategy. The illusion of the security perimeter has been shattered by massive mobility, cloud computing, Software-as-a-Service, and unparalleled Bring-Your-Own-Device implementation as organizations everywhere pivoted from traditional enterprise environments to today's modern digital reality. Today's reality is that the traditional network security perimeter is dead; there is no "outside" or "inside" anymore.

Sadly, many people and organizations, including that naysayer who scoffed at the Jericho Forum's vision, have jumped on the Zero Trust bandwagon. Many declare allegiance to "Zero Trust" yet don't know what it really is or how to practice it. Organizations whose legacy networking gear and methodologies have proven exceedingly complex and vulnerable have their marketing teams miraculously declare their vulnerable capabilities to be "Zero Trust." Despite the great Zero Trust research conducted by Forrester's Dr. Chase Cunningham and Gartner's Neil MacDonald, until this book, there wasn't a practical definitive guide to Zero Trust.

Fortunately, authors Jason Garbis and Jerry Chapman are highly experienced technologists and practitioners who are recognized experts in Zero Trust, enterprise network operations, cybersecurity, and business operations. I encourage you to read their biographies as their credentials are impressive and uninflated. To use military jargon, they've "Been There, Done That."

In the chapters that follow, Jason and Jerry deliver an outstanding book that presents an invaluable explanation of Zero Trust that I believe ought to be used as the definitive reference for students and practitioners everywhere.

The organization of the content is superb. Those who are not familiar with the concept of Zero Trust, and even those who are, will benefit from the first four chapters, which provide a strategic overview of the Zero Trust journey. Chapter 1 provides an insightful discussion that answers the question, "Why is Zero Trust needed?" Those who are just starting their Zero Trust journey will find Chapter 2 invaluable as the authors provide an excellent chronicle of how we got to today's Zero Trust environment and clearly define what Zero Trust is, and isn't. Those seeking to see how to incorporate Zero Trust into their operational architectures will appreciate the practical advice and vivid descriptions presented in Chapter 3. Many people, myself included, prefer to have others "flight test" capabilities before making significant investments or major strategic changes. We're rewarded in Chapter 4 with a fulsome discussion of how organizations such as Google have incorporated Zero Trust into their operations.

The second part of the book provides an outstanding overview of the essential components of Zero Trust, starting with Chapter 5's exceptional discussion on Identity. I contend that Identity is the core component of any successful Zero Trust implementation and was pleased to see Jason and Jerry starting this section of the book with this chapter. The next three chapters provide an important discussion on the impact of Zero Trust on network infrastructure, network access control, and intrusion detection and protection systems. If you find those three chapters provocative, Chapter 9's discussion on virtual private networks in a Zero Trust world likely will change the way you view today's environment and the ongoing movement to a work-from-anywhere future.

Chapter 10's discussion on Next-Generation Firewalls (NGFWs) likewise is provocative as the authors discuss the history and evolution of the subject capabilities and forecast their future in a Zero Trust world. Chapter 11's discussion on Security Information and Event Management (SIEM) and Security Orchestration, Automation, and Response (SOAR) in a Zero Trust model is a must-read for those focused on identifying, managing, and controlling risk. Those who find Chapter 5's discussion on Identity exceptional won't be disappointed with Chapter 12's discussion on Privileged Access Management. Those organizations that are keen to reduce their risk of insider threats ought to pay close attention to it as well!

The next four chapters provide practical analysis and guidance on contemporary technical issues many organizations are wrestling with today. Chapter 13's discussion on Data Protection is exceptional and one my students at Carnegie Mellon University's Heinz College ought to pay close attention to (that's a not-too-subtle hint from the professor!). Chapter 14's discussion on Cloud Resources provides straightforward practical advice on how to properly apply Zero Trust when operating in cloud-based environments. As many organizations embrace technologies such as Software as a Service, Secure Web Gateways, and Cloud Access Security Brokers, Chapter 15 provides an outstanding discussion on how these technologies can integrate into your Zero Trust strategy and provides practical advice on how to "get it right." Finally, I was thrilled to see Jason and Jerry's inclusion of Chapter 16's discussion on Internet of Things devices and "Things." Too many cybersecurity personnel are fixated on information technology devices and ignore the risks associated with organizational operational technology, industrial control systems, and "Internet of Things" devices. Regardless of your organizational role, please pay attention to this chapter and recognize the importance of applying Zero Trust in protecting these important systems.

Wrapping up the book are three chapters crucial to every organization committed to properly implementing Zero Trust across their organizations. Chapter 17 provides an essential discussion on how to create and implement a meaningful Zero Trust policy model. Chapter 18 provides invaluable discussions on the most likely use cases your organization will address as you roll out your Zero Trust implementation. Chapter 19 is a welcome companion to the previous chapter, as it discusses how organizations should approach Zero Trust in order to have the strongest likelihood of success. Those who believe in the mantra "start small, think big, and scale fast" won't be disappointed by Jason and Jerry's practical advice. Finally, Chapter 20 provides a satisfying wrap-up of the book's journey through Zero Trust, with a reminder that security exists to enable organizations to achieve their missions.

Zero Trust isn't just a catchy aphorism, it is within our grasp and waiting to be implemented everywhere. This book will help you achieve your Zero Trust goals with velocity and precision. Nation-state actors and cyber criminals have proven that the perimeter-based security model is no longer valid. So have noteworthy insider villains like Edward Snowden. The time to move quickly and deliberately to the Zero Trust security model is now. Thankfully, due to the insightful work of Jason Garbis and Jerry Chapman, we now have a practical guide to how we can achieve our Zero Trust objectives.

Generals since Sun Tzu and Alexander the Great implemented the perimeter-based security model to defend their assets. They didn't have the Internet, mobile devices, cloud computing, and other modern technology. The Jericho Forum got it right; the perimeter is dead. Now is the time to embrace and implement Zero Trust everywhere. Our national security and national prosperity deserve nothing less.

—Gregory J. Touhill, CISSP, CISM,
Brigadier General, USAF (Ret.)

PART I

Overview

Zero Trust is a security philosophy and set of principles, which taken together represent a significant shift in how enterprise IT and security should be approached. The results can be enormously beneficial for security teams and for businesses, but Zero Trust is broad in scope and can be overwhelming. In Part I of this book, we'll be providing you with a historical and foundational introduction to Zero Trust, explaining what it is (and what it isn't), and depicting Zero Trust architectures in theory and in practice. This will help you make sense of Zero Trust, one piece at a time, and begin to think about how it can be applied to help improve your organization's security, resiliency, and efficiency.

CHAPTER 1

Introduction

Enterprise security is hard. This is due to the complexity of IT and application infrastructures, the breadth and velocity of user access, and of course the inherently adversarial nature of information security. It's also due to the far-too-open nature of most enterprise networks—by not enforcing the principle of least privilege at both the network and application levels, organizations are leaving themselves incredibly vulnerable to attacks. This is true both for internal networks and for public Internet-facing remote access services such as Virtual Private Networks (VPNs), the latter of which are exposed to every adversary on the Internet. Given today's threat landscape, you'd never choose to design a system like this. And yet, traditional security and networking systems, which remain in widespread use, continue to perpetuate this model.

Zero Trust security, the subject of this book, changes this and brings a modern approach to security which enforces the principle of least privilege for networks and applications. Unauthorized users and systems will have no access whatsoever to any enterprise resources, and authorized users will only have the minimum access necessary. The result is that enterprises are safer, more secure, and more resilient. Zero Trust also brings improvements in efficiency and effectiveness, through the automated enforcement of dynamic and identity-centric access policies.

Please note that the "zero" in Zero Trust is a bit of a misnomer—it's not about literally "zero" trust, but about zero *inherent* or *implicit* trust. Zero Trust is about carefully building a foundation of trust, and growing that trust to ultimately permit an appropriate level of access at the right time. It could perhaps have been called "earned trust" or "adaptive trust" or "zero implicit trust," and these would have suited the movement better, but "Zero Trust" has more sizzle, and it stuck. Don't take the "zero" literally, please!

Zero Trust is an important and highly visible trend in the information security industry, and while it's become a marketing buzzword, we believe there's real substance and value behind it. At its heart, Zero Trust is a philosophy and an approach, and a set of guiding principles. This means that there are as many ways to interpret Zero Trust as there are enterprises. However, there are fundamental and universal principles that

3

© Jason Garbis and Jerry W. Chapman 2021
J. Garbis and J. W. Chapman, *Zero Trust Security*, https://doi.org/10.1007/978-1-4842-6702-8_1

every Zero Trust architecture will follow. Throughout this book, we'll be providing guidelines and recommendations for Zero Trust based on our experiences working with enterprises of different sizes and maturities throughout their Zero Trust journeys. Keep in mind, we use the word *journey* deliberately; this is to underscore the fact this is not a one-and-done project, but an ongoing and evolving initiative. And this is why we wrote this book—to share our thoughts and recommendations around how to best approach Zero Trust in your environment, and to be a guide along your journey.

We fundamentally believe that Zero Trust is a better and more effective way to approach and achieve enterprise security. In some ways, Zero Trust has been closely associated with network security, and while networks are a core element of Zero Trust, we're also going to be exploring the full breadth of Zero Trust security, which crosses boundaries into applications, data, identities, operations, and policies.

As a security leader, you have a responsibility to push, pull, and prod your organization into adopting this new approach, which will improve your organization's resiliency, and also help you grow professionally. This book—your guide—is divided into three parts. Part I provides an introduction to Zero Trust principles, and establishes the framework and vocabulary we'll be using to define Zero Trust and align IT and security infrastructure. These are the foundations of what we believe is required to tell the full Zero Trust story.

Part II is a deep dive into IT and security technologies, and their relationship to Zero Trust. This is where you'll begin to see how your organization can start using Zero Trust, and where you can adapt and integrate your current IT and security infrastructure into a more modern architecture. Because Zero Trust takes an identity-centric approach to security, we'll be examining how different technologies can start to incorporate and benefit from identity context to become more effective.

Part III brings everything together, building on where the first two parts of the book provided a conceptual foundation and a deep technology discussion. This part explores what a Zero Trust policy model should look like, examines specific Zero Trust scenarios (use cases), and finally discusses a strategic and tactical approach to making Zero Trust successful.

Also, it's important to note that we're deliberately not evaluating vendors or vendor products within the scope of this book. Our industry moves too quickly—the pace of innovation is high—and any such reviews would have a very short shelf life. Instead, we're focusing on exploring architectural principles from which you can draw requirements and which you can use to evaluate vendors, platforms, solution providers, and approaches.

By the time you reach the end of this book, it should be clear that there is no single right approach to Zero Trust. Security leaders will need to take into consideration existing infrastructures, priorities, staff skills, budgets, and timelines while designing their Zero Trust initiative. This may make Zero Trust seem complicated, but its breadth of scope actually helps simplify enterprise security and architecture. As an overlay security and access model, it normalizes things and gives you a centralized way to define and enforce access policies across a distributed and heterogeneous infrastructure.

Ultimately, the goal of this book is to provide you with a solid understanding of what Zero Trust is, and the knowledge to successfully steer your organization's unique journey to Zero Trust. If you come away with this, we've been successful in our efforts. Let's get started on our voyage.

CHAPTER 2

What Is Zero Trust?

In this chapter, we're going to introduce Zero Trust as a concept, a philosophy, and a framework. In addition to a brief overview of the history and evolution of Zero Trust, we'll also be introducing some guiding principles. We believe there are *core* and *extended* principles common to every Zero Trust initiative, which are important to understand as you embark on your journey. Our goal for this chapter is to provide you with a working definition of Zero Trust based on these principles, and a set of foundational platform requirements.

History and Evolution

Traditionally, security boundaries were placed at the edge of the enterprise network in a classic "castle wall and moat" approach. However, as technology evolved, remote workers and remote workloads became more common. Security boundaries necessarily followed, and expanded from just the corporate perimeter to also encompass the devices and networks from which the remote user was connected, and the resources to which they were connecting. This forced security and network teams to accommodate these business requirements, and to adjust the models by which organizations applied security and access, with mixed degrees of success.[1]

In 2010, Forrester Analyst John Kindervag introduced the term "Zero Trust" in the influential "No More Chewy Centers: Introducing The Zero Trust Model Of Information Security"[2] whitepaper. This paper captured ideas that had been discussed in the industry

---

[1]We're attempting to be diplomatic with this statement. It is an undeniable fact that enterprise network security and data security, as an industry, has failed to effectively protect our organizations from data loss and system breaches. Granted, we are facing sophisticated and motivated adversaries, but we believe that this widespread failure is largely due to the shortcomings of traditional infosec tools and approaches, and that Zero Trust will prove to be far more effective.

[2]Forrester, "No More Chewy Centers: Introducing The Zero Trust Model Of Information Security," September 2010

© Jason Garbis and Jerry W. Chapman 2021
J. Garbis and J. W. Chapman, *Zero Trust Security*, https://doi.org/10.1007/978-1-4842-6702-8_2

for a few years, in particular promoted by the Jericho Forum. The Forrester document described the shift away from a hard perimeter, and toward an approach that required inspecting and understanding elements within a network before they could earn a level of trust and access. Over time, Forrester evolved this concept into what's now known as the *Zero Trust eXtended* (ZTX) Framework which includes Data, Workloads, and Identity as core components of Zero Trust.

About the same time, Google began their internal BeyondCorp initiative, which implemented a version of Zero Trust and put in place foundational Zero Trust elements that effectively removed their enterprise network boundary. Google strongly influenced the industry with a series of articles documenting their groundbreaking internal implementation, starting in 2014. Also in 2014, the Cloud Security Alliance introduced the Software Defined Perimeter (SDP) architecture, which provided a concrete specification for a security system that supports Zero Trust principles.[3] We'll be examining both BeyondCorp and SDP through the lens of Zero Trust a bit later, in Chapter 4.

In 2017, industry analyst firm Gartner revised and refreshed their Continuous Adaptive Risk and Trust Assessment (CARTA) concept, which has many principles in common with Zero Trust. CARTA provides not only Identity and Data elements but includes risk and posture associated with identity and devices accessing the environment.

Further industry-wide emphasis on Zero Trust continued, as the US National Institute of Standards and Technology (NIST) released a Zero Trust Architecture publication[4] and an associated US National Cybersecurity Center of Excellence project in 2020.[5]

Zero Trust continues to evolve as vendors and standards organizations review and refine specifications and implementations of Zero Trust, recognizing it as a fundamental shift in the approach to information security. Ultimately, the industry has agreed that these changes and refinements are necessary, in order to prevent malicious actors from accessing private resources within organizational boundaries, exfiltrating data, and disrupting operations.

---

[3]See the CSA's Architecture Guide for SDP, `https://cloudsecurityalliance.org/artifacts/sdp-architecture-guide-v2/`.

[4]NIST Special Publication 800.207—Zero Trust Architecture, `https://csrc.nist.gov/publications/detail/sp/800-207/final`, August 2020

[5]`https://www.nccoe.nist.gov/projects/building-blocks/zero-trust-architecture`.

We, the authors of this book, work in the information security industry, and both spend much of our time speaking to security professionals about Zero Trust. One common question we hear is "What's new about Zero Trust—how is it different from what's already been done?" It's definitely true that some elements of Zero Trust, such as *least privileged access* and *role-based access control*, are principles that are commonly implemented in current networking and security infrastructure (and must be utilized in Zero Trust environments), but alone they do not complete the picture.

Foundational security elements used prior to Zero Trust often achieved only coarse-grained separation of users, networks, and applications. For example, in most organizations, development environments are separated from production environments. However, Zero Trust amplifies this, effectively requiring that all identities and resources be segmented from one another. Zero Trust enables fine-grained, identity-and-context-sensitive access controls, driven by an automated platform. Although Zero Trust started as a narrowly focused approach of not trusting any network identities until authenticated and authorized, it has rightfully grown in scope to provide a much broader set of security capabilities across an organization's environment.

Let's briefly examine the Forrester and Gartner Zero Trust models, before we introduce what we believe are the key Zero Trust principles.

Forrester's Zero Trust eXtended (ZTX) Model

Forrester released their initial Zero Trust model in 2010, and in the following years, it has been revised and re-released as *Zero Trust eXtended* (ZTX). ZTX provides richer content and a well-rounded model that places data at the center, as shown in Figure 2-1. This reflects Forrester's belief that the data explosion in both on-prem and cloud environments is at the center of what has to be protected. The surrounding elements—Workloads, Networks, Devices, and People—are conduits to data and therefore need protection as well. Let's look at each of these elements in turn.

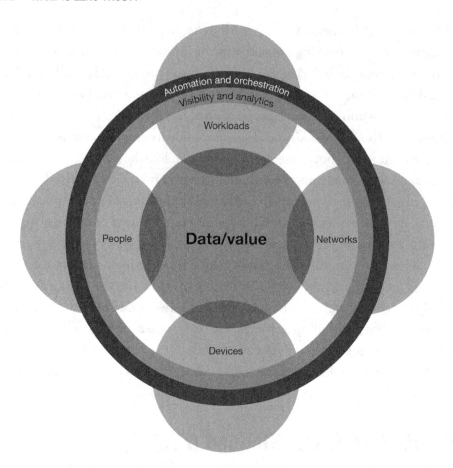

Figure 2-1. *Forrester Zero Trust eXtended Model (Source: The Zero Trust eXtended Ecosystem: Data, Forrester Research, Inc., August 11, 2020)*

Data: *Data* (which Forrester also tags as "value" to highlight its importance[6]) is the center of the ZTX model, and it includes Data Classification and Protection at the core of the requirements to support the Zero Trust Model. Throughout the book, we view data as an element of the *Resources* that Zero Trust systems must protect. Additionally, Data Loss Prevention (DLP) should be a part of a Zero Trust architecture, and tied into the policy model with the ability to enforce contextual access policies where possible.

---

[6]In fact, Forrester states "in truth, what we considered solely as 'data' is now really 'value.' Whatever is of value to your business is the most critical asset to focus your defenses around, and you should defend that value at all costs," The Zero Trust eXtended Ecosystem: Data, Forrester Research, Inc., August 11,2020

Networks: The *Network* pillar of the ZTX model is primarily focused on network segmentation—both from a user and a server perspective—to provide better security based on identity-centric attributes. It's important to recognize that enterprises have many existing components that make up the traditional network security infrastructure, such as Next-Generation Firewalls (NGFWs), Web Application Firewalls (WAF), Network Access Control (NAC) solutions, and Intrusion Protection Systems (IPS). These components generally all have a role to play in a Zero Trust system. We'll introduce these components in a representative enterprise architecture in Chapter 3, and examine their relationship to Zero Trust at length in Part II of the book.

People: The *People* pillar of the ZTX model must include multiple elements of Identity and Access Management (IAM). Role- and Attribute-Based Access Control (RBAC and ABAC) are well-understood models within IAM, and Zero Trust enables the use of these more broadly, and more effectively, across the enterprise infrastructure. Multi-Factor Authentication (MFA) is another requirement and is essential to supporting Zero Trust. Finally, Single Sign On (SSO)—using modern, open standards such as OAuth and SAML—is another core element within the people pillar. As you'll see throughout this book, we're strong proponents of making Identity central to every Zero Trust environment.

Workloads: *Workloads*, as defined by Forrester, consist of the components that make up the logical functions that drive business within both customer facing and backend business systems—containers, applications, infrastructure, processes, etc. Zero Trust requires metadata-driven workload access controls, enforced consistently across hybrid environments. We'll be exploring this further in Chapter 17.

Devices: The security model for *Devices* should include the identity, inventory, isolation, security, and control of the device. In Chapter 3, we'll describe user agents which run on devices, and how they are core to the Zero Trust environment. We'll also see later, in Chapter 4, the ways in which devices were key to Google's BeyondCorp implementation.

Visibility and Analytics: *Visibility and Analytics* within ZTX is the consumption and presentation of data across the enterprise to support informed security decisions based on contextual information. We agree that this is critical, especially the consolidation of data across multiple disparate sources. There is not a single platform that exists today that spans the necessary breadth of functionality, but this is an evolving space. We'll discuss further in Chapter 11.

Automation and Orchestration: *Automation and Orchestration* within ZTX are required to automate manual processes, and to relate them to security policy and actions for response. We believe that this element is critical to the success of a Zero Trust platform—Zero Trust is inherently dynamic and adaptive, and the only way to achieve this is with automation and orchestration, across the enterprise environment. We'll discuss this further in the following, as Automation is one of our key Zero Trust principles.

Gartner's Approach to Zero Trust

Gartner has approached Zero Trust through a model they call CARTA—Continuous Adaptive Risk and Trust Assessment. The premise of CARTA is to provide continuous risk assessment as it pertains to users, devices, applications, data, and workloads, from a perspective of *Predict, Prevent, Detect, and Respond.*

CARTA uses the fundamental process of *Implement a security posture, Monitor the posture*, and *Adjust the security posture* through different planes of security. Gartner believes that these principles should be enforced across the entire enterprise and include security, policy, and compliance requirements throughout.

Gartner tends to view Zero Trust a bit more narrowly, using the terms *Zero Trust Network Access* (ZTNA) for user-to-server security, and *Zero Trust Network Segmentation* (ZTNS) for microsegmentation/server-to-server security. Their overall security framework is built around *CARTA*, and its principles are well aligned with the ones we're espousing here. Ultimately, it doesn't matter whether your strategic initiative is named *Zero Trust, CARTA, Earned Trust*, or something else.[7] The principles and goals of Gartner's CARTA are sound and we believe are in harmony with the ones we're exploring in this book.

Our Perspective on Zero Trust

Zero Trust is a holistic model for securing network, application, and data resources, with a focus on providing an identity-centric policy model for controlling access. All enterprises have a set of IT and security tools in place in their environments, but Zero Trust demands that they be viewed and operated holistically, with identity at the core, and with the ability to enforce attribute- and context-sensitive policies throughout the environment. This should become clear as we next examine the underlying principles of Zero Trust, which we've grouped into *Core* and *Expanded* principles.

Core Principles

Across the industry, there are three core Zero Trust principles that are generally accepted as being foundational and essential. These were initially defined in the "No More Chewy Centers" paper published by Forrester, and we believe that they must hold true in any Zero Trust implementation. In addition to these core principles, we have incorporated the tenets described within the NIST Zero Trust Architecture document. We're providing our interpretation here, viewed from a current industry perspective.

Ensure all resources are accessed securely, regardless of location.

This is a powerful, compact statement, and one which encompasses multiple dimensions. First, it requires that *all* resources be included in the scope of a Zero Trust solution. Implicitly this demands that organizations take a holistic approach with Zero Trust and that they should eliminate silos and barriers which have historically existed between security tools and teams.

---

[7]In fact, we've spoken with several enterprises who deliberately avoid using the term "Zero Trust" internally. They believe it's somewhat misleading and potentially can be negatively interpreted by end users as a message from the security team that "we don't trust you."

Second, this principle requires that Zero Trust secure access by all identities (human and machine), to all resources (data, applications, servers)—regardless of the location of the identity, and regardless of the location or technology of the resource being accessed. It's this principle which effectively mandates the dissolution of the traditional corporate perimeter, and its replacement with an alternative security paradigm. It also means that not only must the network traffic be encrypted as it transits untrusted network areas[8] but that all access must be subject to an enforced policy model—which is the subject of the second principle.

Adopt a least privilege strategy and strictly enforce access control.

The concept of least privileged access to resources is not new, but it has been difficult to enforce broadly prior to Zero Trust. Least privilege must be consistently managed across locations and resource types, and at both the network and application layer, using security and identity context.

Historically, security solutions have been unable to bridge the disconnect between network and application level security. Traditionally, users (and their devices) obtained broad access to networks, and applications relied upon authentication-only access control. Anyone in the company could access the login page on the Finance server, but only Finance users had accounts and passwords. This is no longer a sufficient level of security. There are far too many known and critical vulnerabilities which don't require authentication and can be remotely exploited. We'll state this loud and clear—the ability to send network packets to a system is a privilege, and must be managed as such. If users are not authorized to access a given service (e.g., having credentials to SSH into a server, or to authenticate to a VPN), they must not have the ability to connect to that service at a network layer.

Inspect and log all traffic.

Networks represent a particularly interesting place in the security and IT infrastructure, since they are the means by which distributed components connect and communicate with one another. It's for this reason that the final core principle requires inspection and logging of network traffic. Zero Trust systems are well suited to this—as we'll see in Chapter 3, they are typically made up of a distributed set of network enforcement points. It's important to note that Zero Trust systems should broadly examine and log network traffic metadata, but be more judicious in the inspection of network traffic content due to processing and storage costs. (We'll talk about this further in Chapter 8).

---

[8]In Chapter 3, we'll introduce the concept of an implicit network trust zone, which is a byproduct of certain Zero Trust deployment models. Encrypted application protocols will reduce the risk of such zones.

The network traffic information should be enriched by the Zero Trust system—adding identity and device context—and fed into Next-Generation Firewalls, network monitoring tools, and SIEMs, to enhance their ability to make decisions to detect, alert, and respond, as well as support incident response and other alerting mechanisms.

Expanded Principles

In addition to the core Zero Trust principles discussed, we believe that there are three additional principles that are equally important and necessary in any enterprise-class Zero Trust environment.

Ensure all components support APIs for event and data exchange.

Zero Trust must provide a holistic security policy and enforcement model that encompasses broad areas of the IT ecosystem—which links back to the first core principle. As such, it must be able to integrate with many (ideally all) components of this ecosystem. The integration of previously siloed security products, infrastructure, and business systems is essential. As you will see throughout our discussions, integrating identity and security tools enables a holistic security context with which Zero Trust can provide a more secure environment. These integrations will be used for both initiating and responding to events, as well as for exchanging data and log information, and enabling our next principle. One corollary to this principle: Every security and IT component that's integrated into your Zero Trust platform adds to its value, effectiveness, and reach. Conversely, every siloed (un-integrated) component adds friction, diminishes your Zero Trust system effectiveness, and can impede security.

Automate actions across environments and systems, driven by context and events.

Automation is a key element for a successful Zero Trust environment, and necessary for operating at even small scale. Zero Trust is predicated on a set of dynamic access control rules, which change in response to identity, device, network, and system context. As we'll see in Chapter 3, Zero Trust models all require a centralized Policy Decision Point (PDP) connected with a distributed set of Policy Enforcement Points (PEPs) via a logical control channel. This channel is used to automate changes to the enforced policies via integration/APIs and is critical for a Zero Trust system to work.

Automated changes to access can take many forms in a Zero Trust system, including granting access through an identity management system, access management system, or a network access control system. Other automated activities could include temporary or permanent removal of access to a given resource, for example, driven by a lifecycle management event or context change.

Note that while automated actions are fundamental in an operational environment, this doesn't eliminate the ability to utilize manual intervention or to include explicit manual steps in a workflow prior to initiating an automated response. That is, automation doesn't mean "automatic." For example, many access request processes require manager approval, to meet security and compliance guidelines. This workflow requires a human being to read some information, make a decision, and submit that decision to the system. That should be the only manual step in this process—the rest of the workflow, including the provisioning of any access changes, should be automated.

Deliver tactical _and_ strategic value.

Ultimately, core initiatives around Zero Trust must be tied to business value. Zero Trust projects can (and typically do) have significant impacts on infrastructures, teams, operations, and end-user experience. The outcomes are positive, but even so, changes are often difficult to achieve, technically, culturally, and politically. And the changes associated with a Zero Trust project can be broad-reaching—there are many components within your environment that will be changed or integrated into your Zero Trust environment as an enforcement point or policy driver.

Zero Trust is a journey, and an investment of time and money. An understanding of your organization's business drivers and priorities will help you justify and execute on your strategic vision for Zero Trust in your enterprise environment. As you start your journey, incremental deployments and tactical wins must be realized. Doing so will simplify your Zero Trust journey, and build momentum and support internally. That is, by delivering early tactical wins—within the framework of your strategic Zero Trust architecture—you'll enable your organization to realize its full strategic value. Each successful new project further opens pathways and builds support for your Zero Trust initiative.

A Working Definition

As we work through this book and introduce concepts of Zero Trust principles, architectures, and working examples, it's important to understand what Zero Trust is. We find it useful to treat Zero Trust as a lens by which you can view and interpret security initiatives and components. To that end, we propose the following concise definition:

A Zero Trust system is an integrated security platform that uses contextual information from identity, security and IT Infrastructure, and risk and analytics tools to inform and enable the dynamic enforcement of security policies uniformly across the enterprise. Zero Trust shifts security from an ineffective perimeter-centric model to a resource and identity-centric model. As a result, organizations can continuously adapt access controls to a changing environment, obtaining improved security, reduced risk, simplified and resilient operations, and increased business agility.

This core definition, in addition to the principles we defined previously, allows us to provide an initial set of Zero Trust requirements, which we discuss next.

Zero Trust Platform Requirements

In this section, we provide a baseline set of platform requirements that stem from the Zero Trust principles previously discussed. Our goal in this section is not to simply restate the principles, but to attempt to highlight relevant aspects from a platform perspective. Some of these principles (especially APIs and Integration) are best expressed as requirements associated with specific IT and security functions, but in general, we've defined these requirements broadly:

1. Data plane communications must be encrypted. Any exceptions must be deliberate (e.g., DNS).

2. System must be able to enforce access controls for all types of resources. Access control mechanisms must be driven by identity-centric and contextual policies.

3. Data resource protections should be able to use identity and contextual policies to control access.

4. System and policy model must support securing all users in all locations. Policy model and controls must be consistent for remote and on-premises users.

5. Devices must be able to be inspected for their security posture and configuration prior to being granted access, and periodically thereafter.

6. It must be possible to distinguish BYOD from corporate-managed devices, and control the level of access accordingly.

7. Access to any network resource must be explicitly granted by policy. No user or device should inherently have broad network access.

8. Access controls must be able to distinguish between different services on the same network resource. For example, access to HTTPS must be granted separately from access to SSH.

9. Access to specific data elements contained within applications or containers that have different classifications must be enforced based on business policy.

10. Network traffic metadata must be logged and enriched with identity context.

11. Network traffic must be able to be examined for security and data loss purposes.

12. Workloads transferred into the cloud should include the same access control policies as defined by on-premises solutions.

13. Automation must include identity-centric details to provide efficient and effective incident response.

14. Logs must be included in analytics tools for effective and dynamic enforcement of policies.

Summary

In this chapter, we highlighted the history of Zero Trust, beginning with the term's introduction by Forrester in 2010, followed by its continued evolution by different organizations, including Google, NIST, CSA, and others. Based on this historical background, we explained and refined three core Zero Trust principles, and added three extended principles. Taken together, we believe that this set should be fundamental to every Zero Trust initiative.

In our next chapter, we'll be introducing a representative enterprise architecture model. It won't be all-inclusive, but will provide common ground to work from while introducing Zero Trust deployment models, and how these models fit within the enterprise. Later, in Part II of the book, we'll be providing an in-depth examination of how IT and security technologies are affected by Zero Trust.

CHAPTER 3

Zero Trust Architectures

So far, we've introduced the history of Zero Trust, provided our perspective on it, and introduced its core set of principles. Zero Trust is a philosophy that can support many different types of architectures (and many, many different types of commercial products). It will become clear that there is no single right architecture and that each organization needs to evaluate its own distinct requirements to thoughtfully develop the right approach its journey to Zero Trust.[1]

Given the wide variety of approaches and the uniqueness of each organization's starting point, it's not possible to create a "one-size-fits-all" Zero Trust architecture. Nevertheless, we've taken on this challenge and are approaching this by doing two things. First, we're creating a simplified but representative enterprise architecture, which we'll be introducing and exploring in this chapter. This architecture is intended to be illustrative of a typical enterprise, but not be an exact or detailed technical model of any specific organization or network. Its goal is to show an architecture that has many elements in common with most organizations, and to show connections and dependencies between these various components, within a simple visual model.

After we introduce the enterprise architecture, we'll briefly explain each of the IT and security components in use. This lets us tee them up for our in-depth examination of each in Part II of the book. For each, we'll be exploring how they map to, integrate with, and should be thought of from the perspective of a Zero Trust architecture.

Second, we'll be introducing a conceptual model of a Zero Trust architecture in this chapter. This is also a challenge, since there are varied approaches to Zero Trust which are dependent on the underlying enterprise architecture and the choices made by enterprise security architects. For our Zero Trust architecture, we'll be starting with the US National Institute of Standards and Technologies (NIST) Zero Trust Architecture, from Special Publication 800-207. However, we're extending and refining

---

[1]Ultimately, the aim of this book is to provide you with the knowledge to do exactly this!

© Jason Garbis and Jerry W. Chapman 2021
J. Garbis and J. W. Chapman, *Zero Trust Security*, https://doi.org/10.1007/978-1-4842-6702-8_3

that architecture to make it more relevant for enterprises, and to better align with our approach. That is, we'll be using these architectural concepts throughout the course of this book to make Zero Trust concepts concrete and relatable to your enterprise.

Think of it this way—your enterprise network and security infrastructure has many elements such as Firewalls, NAC, IDS/IPS, etc. Most of these will continue to exist in a Zero Trust architecture (although some may not). But in all cases, the way in which your infrastructure elements are configured and operated should change with Zero Trust, resulting in improved security and streamlined operations. Let's get started by introducing the enterprise architecture.

A Representative Enterprise Architecture

Figure 3-1 shows an enterprise architecture containing the most common IT and security infrastructure elements, depicting logical connections between relevant networking components. For clarity, we've omitted a great deal of detail from this diagram—we'll be examining each of the components, as well as their dependencies and connections, in the relevant chapters in Part II of the book. For now, we'll provide a brief introduction to each of the elements, highlighting its role in the architecture, how our fictional enterprise is using it, and how they wish to improve it.

Let's briefly introduce the graphical elements we're using throughout the book: Logical connections between objects are portrayed with a dashed line. A secure (encrypted) connection between objects will be shown as a solid bolded line. A solid line (non-bolded) represents the data flow between objects in the diagram using native application protocols (which may or may not be encrypted). Resources being accessed (workloads, services, or data) are represented as an "R." Finally, ellipses between resources signify a common set of resources in a collection.

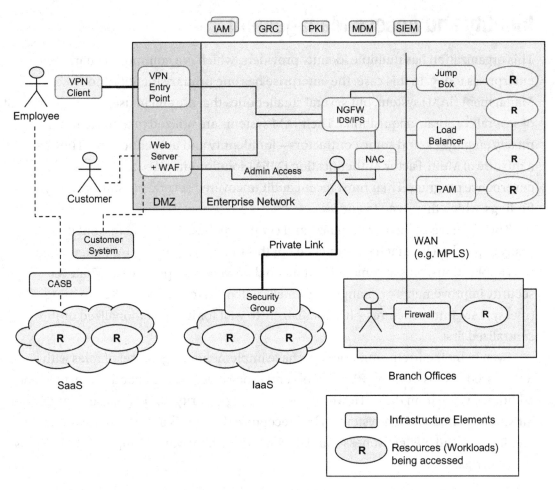

Figure 3-1. *A Representative Enterprise Architecture*

The enterprise in our architecture operates a primary headquarters enterprise network and multiple branch offices. These physical locations each house a number of networked resources (workloads) that users must be able to securely access, depicted as R. This enterprise also has workloads running in private networks running on a public Infrastructure as a Service (IaaS) provider, as well as multiple Software as a Service (SaaS) resources accessed by different user groups.

Like most enterprises, this one has a variety of access control and networking mechanisms of different types, as well as an ecosystem of IT and security infrastructure elements. In the following sections, we'll be briefly discussing why and how they're using each of these, as well as the ways in which they are looking to improve.

Identity and Access Management

This organization has multiple identity providers, which is a common scenario for enterprises today. In this case, the enterprise has one primary Identity and Access Managment (IAM) system, but several smaller ones that are still in use, largely as a result of several corporate acquisitions. Their IAM systems are utilized to manage users—mostly employees, and some contractors—for identity and authentication. They have a mixture of Multi-Factor Authentication (MFA) solutions in place and a basic identity governance program. Their most recent audit uncovered several medium-priority findings, which they need to address.

They do have a plan to rationalize and centralize these IAM systems, but there are many dependencies that have stretched out this process, including IAM integrations with applications, plus automated and manual provisioning processes. Whatever security improvements or changes they make will need to work with their existing (messy) IAM infrastructures—it's not realistic to wait for it to be rationalized or centralized first.

Even in their current situation, they have implemented a good set of roles with Role-Based Access Control (RBAC) tools and processes, and they naturally want to get additional value from these. However, their existing security infrastructure is largely not integrated with their IAM systems. They recognize that this is a source of friction, cost, inefficiency, and ineffectiveness—and it's something they want to improve as they move to Zero Trust.

Network Infrastructure (Firewalls, DNS, Load Balancers)

This enterprise has a fairly typical network infrastructure, including a wide variety of traditional firewalls and a private DNS server for resolving internal server hostnames. They also make use of several types of load balancers, including both network and application load balancers. Many of these elements have been in place for years and are used to protect services, segment the network, and control access to private resources.

However, as is often the case, these elements and the teams that manage them have struggled to keep up with the changes in the way that applications (workloads) are developed, deployed, and accessed. Specifically, the adoption of more dynamic (ephemeral) workloads running in on-premises containerized or virtualized environments, coupled with an increase in remote user access, has made these solutions less effective overall. Essentially, they're forced to grant too-broad network access, since these traditional security tools—designed and built to secure a more static and deterministic IT infrastructure[2]—are increasingly unable to properly distinguish different users and different target workloads.

This open network access is now a priority for them to eliminate—they recently suffered from a malware attack, which was able to spread broadly throughout the network and impact a considerable number of systems. They're also looking to Zero Trust to better align the access controls across different parts of their network.

Jump Boxes

This enterprise has been using jump boxes (sometimes referred to as jump hosts, or jump servers) as hardened access points to control admin access to certain high-value assets on the network, such as production systems and backup systems, which are isolated on a separate network segment. Although a recent audit identified and forced them to overcome some security issues with their jump boxes (e.g., shared credentials and a lack of MFA), they still have a number of issues they want to address.

These include the fact that the jump boxes have full network access to the high-value systems, their inability to enforce the desired business process (request and approval) for temporary access, and their lack of integration with Identity systems. They'd also like to rationalize and align their jump boxes with their privileged access management system, discussed next.

Privileged Access Management

This enterprise is using a Privileged Access Management (PAM) solution to support password vaulting and provide session recording for access to several high-value systems. Although this does provide a secure solution to obfuscate passwords and secure access to specific systems within the enterprise, PAM is only used sparingly across the enterprise, due to its cost and complexity.

Currently, the PAM solution provides limited contextual awareness without any connection to their core Identity solution. This limits its ability to provide a role-based solution to control who should have access to the high-value systems within the PAM solution.

---

[2]Specifically, these new deployment models now house multiple workloads that require different access controls behind a single, shared IP address. Likewise, remote users now appear to share IP addresses, due to the NATting being performed by the VPN Gateway.

Ideally, the PAM solution would be able to use contextual information to make access control decisions in alignment with policy and compliance requirements. Integrating it with their IAM solution is also a priority, as part of their overall re-evaluation of their use of jump boxes and PAM for access to high-value resources.

Network Access Control

This organization uses a Network Access Control (NAC) solution to manage network access for on-premises users in their headquarters office, as well as guest Wi-Fi access. This hardware-based system—which is part of the networking infrastructure—uses enterprise-issued certificates to identify valid devices and assign them to VLANs.

Initially, this worked reasonably well for the enterprise headquarters, although because NAC is operationally complex, it hasn't kept up with networking changes, and users have access to a broader set of workloads and data than desired. This "drift" was in fact the root cause of a recent audit finding around network access to production systems.

In addition, their NAC solution is a silo, in several dimensions. First—largely due to cost and complexity—they chose not to deploy NAC into their branch offices. As a result, users in those offices have different types of access controls applied to them. Second, NAC obviously can't be used for remote access or cloud environments either. Those environments have separate access policy models, which are coarse-grained and static.

Finally, their NAC hardware is approaching end-of-life support. Taking all these aspects into consideration, the enterprise's security leaders have decided to eliminate the NAC. This will let them reallocate the NAC budget to fund their Zero Trust initiative while also modernizing their infrastructure and reducing complexity and operational cost.

Intrusion Detection/Intrusion Prevention

Like many enterprises, this organization has a network-based Intrusion Detection System/Intrusion Prevention System (IDS/IPS) in place, deployed through a combination of modules running within their Next-Generation Firewalls (NGFWs), as well as some deployment of an open source IDS/IPS. These systems are used to sense anomalous behavior, and respond to it, through a combination of automated and manual responses by their Security Operations Center.

However, their IDS has become less effective over time, largely due to growth in the size and complexity of the network, the adoption of cloud-based resources where their IDS cannot be an inline "chokepoint," and increased use of encrypted protocols.

They want a more comprehensive and holistic way of detecting and responding to indicators of compromise across their heterogeneous environment. They feel that they're spending too much time and money and achieving only limited results. Ideally, they'd have a single place to define IDS policies, and multiple places to enforce them across their network, user devices, and workloads. They also want to obtain quantitative benefits (reduced noise and false positives) as well as qualitative ones (enhanced context for better security analyst decision-making).

Virtual Private Network

Their Virtual Private Network (VPN) is the only system currently used for remote access within this environment. This VPN has been in place for remote workers to access the enterprise environment. However, with an increased remote workforce and growing security concerns, the organization has experienced performance and reliability issues, and the VPN provides no context about identities within the environment. Additionally, the organization is concerned about the rudimentary level of access controls within the VPN solution—remote users can move throughout the network with few controls in place.

The organization would like to increase the security context and decrease the potential service and performance impacts to the business. In order to provide this security, they wish to integrate remote access with their identity provider, and utilize user and device attributes for access decision-making and enforcement.

Next-Generation Firewalls

This enterprise's Next-Generation Firewalls (NGFWs) consist of traditional firewall capabilities, IDS/IPS, some application awareness and control capabilities, and a remote access VPN (discussed separately earlier). They are not dissatisfied with their primary NGFW, but do struggle with a hybrid infrastructure—they have two enclaves of different vendor NGFWs, and have never been able to justify the capital and operational expenses to rationalize this into a single vendor.

As a result, they have differing capabilities between these two enclaves, which causes operational friction, misaligned policy, and control models, and has caused technical issues when traffic needs to transit between these security domains. They'd like to find a security and operational solution which provides them a unified policy model, and operates consistently across these hardware infrastructures. They would like to avoid the expense of replacing this hardware, because they still have multiple years left of capacity and depreciation. They'd also like to begin incorporating threat intelligence into their security platform.

Security Information and Event Management

This organization is using a combination of a traditional on-prem Security Information and Event Management (SIEM) and a newer cloud-based SIEM. They are planning to fully migrate to the cloud-based SIEM, but they have some on-premises systems that they've customized and integrated. This integration, while important to them operationally, is inflexible and difficult to maintain.

Migrating to the cloud-based SIEM will provide them with better performance and ability to scale, and enable them to use capabilities present in that more modern platform, such as the ability to better integrate log data from a wider variety of sources. They'd like to enrich the information that the SIEM can use and leverage it as a way to influence user access via a risk scoring measurement. Overall, they are pleased with their cloud-based SIEM, but want it to have more "teeth"—namely, the ability to automatically affect user access. They are looking to improve this through a combination of their Zero Trust initiative and the introduction of a Security Orchestration, Automation, and Response (SOAR) system.

Web Server and Web Application Firewall

A significant part of this enterprise's revenue is driven by a web-facing system used by their enterprise customers—via a web portal as well as a set of web APIs. This system sits in their DMZ, and is connected to a number of production systems inside the enterprise network. It's protected by a Web Application Firewall (WAF), which provides the web portal and the API with protection against application and network-level attacks such as SQL injection and cross-site scripting.

There are several components to this web application that are relevant here. There's a public component, which is essentially part of their public website. This needs to remain accessible to everyone, including unauthenticated and anonymous users. They also provide a free hands-on demo of their service, running in a sandbox demo tenant of their system. This has proven to be a valuable business-generation tool.

The other parts of the website are more private, and are only accessible to identified and authenticated users. There is a rich web UI, where customers log in and use the application to transact business with this enterprise. This application also houses an API that is heavily used by customer systems to transact business—in fact, in recent years, the API has overtaken the UI, and now generates 75% of their online business versus 25% for the web UI. They are satisfied with the level of external security for this system, and do not have an urgent need to improve it. Internally, of course, system admins have administrative access to the system. They have a relatively immature set of access controls for these admins, which they wish to improve as part of their Zero Trust initiative.

Infrastructure as a Service

This organization has enhanced its compute and networking capabilities by utilizing Infrastructure as a Service (IaaS), and has created a "private link" tunnel between the on-premises network and the cloud infrastructure; the same flat network approach is maintained even though the infrastructure is now deployed in the cloud. Although this provides connectivity, it doesn't provide additional security. In fact, this connection increases complexity because they have one network but two disparate security models and tools.

Although the organization has the ability to utilize additional monitoring and networking services the Cloud Service Provider (CSP) supports, their on-premises infrastructure is still built based on legacy networking services, including some elements that operate at Layer 2. These components cannot work in a cloud environment, which is forcing the organization to reconsider how they should approach security with IaaS.

The organization is looking to provide a dynamic and context-sensitive security, in a way that's consistent with and aligned with their on-premises security models. It should be identity-centric, and give them a holistic way of controlling and monitoring access across both on-prem and cloud environments. Finally, they want to replicate the kind of control and automation that they have in IaaS across their heterogeneous environment, without having to migrate everything into the cloud.

Software as a Service and Cloud Access Security Brokers

The organization has grown significantly, and naturally adopted Software as a Service (SaaS)–based applications to support primary business functions, including HR and other functions. Additionally, there has been significant growth of resources not being completely protected, as business units have purchased their own SaaS applications to support growth (shadow IT). With all of this rapid growth, the organization has deployed a Cloud Application Security Broker (CASB), which has helped them find resources being utilized, and secure them.

The enterprise would like to further the adoption of the CASB to not only prevent further shadow IT but also to better (and more broadly) enforce Data Loss Prevention (DLP). Also, they would like to realize a more secure and identity-centric approach to managing their use of SaaS applications.

This concludes our introduction to this enterprise's existing architectural elements and the ways in which they want to improve them. Note that we'll be examining each of these components further in Part II of the book, from a Zero Trust perspective. Now, let's introduce the structure and makeup of the Zero Trust architecture.

A Zero Trust Architecture

In this section, we'll be presenting a conceptual Zero Trust architecture that builds on the work presented in the NIST document, while refining and extending it. In this chapter, we've taken on the same challenge as the NIST authors—namely, that Zero Trust starts with a set of principles and a philosophy and that there are many different enterprise security architectures that could be used to achieve the goals of Zero Trust. We acknowledge that it's impossible to create or depict a single architecture that's universally applicable—our goal is to introduce a set of architectural components and a set of requirements, which you can use to construct a relevant and valuable architecture for your specific organization.

The NIST Zero Trust Model

As we mentioned in the previous chapter, NIST introduced a logical set of Zero Trust components, shown in Figure 3-2. This diagram contains some of the core concepts and components which we'll be using throughout this book.

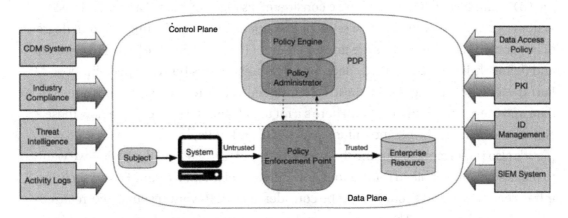

Figure 3-2. *Logical Zero Trust Components (Source: NIST: Zero Trust Architecture, SP 800-207)*

First, there's the notion of a **Subject**—defined by NIST as either a user, application, or device—operating on (or with) a computer system, and which has access to an **Enterprise Resource**. This resource may be an application, data, document, or workload that's under the control of the enterprise and protected by the Zero Trust system. We generally refer to this as a *Resource* throughout this book.

The subject is presumed to be operating in an untrusted environment on an untrusted network, and is only permitted to access the Resource by way of a **Policy Enforcement Point** (PEP). The PEP controls the subject's access to the resource via what NIST terms the *implicit trust zone*, which we'll be discussing further later. The PEP doesn't store or make policy determinations—that work is done by the **Policy Decision Point** (PDP).[3]

---

[3]Note that NIST includes a logical separation between two components that make up a PDP—a Policy Engine and a Policy Administrator. For this book, we don't consider this distinction to be relevant, and just refer to the PDP as a unit.

Notice that the Subject communicates with the Enterprise Resource across what is termed the *data plane*, which is distinct from the *control plane*—as NIST states, the PDP and PEP "communicate on a network that is logically separate and not directly accessible by enterprise assets and resources. The data plane is used for application data traffic."

The additional elements depicted previously as sitting outside the system (e.g., the CDM and PKI) actually need to be considered as logically part of any Zero Trust system—or at the very least with a set of bidirectional arrows indicating different degrees of integration. These elements are important input (context) into the Zero Trust system, and definitely influence its policy decisions. Throughout this book—especially in Part II—we'll be arguing that all these systems need to be producers and consumers of data and events, meshed together. There's a lot to talk about, as we explore how these elements can interact with and influence the PDP and PEPs.

It's also important to examine the key concepts of the PDP and the PEPs—we want to make sure you're able to think about how different elements of your IT and security infrastructure can and should in fact be considered as PEPs within your to-be-realized Zero Trust architecture. This is the reason that in the architecture diagram shown in Figure 3-3, we have many different conceptual PEPs in place across the enterprise that will likely be doing different things and serving different roles. In fact, as we introduce later in this chapter, we believe that there are several different types of PEPs. Let's now examine this conceptual architecture.

A Conceptual Zero Trust Architecture

In Figure 3-3, we introduce a conceptual Zero Trust architecture, depicting the security and IT infrastructure from our representative enterprise, but re-imagined from a Zero Trust perspective.

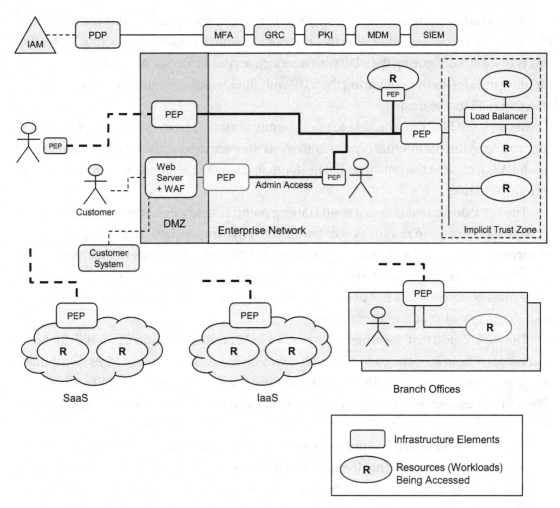

Figure 3-3. *Conceptual Zero Trust Architecture*

The first thing to note is that there's a logically centralized Policy Decision Point, which acts as the heart of any Zero Trust system. In practice—in a real-world enterprise system that's being evolved to support Zero Trust—the PDP will likely be a combination of different technical systems, glued together by integrations and business processes.

Zero Trust is, of course, very much an identity-centric system, and any PDP must have a tight, trusted relationship with the organization's identity providers. Technically, the PDP may have a direct network connection with the IAM provider (i.e., if it's using LDAP or RADIUS), or an indirect connection (i.e., if it's using SAML).

What's more important is that first, the PDP must be configured so that it can trust the data that it receives, either directly or indirectly, from the identity provider. Typically, this is done by configuring the PDP with a service account to make API calls into the identity provider, or by configuring the PDP with the identity system's public certificate so it can validate the data.

Second, the PDP must be able to map identity attributes from the identity provider (or providers) into its internal representation, as they are used within the PDP's policy model. We'll explore the policy model in-depth in Chapter 17, but we will provide a light introduction here.

The NIST document makes a good starting point: It states, as one of the basic Zero Trust tenets, "Access to resources is determined by dynamic policy—including the observable state of client identity, application, and the requesting asset—and may include other behavioral attributes." Put another way, if a subject can access a resource, there must be a policy that has been evaluated which grants the subject access to the resource in question at the current time.

The NIST Zero Trust document also states that "Enterprise resources should not be reachable without accessing a PEP," which is why in Figure 3-3, there are PEPs distributed throughout the enterprise architecture. In our diagram, also note that the PEPs are in different places, and perform different functions. Even though they are all PEPs, they are of different types, and have different roles and functions in enforcing policies.

Our perspective is that an effective Zero Trust system will have a set of PEPs that are centrally managed while being distributed across the enterprise ecosystem. The system must control PEP behavior through a set of policies, which are dynamic and context sensitive and enforced throughout the environment. As we noted earlier, however, these PEPs can be of different types, with different roles and functions.

For example, the PEP sitting in the DMZ has the responsibility to permit only authorized and authenticated users with access to the appropriate set of internal resources. It must do so—with enforcement at the network layer—based on the set of permissions given to it by the PDP, which the PDP derives from policies, based on various inputs including user and system context. We'll explore the mechanisms by which this can happen later in the book.

Here's another example—the PEP running within the Resource in the upper right of the diagram must enforce the set of permissions given to it by the PDP. This PEP may be responsible for controlling inbound (and potentially outbound) network traffic, or may be responsible for enforcing role-based permissions within the application.

In both cases, the PEPs receive their instructions—the policies that they are responsible for enforcing—from the PDP. We'll be exploring policies in depth in Chapter 17, but it's necessary to frame things up here. We're being more specific on this than NIST is, because we believe that this additional structure is worthwhile, and will provide you with a useful framework with which to think about, design, define requirements, select solutions, and ultimately deploy a Zero Trust platform in your enterprise.

Policy Components

We define a policy as a declarative statement specifying that a **subject** is permitted to perform an **action** on a **target**, if and only if certain **conditions** are met. This is shown in Table 3-1.

Table 3-1. *Policy Components*

Component	Description
Subject Criteria	Subjects are the entities performing (initiating) actions. Subjects must be authenticated identities, and policies must contain *subject criteria* which designate the subjects to which this policy applies.
Action	The activity being performed by the subject. This must contain either a network or an application component, and may possibly contain both.
Target	The object (resource) that the action is being performed upon. This may be statically or dynamically defined within the policy, and may be broad or narrow in scope, although narrow is preferred.
Condition	The circumstances under which the subject is permitted to perform the action upon the target. The Zero Trust system must support the definition of conditions that draw upon multiple types of attributes, including subject, environment, and target attributes.

Let's examine this policy structure. *Subject criteria* are used to define the set of identities (subjects) to whom this policy applies. Subjects—which may be people or Non-Person Entities (NPE)—must be authenticated entities, and must exist in some identity management system. Subjects have many attributes associated with them, drawn from sources such as their authenticating identity system, device profile, and network or geolocation information, among others. These attributes are used in the subject criteria

33

to determine whether a policy should be assigned to a given identity (note that attributes are also used in Conditions, which we'll discuss shortly). It should be clear, even based just on this brief introduction, that a Zero Trust policy model enforces Attribute-Based Access Control (ABAC) in many ways.[4]

Actions define the actual activity that this policy allows the subject to perform. It must contain either a network or application action, and may contain both.

Targets are the system or component that are being acted upon. These may be defined statically (e.g., with a fixed hostname or IP address[5]), or dynamically via attributes such as hypervisor or IaaS labels or tags, which get resolved at runtime. They may be narrowly defined (e.g., a single service running on a single server) or more broadly defined (e.g., access to a class of servers, or a subnet). *Conditions* dictate when the subject is allowed to actually perform the action on the target and can include a very wide variety of circumstances. Let's introduce an example to make this concrete, and to help you think about how they are interpreted by the PDP and how different types of PEPs may work.

Table 3-2 shows a sample policy, controlling access to an internal web application. We'll be exploring this and other examples in depth in Chapter 17.

***Table 3-2.** A Sample Policy*

Policy: Users in the Billing department must be able to use the Billing web application

Subject Criteria	Users who are members of the group `Dept_Billing` in the Identity Provider.
Action	Users must be able to access the Web UI on port 443 over HTTPS.
Target	The billing application with the FQDN `billing.internal.company.com`.
Condition	Users may be on-premises or remote.
	Remote users must be prompted for MFA prior to access (at time of authentication).
	Users must be accessing this application from a company-managed device with endpoint security software running.

---

[4]In fact, NIST SP 800-162 on the topic of ABAC, published in 2014, is in many ways a precursor to this Zero Trust model, stating "when a subject requests access, the ABAC engine can make an access control decision based on the assigned attributes of the requester, the assigned attributes of the object, environment conditions, and a set of policies that are specified in terms of those attributes and conditions."

[5]Yes, hostnames are actually dynamically resolved via DNS, and may resolve differently via the use of load balancers. For our purposes, we consider them to be static.

Types of Policy Enforcement Points

Now that we've briefly introduced policies, let's take a deeper look at the PEPs. As we mentioned before, policy enforcement is performed by PEPs at different levels and of different types—depicted in Figure 3-4.

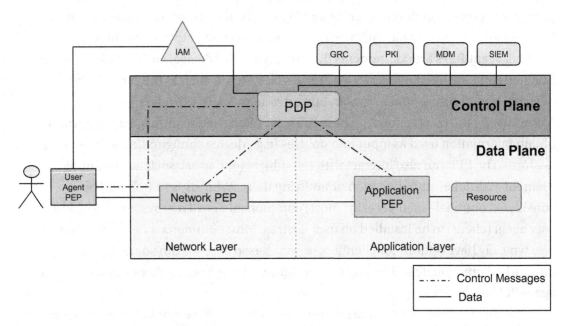

Figure 3-4. *Control Plane, Data Plane, and Policy Enforcement Layers*

We believe that there are actually three types of PEPs, as depicted in this figure: user agent PEPs, network PEPs, and application PEPs. Network PEPs are perhaps the simplest, conceptually, in Zero Trust models, since Zero Trust networking typically is the most common starting point and is largely the orientation of the NIST document. Network PEPs are also already in place in many organizations—to some degree, enterprise firewalls (Next-Generation Firewalls) can be thought of as Zero Trust PEPs, although with some caveats as we'll discuss later. Because these PEPs operate at the network layer, they can perform inline enforcement of network traffic, which is why they are natural enforcement points. They may also perform inspection of traffic, either metadata or the actual traffic data.

Application PEPs may be external to applications (e.g., a PAM or DLP system) or internal, such as an agent running on a workload. In the latter case, the PEP can be used to enforce policies locally on the host, such as local OS firewall rules. Additionally, the PEP might logically be part of the application itself, relying on external attributes or actions to affect the application. This is an important aspect—PEPs must have some level of integration with the PDP and be able to enforce elements of the policies that are provided to it by the PDP. This enforcement may be scoped solely within the application (e.g., ensuring that a given identity has an account with a certain application role). We've seen examples of this in modern applications, for example, that support just-in-time provisioning based on the contents of a SAML assertion. This provisioning can take the form of new account creation with an initial role, or a change to a user's roles.

User agent PEPs are components that run on a user's device, and provide functions that are often necessary for Zero Trust systems, such as the establishment of an encrypted connection across an untrusted network (NIST refers to this as "coordinating the connections"). These PEPs are often used to introspect the device to obtain information used as input into policies (e.g., device configuration and security posture). The PEP can also interact with the subject (end user), such as prompting them for additional authentication or notifying them. While this PEP should be considered optional—many (really, most) commercial Zero Trust systems provide a user agent (client) to be installed on user devices. Most commercial Zero Trust systems *also* typically have options for clientless or web-based access, with some degree of diminished functionality.[6] Throughout the figures in this book, we'll be depicting a user agent PEP in place.

Note that in some cases, there's a fuzzy line between these types of PEPs and may be some overlap in the functions performed by them. For example, our industry is well aware that IDS/IPS can be network-based or host-based. Likewise, DLP functions may be implemented within a network device, such as an NGFW, or on a host. Whether specific enforcement points, such as DLP and PAM, act at the network layer or the application layer (or both) is not that important. What is important is that both DLP and PAM should be considered part of the Zero Trust PEP, and their policies should logically be part of the Zero Trust model. Ideally, there'd be integration between them and the Zero Trust system to drive this. It might be driven by identity attributes/roles or via a separate Zero Trust policy model—this really depends on the implementation.

Ultimately, the functionality and behavior of your PEPs will be dependent on the platform you choose, and on how you choose to deploy it. Throughout this book, the heart of what we're doing is describing how your current infrastructure and architecture should be thought of as a set of Zero Trust PEPs. A successful Zero Trust journey means

---

[6]And some commercial systems split the difference, deploying their user agent software as a browser extension.

that all your PEPs are integrated, share a policy model, and are operationally connected. But this is a goal, not a starting point, and you should keep in mind that there will still be many existing infrastructure elements in place that are not PEPs, and not logically connected into your Zero Trust policy model.

For example, Figure 3-3 still depicts a load balancer, which continues to serve a useful function, even within the Zero Trust architecture. In this case, the load balancer is operating at a simple network level, and can continue to perform its function without change despite the adoption of Zero Trust throughout the rest of the architecture. There's no reason to overly complicate it, and its function doesn't need to be changed by user or system context. This will be the case for many elements of your infrastructure— so while Zero Trust can and should give you the opportunity to re-think your security and integration architecture, it doesn't mean that every element must be changed. Put another way, it's realistic to incrementally adopt Zero Trust and begin enforcing policies at key points across your infrastructure while avoiding disruptive change. This leads us to our next topic: policies.

What Is a Policy Enforcement Point?

Policies are at the heart of every Zero Trust system, and are continuously being evaluated by PDPs, and enforced by the PEPs. But this raises an interesting and somewhat philosophical question—what makes a security component a Zero Trust Policy Enforcement Point? For example, can a 5-year-old, basic firewall be considered a PEP? Like most interesting questions, the answer is "it depends," and insight stems from the thought processes involved in examining the dependencies, so let's dive in.

Our basic firewall is of course a "network enforcement point" in the sense that it has access control rules that it enforces, such as "Allow TCP traffic on port 443 from source subnet 10.5.0.0/16 to reach destination subnet 10.3.0.0/16." However, we argue that this firewall is not a Zero Trust PEP—it fails to meet the following requirements:

- Have the ability to enforce the PDPs' identity-centric and context-sensitive policy model

- Automatically respond to policy changes driven by PDP

- Utilize a control channel for communication with the PDP

It should be clear that a traditional firewall doesn't meet these requirements—in fact, as we'll explore later in the book, the ability for a PEP to be programmatically driven by the PDP and to be able to adjust its policies in an automated way is a key capability in realizing Zero Trust. That is, our fundamental premise is that a Zero Trust system must be able to enforce identity and context-sensitive dynamic policies. The implication of this is that every PEP must be able to receive ongoing updates from the PDP, and automatically adjust the policies it's enforcing in near-real time and without human intervention. This is the only way to achieve the responsive, dynamic nature of Zero Trust, even at a small scale.

So, let's continue our thought experiment. What if our 5-year-old firewall, sitting in a wiring closet and covered with dust, has a policy-driven automation layer that's been implemented on top of it? In this case, we'd argue that now this firewall—in combination with the network security automation software—could be considered a Zero Trust PEP, as long as the network security automation solution is itself tied into the PDP and meets the criteria described previously. That is, the essence of a Zero Trust PEP is that it has automated integration with the PDP and can respond quickly to policy changes. Zero Trust Policy Enforcement Points cannot be siloed from either a policy model or operational perspective.

Note that we used the term *automated* here. Automated doesn't necessarily mean *completely* automatic—it's perfectly fine to have manual steps involved, such as a business process approval for certain changes, or manual approval of exceptional "breakglass" situations. But there must be automatic changes for the day-to-day (or hour-to-hour, or even minute-to-minute) changes that this enforcement point controls.

For example, recall our sample Policy from Table 3-2. Consider what happens when user Jane is added to the `Dept_Billing` directory group. Soon thereafter, she must be able to access the Billing app at a network layer, and have an active account at the application layer. Now in reality, provisioning the account for Jane may be a manual process, but we believe that the network access changes must be automated. To illustrate this, imagine that a few days later, Jane inadvertently clicks a phishing link and installs malware on her laptop, which starts performing network reconnaissance. The enterprise's security systems recognize this as an indicator of compromise, and respond by automatically blocking her network-level access to the business-critical billing system, to prevent the malware from potentially compromising it.

This response must be done quickly and automatically by the network PEP—this cannot wait for a business process. Note that in our example, it's very likely that this access will only be blocked at the network layer, by the network PEP. There's no reason to make any changes within the application PEP—this is a transient issue with Jane's laptop. In fact, a well-designed Zero Trust system would continue to allow Jane to access the billing application from a different device (e.g., a desktop computer) while continuing to block the laptop. We'll be exploring these topics further in Chapter 5 and Chapter 17.

Zero Trust Deployment Models

Next, we'll be exploring several Zero Trust deployment models—including two from the NIST Zero Trust document, plus two more for completeness. These models provide us with the next level of specificity about how Zero Trust systems might actually be deployed, although of course real-world deployment architectures will be dependent on the capabilities of the chosen technology. We believe that many of the vendor-provided enterprise Zero Trust models will align with one or more of the deployment models depicted in the following text. That is, these deployment models will serve as a useful framework with which you can evaluate potential vendors, and examine their pros and cons. These aren't intended to be exhaustive, but they are intended to be representative. They're also not necessarily mutually exclusive—some systems may well combine elements of several of these models. Note that in the discussions to follow, we're focusing on the contrast between these models, rather than what they have in common.

Finally, note that for clarity in the following diagrams, we're omitting the PDP's connection to identity management and other enterprise security systems as depicted previously. Those connections still must exist, no matter which Zero Trust deployment model you choose.

Resource-Based Deployment Model

Our first model is the *resource-based deployment model*—depicted in Figure 3-5.[7]

---

[7]Note that NIST refers to this as the somewhat verbose *device agent/gateway model*.

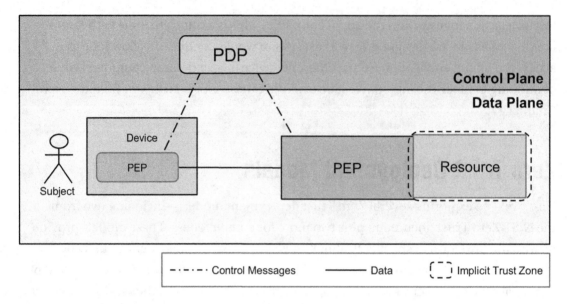

Figure 3-5. *Resource-Based Deployment Model*

What's important about this model is that, first, there's typically a user agent deployed onto the subject's system, acting as the user agent PEP.[8] Second, that there's an inline PEP (the gateway), which is deployed (per NIST) "**on** the resource or as a component **directly in front** of a resource" (emphasis ours).

This diagram also introduces a visual representation of the *implicit trust zone*, which is an area behind a given PEP, within which all resources (entities) are trusted to the same degree. This represents the boundary of the security domain for which that PEP is responsible. By definition, any interactions between components that stay within the implicit trust zone occur outside of the control of the PEP. In the preceding example, if the PEP is running on the local resource Operating System, the implicit trust zone comprises the set of local processes and their interactions within the local OS. Naturally, you want to minimize the size of the implicit trust zone—understanding that there are trade-offs involved with each of the deployment models.

Resource-Based Deployment Model: Pros

- End-to-end control of application access and network traffic

- Very compact implicit trust zone that's "behind" the gateway

---

[8]As we noted previously, this agent is a component of most commercial Zero Trust solutions, although strictly speaking, it's optional. Most vendors support a "clientless" option, with some associated trade-offs in functionality.

This model ensures that all network communications between user devices and the target resource are encrypted and that access control policies are enforced. It also ensures that *all* network communication with the resource is enforced by the PEP (and therefore, by the organization's Zero Trust security model). However, this model also has a number of cons, which must be considered.

Resource-Based Deployment Model: Cons

- Requires deployment of the PEPs on both user devices and resources.

- Potential for technical conflicts between resource components and PEPs.

- PEPs must be deployable onto a wide large variety of perhaps outdated/legacy OSs.

- Potential for pushback from application resource owners.

- Requires a 1:1: relationship between PEPs and Resources.

- End-to-end secure tunnel can blind existing inline security controls.

- PEP must be visible and available to remote users.

First, this model requires that a PEP be deployed on every resource in the environment, which is potentially problematic. In any environment of more than minimal size, it'll likely require a high degree of automation, especially for virtualized or cloud environments. Locally deployed PEPs also have the potential for technical conflicts within the same OS, for example, with components that take control of network or disk I/O, such as web servers or databases.

This model also requires that PEPs be deployed on 100% of protected resources. This often represents a multi-dimensional challenge. First, technically, it requires that the PEP software be supported and deployable on all workloads. Many organizations have legacy applications running on mainframe or minicomputers, which likely cannot support a PEP. Arguably—and ironically—these legacy applications are often the ones that are in most dire need of being better secured!

And second, many security teams will encounter pushback from application owners who will be reluctant to deploy any additional software onto their revenue-generating or business-critical applications.

From an operational perspective, this model requires one PEP deployed for each managed resource, which can impose considerable management load on the Zero Trust system, and the team responsible for it. For example, if a virtualized or cloud environment consists of many ephemeral workloads, the constant onboarding and offboarding of these resources is something to be wary of. In this case, you'd need to ensure that the Zero Trust system is sufficiently automated to be able to manage this churn.

As a core Zero Trust tenet, this model ensures that network traffic is encrypted from the user agent PEP to the resource PEP.[9] In many commercial Zero Trust systems, this is achieved by the use of an encrypted tunnel. This is secure and effective, but typically has the side effect of rendering all that traffic opaque to any intermediary. This is beneficial if the intermediary is an attacker, but detrimental if it's an enterprise-deployed security component, such as a network-based IDS/IPS.

Finally—and perhaps most importantly—the PEP protecting the resource must, of course, be accessible to subjects, including remote users. Because the PEP in this model is part of the resource, this implies that either all subjects are on the same physical network as each PEP or that all PEPs are directly accessible remotely. The first option is rarely going to be true, and the second option is probably not viable, given that many of these resources are in place on private network segments. In reality, Zero Trust deployments that follow this model will require a separate secure remote access capability—ideally as part of the Zero Trust platform.[10]

We realize that it may seem that we've overly emphasized the negative aspects of this model, but we don't want you to get that impression—there are certainly significant benefits of this approach, for sure. We just want to make sure that you're aware of these *potential* downsides, and to arm you to make informed decisions, and ask intelligent questions about your architecture or Zero Trust vendor. We take a similar approach with the other deployment models, so let's dive in and look at the next one, the enclave-based deployment model.

---

[9]Traffic "behind" the PEP may not be encrypted—it traverses the implicit trust zone in its native protocol.

[10]Commercial Zero Trust platforms typically approach this with a combination of an edge PEP and a required user agent PEP. Be cautious about architectures that solve this outside the scope of the Zero Trust model, such as requiring a traditional VPN.

Enclave-Based Deployment Model

The second model is the *enclave-based deployment model*, depicted in Figure 3-6. In this case, the PEP is sitting in front of multiple resources—termed a *resource enclave*. This collection of resources may be physically located together (e.g., in an on-premises or co-located data center) or logically related (e.g., a set of cloud-based or virtualized servers). Like the previous model, the subject has an optional locally installed user agent PEP.

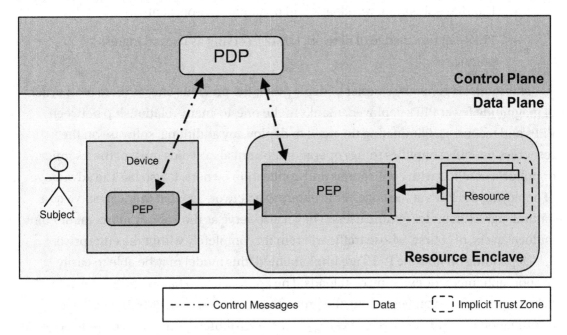

Figure 3-6. *Enclave-Based Deployment Model*

What's important to understand is that in this model, the implicit trust zone contains multiple networked resources which are very likely communicating among themselves. That is, it's critical that in this model, the resource enclave must be running solely on a logical private network that's under the control of the enterprise. We state "logical," since of course this may be running in a public IaaS environment, or a shared colocation environment, but the network traffic at layers three and up must be private to the enterprise.

Although the resources inside the enclave can and may communicate with one another outside the visibility and control of the PEP, the only way for subjects outside the trust zone to communicate into it is via the PEP, and therefore is controlled by policy.

That is, with this model, enterprises need to make sure they thoroughly understand the resources' data and communication patterns. Note also that this deployment model leans toward a "user-to-service" approach to Zero Trust.

Enclave-Based Deployment Model: Pros

- Simpler to deploy PEPs—no changes to resources.

- Fewer PEPs deployed.

- Handles ephemeral workloads and dynamic environments well.

- PEPs can run at edge of network (DMZ), serving as natural ingress points.

This model is generally simpler to deploy than the previous one, as there is an order of magnitude fewer PEPs deployed, thanks to the one-to-many relationship between PEPs and resources. Eliminating the need to deploy any additional software on the resources not only simplifies things operationally, but also avoids most of the technical or political conflicts with applications and application owners. It also has the advantage of deploying the PEPs at the edge of the enterprise network, so that they can serve as a natural ingress point for remote users. They'll also serve as the Policy Enforcement Point for local users, of course, whose traffic will remain completely within the enterprise.

Depending on how the PEPs are implemented, this model may be able to easily support ephemeral or dynamic workloads. The approach is to have the PEPs be able to be responsive to changes among the protected resources, such as by detecting the instantiation of new resources and using resource attributes (metadata) to apply policies to them. For example, a PEP protecting an on-premises virtual environment could receive an API call from the hypervisor, indicating that a new instance has been created. Based on this instance's attributes, the PEP could immediately apply the correct policy, and grant only the authorized set of users with access. A PEP running in an enterprise's IaaS environment can perform exactly the same function.

Enclave-Based Deployment Model: Cons

- Potentially large, opaque, or noisy implicit trust zone.

- PEPs represent a new type of ingress point into the enterprise network.

The biggest challenge with this model is the size and scope of the implicit trust zone, which of course will be dependent on how and where you choose to deploy these PEPs. With a focused set of resources with well-understood and well-managed communications paths, this model is a solid foundation for Zero Trust. Organizations that are working in newer (especially IaaS based) environments or are using programmatically driven infrastructure (such as DevOps) are especially well suited to this model. Organizations with lower operational maturity, lower visibility, or complex legacy networks may need to deploy more PEPs in order to reduce the size and scope of each implicit trust zone. Alternatively, they may adopt a hybrid approach that's supported by some Zero Trust vendors, combining this model with the microsegmentation model we discuss later.

One more potential con of this model is less technical, but oftentimes more political. In this model, the PEP is typically placed in an organization's DMZ, at the edge of their enterprise network. That is, it's deliberately accessible from the Internet, which is the least trusted place in the known universe. This is necessary, in order for remote users to be able to access protected resources, but also—like a VPN concentrator—represents a potential avenue of attack. Security and networking teams should evaluate and scrutinize new edge devices, but sometimes they push back for nontechnical reasons. It's important for Zero Trust teams to be aware of this, and to obtain sufficient management support for their project, so that these new edge devices can be evaluated fairly and objectively. As a side note, some edge PEPs actually offer better network security than traditional edge devices, so forward-looking networking and security teams should actually embrace the opportunity for change.

Cloud-Routed Deployment Model

In this next model, all traffic from the subject transits a cloud environment before ultimately reaching the resource, hence the name "cloud-routed." This model is a common approach, with many commercial vendors operating this as a service. This model is depicted in Figure 3-7.

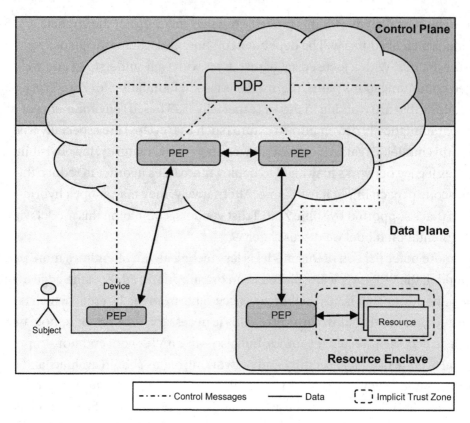

Figure 3-7. *Cloud-Routed Deployment Model*

In this model, the PEPs that sit in front of the enterprise's resource enclaves act similarly to the PEPs in the model shown here. However, these PEPs have one important difference—they don't serve as an ingress point into the enterprise network. Instead, that function has been logically shifted to the PEPs running in the vendor's cloud environment. In this model, the PEPs that sit within the enterprise act as *connectors*, making outbound connections to the cloud-based PEP. Because these on-premises connectors do not require any inbound connections, they often simplify the deployment of this model—in exchange for some limitations as discussed in the following text.

When the subject wants to communicate with the resource, they first authenticate with the PDP, and then their traffic is directed to one of the cloud-based PEPs, typically the one that's geolocated closest to them (or perhaps exhibits the lowest latency). Their traffic then transits the PEPs within the cloud to the PEP that has a connection to the target resource enclave. The on-premises PEP secures a resource enclave in exactly the same way as in the previous model.

Cloud-Routed Deployment Model: Pros

- Simpler to set up for enterprises.

- As-a-Service platform reduces operational overhead for the enterprise.

- Some vendors with this model also provide a Secure Web Gateway (SWG) service.

Because the on-premises PEPs in this model are only making outbound connections, their deployment is typically very straightforward. They can also avoid scrutiny from network and compliance teams, since they don't require any changes to DMZ firewall rules, or deployment of any software into the DMZ. These PEPs can be deployed anywhere inside the enterprise, and provide remote access onto that network. While this is a potential advantage, it's also a potential disadvantage. Teams must not use this technical capability as an excuse or a means to bypass security, network, or GRC oversight. If deployed as "shadow IT," this can represent a significant vulnerability for the organization. Even once approved, of course, security teams must define an appropriate set of policies, and enforce the principle of least privilege. Ease of deployment cannot be an excuse for poor security controls.

Finally, some vendors with this model combine it with a Secure Web Gateway service to secure user access to publicly accessible websites. This combination may be appealing for some enterprises, as it can simplify deployment and operations.

Cloud-Routed Deployment Model: Cons

- PEPs can be deployed without proper security, network, or compliance oversight.

- Adds latency to user traffic.

- Typically supports only limited network protocols.

- Not suitable for on-premises users accessing on-premises resources.

- Potentially large, opaque, or noisy implicit trust zone.

There are several other downsides to this model, in addition to the risk of this becoming a "Shadow IT" remote access too. First, all user traffic needs to transit the vendor cloud, adding latency and potentially reduced throughput. For some use cases and applications, this can be a serious impediment. You definitely need to get a detailed understanding of vendor platform network performance, and do some testing prior to deploying this to production users. Second, cloud-routed models tend to only support a subset of network protocols—most commonly just TCP/IP (and in some cases, just a few application protocols such as HTTPS, SSH, and RDP). If your users and applications require other protocols, such as UDP, or require server-initiated connections to users, this model may not be a fit. And, like the enclave-based model discussed previously, this model shares the same cautions about the implicit trust zone.

Most importantly, this model is generally only well suited for remote users, since all traffic must transit the vendor cloud. If users are on-premises and accessing on-premises resources, their traffic must needlessly be "hairpinned" through the vendor cloud, adding latency, reducing throughput, and increasing the enterprise's bandwidth utilization and costs.

Microsegmentation Deployment Model

The final deployment model is focused on the server-to-server use case, termed *microsegmentation*. This model, as the name implies, approaches the problem from the perspective of *resources* rather than *users*. In fact, as depicted in Figure 3-8, the resources are considered to be the primary subjects (Non-Person Entities, or NPEs) around which policies must be created and enforced. We depict a human subject as well for completeness, and because many of the commercially available solutions support them, but they are typically of secondary importance in this model.

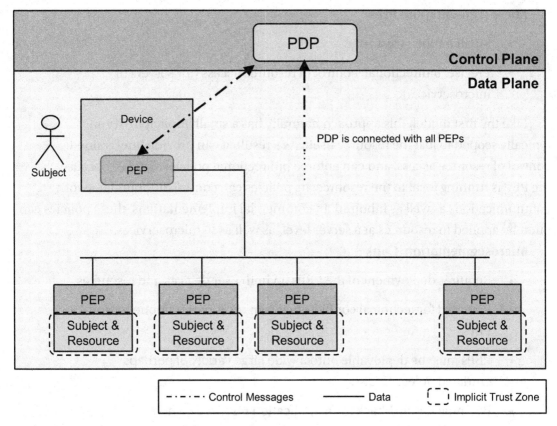

Figure 3-8. *Microsegmentation Deployment Model*

This model is actually a variant of the first model we discussed earlier—the resource-based model—with the important difference that the resources are in fact also subjects (authenticated identities). This has significant implications on the policy model and the PEP enforcement capabilities, as well as on the resource discovery and visualization capabilities that commercial implementations typically provide.

Generally, the NPE subjects will have weaker forms of identity than human subjects—often certificate-based, and obviously based on a single authentication factor.[11] Most frequently, this certificate is generated and managed by the enterprise's certificate authority (PKI).

---

[11]Although you could argue that the fact that they are deployed on enterprise-controlled infrastructure is itself an additional factor.

Microsegmentation: Pros

- Small implicit trust zone

- Precise, bidirectional, control of resource access (for servers or microservices)

Like the first model, this approach naturally has a small implicit trust zone, typically scoped to just the resource itself. As a result, it can provide fine-grained control of resource access, and can enforce bidirectional policies. That is, because the PEP is running local to the resource, its policies can control outbound network communications as well as inbound. In commercial implementations, these policies can often be applied to resources at a server level, as well as to microservices.

Microsegmentation: Cons

- Requires deployment of the PEPs on both user devices and resources.

- Potential for technical conflicts between resource components and PEPs.

- PEPs must be deployable onto a wide large variety of perhaps outdated or legacy OSs.

- Potential for pushback from application resource owners.

- Requires a 1:1: relationship between PEPs and Resources.

- May not be well suited to user-to-resource access.

- No remote access is built in; it requires direct access to PEPs by subjects.

This approach faces the same set of cons as the first model—namely, the deployment and management of PEPs onto every resource requiring protection—so we won't repeat the discussion here. It also has one more possible downside, which is that a vendor (or open source) implementation focused on this area may have functional or architectural shortcomings associated with the user-to-service scenario. This may or may not be the case for any specific implementation, but you should definitely include this in your list of evaluation criteria.

Summary

While the basic concepts of Policy Decision Points and Policy Enforcement Points have been floating around the industry for a number of years, their usage within a Zero Trust security model is relatively new. We encourage you to use this approach to color and inform your thinking and architecture, and drive your requirements and priorities. In order to do this, it's important for you to start thinking about the existing components in your enterprise security architecture as PEPs in your nascent Zero Trust architecture. This book is designed for that purpose—to help you consider them from the perspective of the functions they perform, rather than as distinct components that happen to perform a set of functions. This is somewhat akin to the saying "people don't want quarter-inch drill bits, they want quarter-inch holes"—focusing on the value rather than the means of achieving it.

Bringing this back to security—instead of thinking "I need a firewall," you should be thinking "I need a Policy Enforcement Point that can control network traffic, and a way to define that policy across my infrastructure." Or, from another angle—instead of thinking "I need to deploy an IDS here to examine my web app traffic for SQL injections," you should be thinking "I need to make sure that the web application traffic is scanned for SQL injections before it is processed by the app. I have several PEPs in my architecture that may be able to accomplish this goal." This shift in thinking should help you in your journey.

This chapter provided a lot of background information on Zero Trust architectures—we introduced and examined a representative enterprise architecture, discussed a generalized Zero Trust architecture, briefly introduced a policy model, and explored several different Zero Trust deployment models. In the next chapter, we'll look at three case studies, examining how these enterprises approached Zero Trust in practice.

CHAPTER 4

Zero Trust in Practice

Now that we've introduced the principles of Zero Trust and examined several models, let's look at some real-world examples of Zero Trust systems. Two of these—Google's BeyondCorp and the PagerDuty Zero Trust system—have been publicly described, and are good examples of Zero Trust architectures and systems, implemented internally at two very different enterprises with very different approaches.

We can learn a lot from these case studies, even if we can't deploy a Zero Trust architecture that matches either one of these. Because those first two examples have been well-documented, we'll focus our efforts on contrasting their perspectives, goals, and trade-offs through the lens of the Zero Trust principles and architectures that we've just introduced. Our third example is an enterprise that used the Software-Defined Perimeter architecture to successfully achieve Zero Trust, which will help us examine the benefits of that approach. Let's dive in and look at our first case study, the internal Google project that is arguably responsible for much of the industry attention on Zero Trust.

Google's BeyondCorp

BeyondCorp, Google's internal name for their network security transformation initiative, is a remarkable achievement, and one that deservedly has had significant influence on the industry. Not only did Google reinvent their internal security architecture and provide network access controls for tens of thousands of users, they also publicly documented this in a series of USENIX *;login:* articles, starting in 2014 and continuing across six articles through 2018.[1]

---

[1] See `https://research.google/pubs/` and search for "BeyondCorp."

© Jason Garbis and Jerry W. Chapman 2021
J. Garbis and J. W. Chapman, *Zero Trust Security*, https://doi.org/10.1007/978-1-4842-6702-8_4

These well-written and thorough articles have had outsized influence on the industry, and it's important for us to give Google credit for promoting the concepts behind Zero Trust. We encourage you to read the original articles—we're providing just a brief overview here. Basically, Google created and implemented a complex Zero Trust system over multiple years, at large scale. In their words, they created "a new model that dispenses with a privileged corporate network. Instead, access depends solely on device and user credentials, regardless of a user's network location...All access to enterprise resources is fully authenticated, fully authorized, and fully encrypted based upon device state and user credentials."[2]

The end result of their journey is that the corporate network grants no inherent trust—all access is granted on identity, device, and authentication, based on robust underlying device and identity data sources. Effectively, they replaced *inherent* trust in the network with *earned* trust in the device—they have a true Zero Trust network, and all internal apps are accessed via the BeyondCorp system, regardless of whether the user is in a Google office or working remotely. They also chose to permit access from managed devices only—unmanaged and BYOD devices do not have access to internal applications. It's important to note also that this project was solely focused on controlling user-to-server access, not server-to-server.

These design decisions had several implications for the project—in particular, it's very dependent on high-quality data around device inventory, and to support this, they built a sophisticated device inventory database. They rely on corporate-issued certificates stored in each device's Trusted Platform Module (TPM) as a root of trust, and also utilize a centralized identity system with SSO, which issues short-lived access tokens. Their identity management system is used for group and role information of users, providing their policy decision points with identity context. And their identity system is tied to HR processes, so it's reliable and up-to-date. The BeyondCorp infrastructure components are shown in Figure 4-1.

---

[2]"BeyondCorp: A New Approach to Enterprise Security,";*login: December 2014, Vol. 39, No. 6*

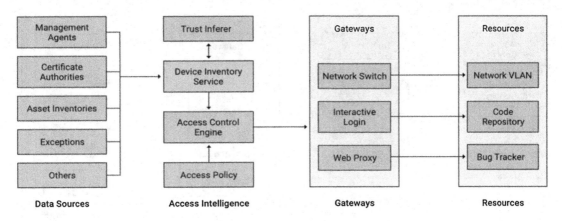

Figure 4-1. *BeyondCorp Infrastructure Components*[3]

The key elements in BeyondCorp are as follows. First, the Data Sources correspond (logically) to the external data sources depicted in the Zero Trust models in Chapter 3. The Resources, of course, correspond to the resources in our model (and are what NIST terms Enterprise Resources). Google has taken an interesting hybrid approach with the other two sections. Effectively, their *Access Intelligence* components make up the Policy Decision Point (PDP), and their *Gateways* comprise the Policy Enforcement Point (PEP)—however, their Access Control Engine is also technically part of their PEP. Their resources may also act as Application PEPs, enforcing fine-grained access, depending on the application. We depict this overlaid view in Figure 4-2, which combines Figure 4-1 with the Zero Trust architectural components that we introduced in Chapter 3.

---

[3]BeyondCorp: Design to Deployment at Google, :login; Spring 2016 Vol. 41, No. 1.

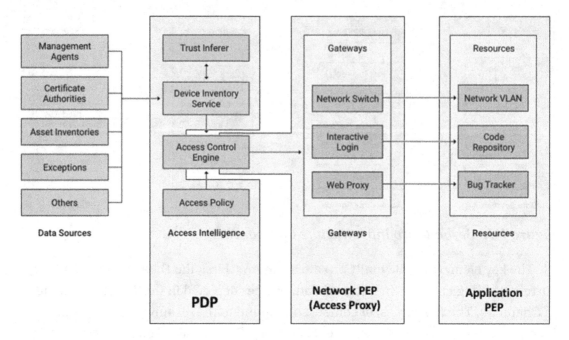

Figure 4-2. *Annotated BeyondCorp Infrastructure Components*

The BeyondCorp Access Proxy (made up of the Gateways and part of the Access Control Engine) acts as a PEP that's globally accessible to both remote and on-premises users. The system utilizes multiple data sources to establish a trust level, with dynamic enforcement within the Access Proxy at the time of access. This is a great example of dynamic behavior, and well aligned with the NIST tenets—for example, policies using group membership and device attributes. Google's articles describe the Access Control Engine making decisions on a per-request basis. This is interesting—one of two areas in which the BeyondCorp implementation blurs the lines between some of the components that are logically distinct in the Zero Trust architecture model (this is common—we'll likewise see some blurry lines later in this chapter when we talk about the Software-Defined Perimeter).

Google describes the Access Proxy as providing coarse-grained enforcement at the front end, with authorization enforced at the back end (within the resource), although the Google articles do not specify to what degree the application PEPs are tied into the access policy, or to data sources such as IAM. It's interesting to note that their on-premises Network Access Control system uses dynamic VLAN assignment based on device certificates, to distinguish managed devices from unmanaged devices. Although very coarse-grained, this is an effective way of integrating their 802.1x-based NAC into their Zero Trust network.[4]

BeyondCorp is also interesting because it combines the enclave-based model with the resource-based model. The Access Proxy uses HTTP headers to propagate additional security metadata to the resources being accessed. The beauty of using HTTP headers to propagate this metadata is that it's silently ignored by any resources that are not expecting it, or cannot process it. This approach reduced the effort required to roll this out across many hundreds of applications at Google—making it possible for most applications to be onboarded without change while optionally enabling the use of this data for improved security in some applications. Note that this approach actually mixes control messages into the data plane. This isn't "wrong"—it's a smart design choice that makes a lot of sense within the BeyondCorp architecture, and serves as an example of the ways in which the conceptual Zero Trust model can be adapted across many different implementation architectures.

The Google team freely admits that BeyondCorp was a complicated, comprehensive, multi-year deployment and organizational transition. Part of the reason was the sheer scale and complexity inherent in Google's organization and network. Another aspect was that this team was, quite simply, a pioneer—inventing, learning, making mistakes, and iterating throughout the process. The good news for the rest of the security industry is that they've shared so much about their implementation, and that as a whole, we've created an ecosystem of commercial and open source tools, technologies, platforms, and approaches that help enterprises quickly achieve many of the same benefits, based on more structured, predictable, and repeatable approaches.

This leads us to the next, obvious question—*Can I deploy BeyondCorp for my organization?* The answer to this is "No, and Yes." Clearly, BeyondCorp is an internal Google program and platform, and it's not available for licensing or re-use. Their published articles explain how deeply integrated BeyondCorp is embedded as part of Google's enterprise architecture, technical infrastructure, and HR processes. So, if your question is *"Can I deploy the BeyondCorp platform for my organization?"* the answer is "no." But a better question is *"Can I deploy a security system that provides similar benefits to BeyondCorp for my organization?"* for which the answer is a resounding "yes."

---

[4]We discuss NAC and 802.1x later, in Chapter 7.

There are numerous commercial and open source Zero Trust solutions available for use, which are designed to deliver these benefits. Educating and preparing you for this initiative is of course the primary goal of this book.

In fact, Google has commercialized some elements of BeyondCorp—not the entire platform, but some elements—and made them available as part of their Google Cloud Platform (GCP) via the Identity-Aware Proxy and BeyondCorp Enterprise services. We anticipate that Google will continue to innovate and add new capabilities to their commercial offering over time, so they bear consideration as part of your Zero Trust evaluation.

If you're interested in the details and thought processes of the Google team—in much more depth than we have covered here—we encourage you to read the original BeyondCorp articles. Next, we'll look at another internal enterprise Zero Trust implementation, from a very different perspective.

PagerDuty's Zero Trust Network

The PagerDuty case study, which was first publicized in the well-regarded *Zero Trust Networks* book,[5] provides a solid contrast to the BeyondCorp example. First and foremost, PagerDuty's network is focused on securing server-to-server access, compared to BeyondCorp's focus on the user-to-server scenario. Second, rather than protecting access to resources running on an enterprise network, PagerDuty needed to secure access between resources running on multiple public cloud environments. Because these disparate cloud platforms provided a wide variety of security capabilities (ranging from good to poor), their Zero Trust system simplified things by acting as a normalization layer. We've seen Zero Trust systems within enterprises provide a similar positive effect, simplifying operations and configuration via a uniform policy model across multiple heterogeneous and hybrid environments.

The PagerDuty system is heavily reliant upon their configuration management system, which was in place prior to their Zero Trust initiative, to automate and control their virtual servers. This was an important foundation for them—it served as the "source of truth" for all their resources and also as an automation platform. Effectively, this is a combination of the Policy Decision Point and the control channel. What's interesting to note about this is its parallel with BeyondCorp, where the source of truth

---

[5]Evan Gilman and Doug Barth, *Zero Trust Networks* (O'Reilly, 2017)

was a combination of their rigorous device management system and their identity systems. Server-to-Sever Zero Trust systems do tend to require a solid Configuration Management Database (or rely on network discovery capabilities) in order to have an authoritative resource catalog. In contrast, user-to-server systems generally rely on identity management as their authoritative systems.

PagerDuty's model uses a central PDP, based on their configuration management and automation system.[6] They have a distributed set of PEPs, which actually use local *iptables* firewall rules on hosts, giving them a consistent mechanism for enforcement across disparate cloud environments. This approach should seem familiar—it's essentially the microsegmentation deployment model from Chapter 3. In this case, the built-in host-based local firewalls act as the PEPs, under the direction of their configuration system (the PDP). Their platform uses a mesh of IPsec connections between all servers on their network, in order to obtain network privacy.

This model and architecture by all accounts worked well for PagerDuty, although it was not without hiccups, as would be expected in any newly built and complex system. They haven't shared a great deal of detail about their policy model, but essentially they assign each server a role, which controls access rules, and all servers in a given role have identical configurations. This approach makes sense for a server-to-server environment—servers are very different from user devices because they're generally deployed into fixed locations, and are 100% under the control of the enterprise. That is, a well-run system—especially one driven by an automated config system such as Chef—will have complete control over each server's image, configuration, and network. This stands in sharp contrast to user devices, which are typically mobile, run on untrusted networks and in untrusted environments, and are often a "wild west" of arbitrary and unique configurations. (BYOD makes user-to-server access control even more challenging).

We commend PagerDuty for their innovation, and want to thank Evan and Doug for sharing it with us in their book. This was a successful initiative for PagerDuty, and an interesting contrast to the design decisions and problem space compared with BeyondCorp, given their different focus on the server-to-server use case. We especially like their approach of defining policies based on data from within their configuration management system, to be read in, evaluated, and rendered into firewall rulesets enforced by the PDPs. Policies that use target resource metadata as input is a common (and recommended) pattern, which we explore in depth in Chapter 17.

---

[6]Initially they used Chef, but later they transitioned this to a separate system.

The Software-Defined Perimeter and Zero Trust

The Software-Defined Perimeter (SDP) is an open security architecture, initially published by the Cloud Security Alliance in 2014, and enhanced with additional related publications.[7] The architecture itself is new, but is composed of well-proven security elements. In fact, the team who authored this original SDP specification drew from their experiences securing classified ("high-side") networks in the US intelligence community.

SDP is designed to solve multiple problems in enterprise security, and has much in common with the goals of BeyondCorp and the principles of Zero Trust that we've introduced already: "SDPs require endpoints to authenticate and be authorized first before obtaining network access to protected servers. Then, encrypted connections are created in real time between requesting systems and application infrastructure."[8] SDP has many potential uses, including identity-driven network access control, network microsegmentation, and secure remote access (for a full list, see the *Software-Defined Perimeter Architecture Guide*[9]).

SDP is an architecture, with multiple deployment models (and with multiple commercial implementations available). These deployment models largely align with the Zero Trust models described in Chapter 3, and the Zero Trust concepts. The high-level SDP conceptual model is shown in Figure 4-3, depicting the Client-to-Gateway SDP deployment model, which is most relevant for our discussions here.[10]

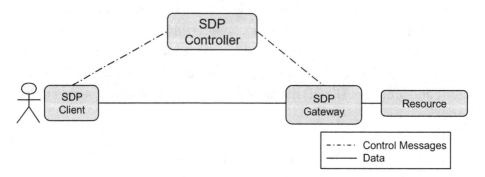

Figure 4-3. *Software-Defined Perimeter Architecture*

---

[7]One of this book's co-authors, Jason, is currently Co-chair of the SDP Zero Trust Working Group at the CSA. He joined the working group in 2015, after the publication of the initial specification.

[8]Software-Defined Perimeter Specification 1.0, Cloud Security Alliance, 2014

[9]Software-Defined Perimeter Architecture Guide, Cloud Security Alliance, 2019

[10]For an introduction to all the SDP deployment models, see the Software-Defined Perimeter Architecture Guide.

There are several things to note. First, like Zero Trust, SDP relies on distinct *Control* and *Data* Channels. The SDP Controller acts as a Zero Trust Policy Decision Point, and the SDP Gateways are Policy Enforcement Points. You'll immediately notice that this SDP model is essentially identical to the enclave-based Zero Trust model introduced in Chapter 3. This is not a coincidence; the NIST Zero Trust team leveraged ideas and approaches from SDP as they created their architecture document.

SDP requires two security components that we believe should be included in every Zero Trust deployment—*Mutual TLS Communications*[11] and *Single-Packet Authorization*, which we'll discuss next.

Mutual TLS Communications

Mutual TLS Communications, or *mTLS*, is simply an approach that requires both the client (connection initiator) and the server (connection acceptor) to validate each other's certificates. This is a significant improvement compared with standard TLS (such as that initiated by a browser connection to a web server), in which only the client validates the server's certificate, but not the reverse.

mTLS provides significantly improved security for the system, essentially eliminating the possibility of a Man-In-The-Middle attack and enabling secure communications even across the most untrustworthy of networks. Of course, it relies upon the establishment of a mutual root of trust for the communicating parties—a Certificate Authority that both components trust, for issuing the certificates. Mutual authentication such as mTLS must be present in Zero Trust implementations, as a foundational element for secure communications.

Single-Packet Authorization

TCP/IP is a fundamentally open network protocol, designed to facilitate the easy connectivity and reliable communications between distributed computing nodes. It has served us well, in terms of enabling our hyper-connected world, but—for a variety of

---

[11]SDP specifies that using IPSec via IKE with mutual authentication is also acceptable.

reasons—doesn't include security as part of its core capabilities.[12] Interestingly, much of the discussion and debate about network security focuses on encryption, rather than another gap—the "connect before authenticate" model.

By design, any device that can exchange IP network packets with any other device can establish a TCP connection, as long as the listening device has what's termed an *open port*. This occurs via TCP's somewhat famous three-way handshake. From a security perspective, the most important thing to understand is that this connection establishment occurs purely at a network layer, with no identity, authentication, or authorization. The beauty of this model is that it enables anyone with a browser to easily connect to any public web server on the planet, and be served up a web page, without requiring any upfront registration or permission. This is a perfect approach for a public web server, but a terrible approach for a private application, and a horrendous idea for an entry point with broad access to enterprise networks. And yet, this is exactly how enterprise VPNs operate—with open ports, inviting malicious users to connect and exploit vulnerabilities. Sadly, this is not a theoretical vulnerability—attackers have successfully achieved this time and time again,[13] and successfully breached enterprise networks in large part due to the open nature of TCP.

SDP overcomes this weakness through the clever use of a one-time password algorithm based on a shared key, in what's called *Single-Packet Authorization (SPA)*. Essentially, the systems use an OTP generated by an algorithm,[14] and embed the current password in the initial network packet sent from the client to the Server. The SDP specification mentions using the SPA packet after a TCP connection has been established, while the open source implementation from the creators of SPA[15] uses a UDP packet prior to the TCP connection. Commercial SDP implementations may take either approach.

---

[12]For a fascinating and nuanced analysis of the history of the Internet and its security challenges, we recommend the Washington Post eBook *The Threatened Net: How the Web Became a Perilous Place* (in particular, Part I). The talented and dedicated people who invented these internetworking protocols deserve tremendous credit for creating something amazing with very limited technology in the 1960s and 1970s. Building in encryption would have been technically impossible, given the limited compute capacity of the time, and even now, 50 years later, there's no good, general solution to the key distribution problem.

[13]Here's just one recent example: www.zdnet.com/article/iranian-hackers-have-been-hacking-vpn-servers-to-plant-backdoors-in-companies-around-the-world/.

[14]SDP uses RFC 4226—HOTP: An HMAC-Based One-Time Password Algorithm: https://tools.ietf.org/html/rfc4226.

[15]See www.cipherdyne.org/blog/2012/09/single-packet-authorization-the-fwknop-approach.html.

In either case, the effect is dramatic, especially with UDP-based SPA—the servers in question become invisible to unauthorized clients. Clients that do not present a valid HOTP are unable to establish a TCP connection, and (depending on the implementation) won't receive any acknowledgement that there's even a server listening on the port. Authorized clients—who have the shared key—can generate a valid HOTP, and the server will permit the establishment of a TCP connection (followed, of course, by an mTLS connection). SPA has an added benefit—it's very computationally lightweight for servers to evaluate and reject unauthorized clients. It consumes orders of magnitude fewer server resources to evaluate a 64-bit HOTP in a UDP packet, versus examining authentication after establishing a TCP and TLS connection. This makes SPA-protected servers more resilient to DDoS attacks.

Finally, keep in mind that while SPA is an excellent first line of defense, it's only the first layer. After SPA, which is used to prove that the client possesses the shared secret, the SDP system still requires the establishment of a mutual TLS connection with certificate validation, and identity authentication prior to permitting access to any protected resource.

SDP is a sound architecture, which aligns well with Zero Trust. That is, you can achieve Zero Trust principles with a solution based on the SDP architecture. Although SDP (as a specification) is limited in scope, there are commercially available SDP implementations that fill in the gaps and provide an enterprise-ready platform. Next, we'll examine how one enterprise used SDP for their Zero Trust journey.

SDP Case Study

In this case study, we'll be exploring how a US-based multinational enterprise approached their Zero Trust journey using SDP. This company, which has been in business since the 1970s, provides consumer-facing services, and has over 14,000 employees worldwide. Frustrated with their traditional security infrastructure and inspired by BeyondCorp, their CISO launched a strategic Zero Trust initiative. His goal was to better secure sensitive customer data, reduce costs, and enable the business to take advantage of new digital platforms for media and customer care.

Their infrastructure was composed of 2 primary data centers (one each in the United States and Europe), 4 US branch offices in addition to headquarters, 8 international regional branch offices, and over 700 retail locations worldwide. The organization supported approximately 2,000 workers in their headquarters office, another 2,000 users total across all 12 regional branch offices, and approximately 10,000 part-time workers in the retail locations. The organization had been embracing IaaS, with several dozen internally built applications migrated from on-premises, which were currently running in production in the cloud.

Their initial IT infrastructure suffered from a number of shortcomings, all of which they intended to address with their strategic adoption of Zero Trust. However, it's important to note that they approached this project incrementally, obtaining nearly immediate value from their efforts. In fact, part of this enterprise's evaluation criteria was the ability for their chosen vendor's security platform to be able to quickly integrate into their existing infrastructure, and be able to smoothly support its evolution to Zero Trust over time. For example, the organization was in the early stages of migrating from an on-premises Active Directory to a cloud-based SAML identity provider, and needed their SDP platform to support both providers concurrently.

A key element of the Zero Trust initiative and vision was to move everyone "off net," and use a distributed set of SDP Gateways (PEPs) across their heterogeneous enterprise infrastructure. The security team evaluated a number of different Zero Trust vendors and solutions, and chose an enterprise-class SDP implementation, following the enclave-based model.

Their initial phase was for a tactical replacement of their aging and troublesome VPN, which was causing connectivity problems and generating complaints across two sets of users. The first group was approximately 750 general corporate users who needed remote access to resources on the company's office network and in the main data center. The second group was around 250 developers, who needed SSH, RDP, and database access to dev, test, and production resources running in an IaaS cloud environment. Even though this initial deployment utilized simple, wide-open policies, it still provided immediate benefits by improving the user experience, increasing connectivity speeds, and gave the security and network teams confidence and experience with their Zero Trust platform. It also gave the developers concurrent access to multiple IaaS accounts and locations while maintaining security.

Once this phase had been successfully rolled out, the security team began using group membership from their cloud-based identity provider to limit access for corporate users on the network. They devised just a few basic roles, including General Employee, IT, Finance, Network Admin, and Database Admin. All employees received access to standard services (e.g., DNS, print, file shares), while the other groups granted access to resources specific to each role.

Next, they began removing their 2,000 regional branch office workers from the enterprise network, shifting things so that all their access was controlled by Zero Trust policies. Essentially, all the network and security software, hardware, and cabling that had been deployed into these 12 branch offices were removed, replaced with commodity business broadband Internet and Wi-Fi. Because the vast majority of their production systems were housed in a single data center in the Northeast United States, and corporate users already needed a secure tunnel to that data center to access business applications, they were able to leverage already in-place security software performing IDS and SWG functions for users' Internet-bound traffic in the data center. This had an additional side benefit of reducing their infrastructure and communications costs by over $500,000 annually.

For each of their branch offices, they deployed a local SDP Gateway (Zero Trust PEP), which enabled users to access local file shares, controlled by policy. With their SDP system architecture, users obtained a direct, secure connection to the local PEP for access to these file shares. This architecture enabled in-office user traffic for the file share to remain wholly on the local network.

Like all organizations, this one was significantly impacted by the onset of the COVID-19 pandemic in early 2020. All of their 700+ worldwide retail locations, with over 10,000 part-time employees, had to be closed temporarily. Prior to COVID, these retail workers connected via the in-store local wireless network, which in turn connected them to centralized application servers through a site-to-site VPN from each store to the main corporate data center. The security and network team quickly pivoted, and deployed the SDP client onto all these workers' devices, which were a combination of corporate-managed and BYOD devices. These part-time users were immediately able to begin working from home, and support the organization as it rapidly shifted to providing their services virtually. One interesting benefit for this organization was that they were then able to begin the process of decommissioning the 700+ site-to-site VPNs, since now all user access occurred via the secure SDP tunnels. This is anticipated to generate additional cost savings for them, as another side benefit.

The next step for this organization in their Zero Trust journey is to begin deploying the SDP client onto their Linux servers, using the microsegmentation deployment model for better access control across their server environments.

Overall, this organization has obtained clear and compelling benefits, both security and financial, from adopting Zero Trust through a Software-Defined Perimeter architecture. Their corporate environment is much more secure, as all users are "off net" and the entry points into their enterprise network are cloaked from unauthorized users. The pandemic had almost no impact on their full-time corporate users, since by that point, nearly all of them were using the Zero Trust solution, and were, from a network perspective, already always "remote."

Zero Trust and Your Enterprise

Despite the first two case studies depicting internally-developed platforms, we want to make it clear that most enterprises, especially in today's Zero Trust security market, follow the approach taken by the organization in the SDP case study. That is, they license and use commercial software, rather than implementing it themselves the way that Google and PagerDuty did. As a sophisticated, highly profitable, and technically advanced organization, Google is clearly in a league by itself, while PagerDuty's core business and skill sets revolve around running a complex, dynamic network. Perhaps most importantly, these organizations both started their journeys before there were widely available commercial Zero Trust platforms.

Today's world is different. Both of us authors work closely with small, medium, and large enterprises on their Zero Trust approach every day—and they almost without exception look to utilize commercially available or open source security solutions as the core of their platform, rather than build their own. There are a wide variety of capable offerings available today, and enterprises can and should evaluate a combination of platform, best-of-breed, and on-premises, cloud-based, or hybrid models.

Also note that this book is not the right vehicle to analyze or critique vendor or open source offerings—these products and platforms are constantly changing as vendors introduce new products and innovations, or acquire complementary technology. But this book *is* the right vehicle to provide you with a solid foundation of Zero Trust principles, an understanding of how it can be deployed in your environment, and a set of requirements from which you can draw, shape, and consolidate. Ultimately, the requirements in this book will enable you to make the right decisions for your enterprise.

Summary

In this chapter, we explored three different Zero Trust implementation case studies, each providing a unique perspective on Zero Trust. Google's internal BeyondCorp not only secured their enterprise but, thanks to the stellar efforts of the team to publish their experiences, had a significant and positive impact on the industry. The PagerDuty case study provided another perspective on how a service and network-centric organization met their server-to-server security challenges. Finally, we introduced the Software-Defined Perimeter, an open architecture that delivers on Zero Trust principles. After describing how SDP works, we presented a case study on an organization that used this architecture to provide security and operational benefits across their multinational enterprise. All three of these examples provide practical guidance and visionary elements that show how Zero Trust security has been an integral part of these different types of organizations. They should serve as inspiration, and be a source of ideas for how your organization can proceed on its Zero Trust journey.

PART II

Zero Trust and Enterprise Architecture Components

In Part I of the book, we introduced the history and background of Zero Trust, compared a representative enterprise architecture with a Zero Trust architecture, and explored three different Zero Trust case studies. In Part II, we'll be examining the major functional areas of IT and security infrastructure through our Zero Trust lens. For each, we'll be discussing its goals and functions, and exploring how these should change and be integrated into your new Zero Trust world.

As we go through this analysis, we'd like you to think about this from the perspective of how Zero Trust can be adopted within your enterprise. Identify the technical and nontechnical constraints within your organization that could prove to be impediments, and think about how to overcome them. And, make certain you understand the implications of Zero Trust on networks, management systems, and infrastructure. If you do those things, you'll be well prepared for your journey to Zero Trust.

CHAPTER 5

Identity and Access Management

Identity and Access Management (IAM) is a broad area within information security, comprising both the technical and business process aspects of controlling access by providing the right access at the right time to the right person. In many ways, identity—and a reasonably well-run identity management program—is the key to success with a Zero Trust program. Zero Trust at its heart provides an identity-centric approach to security, and therefore understanding and managing identity is an incredibly important factor in any Zero Trust program. And yet, organizations should not and cannot hold themselves to an unreasonable standard, or require perfection from their identity teams and systems before embarking on their Zero Trust journey.

Identity management systems should serve as the authoritative source of information about identities (person and non-person entities) and be used as the "keystone" system for many technical integrations as well as business processes. This is not easy—today's enterprises are complex, and may not have a single, centralized identity system. That's okay, and should not be seen as an impediment to adopting Zero Trust. In fact, Zero Trust, by its very nature as an overlay system, can help bridge the gaps between multiple identity systems. We'll be discussing this a bit later in this chapter, in the *IAM and Zero Trust* section. But first we'll provide a review of the primary components of IAM, which are foundational for discussions about Zero Trust throughout the book.

© Jason Garbis and Jerry W. Chapman 2021
J. Garbis and J. W. Chapman, *Zero Trust Security*, https://doi.org/10.1007/978-1-4842-6702-8_5

IAM in Review

While every identity management system is different, based on the unique combination of each enterprise and its chosen set of technologies, identity management systems do contain common elements, depicted in Figure 5-1. Let's explore each of the areas, for a tour across the breadth of IAM programs.[1]

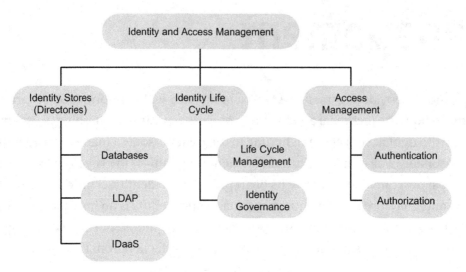

Figure 5-1. *Identity Management System Scope*

Identity Stores (Directories)

The core element of any identity management system is its identity store, often referred to as a *Directory* (more formally, a *Directory Service*). This is logically where the authoritative information about entities[2] are stored—attributes that describe the entity and provide meaningful data about the entity intended for use by human and automated consumers of this information.

---

[1]Note that some organizations refer to this as ICAM—Identity, Credential, and Access Management.

[2]Directories store entities and attributes. Keep in mind that entities can be (human) users, as well as non-person entities such as servers or services, which will also be authenticating and receiving authorizations. We discussed this briefly in Chapter 3.

Directories began to be formalized in the late 1980s, driven partially by enterprise IT adoption of PC-based local area networks. These directories existed to authenticate users for network access, serving as a searchable and authoritative list of information about users. This included user credentials, making directories a centralized, and centrally managed, source against which users were authenticated.

We think it's fair to state that it's from this core directory function that the entire modern IAM ecosystem has grown. Like many areas, it's also become more standards-based as it has matured. For directories, this process began with the X.500 specification to store entity information, with initial connectivity through the Directory Access Protocol (DAP). This was not based on TCP/IP networking and was very complex for clients to utilize, which resulted in limited adoption. In response, a "lighter" version of DAP was created: Lightweight Directory Access Protocol (LDAP), which we discuss shortly.

Directories, and the identity management systems that surround them, have clearly grown in capability and scope over the past few decades. Today's directories support many different and complex scenarios, including metadirectories and federated directories, which tie together multiple disparate directories (albeit in different ways). Next, we introduce the three primary types of directories in use today.

Databases

Databases can, technically, provide a centralized identity store which can be accessed across a network. However, most modern enterprises have steered away from using raw databases as their directories for a number of reasons. Giving remote applications database access to user information (especially credentials) is not good design, even if it's read-only.

Ultimately, even standards-based directories do, of course, rely on an underlying database. But there is a significant difference between raw database access, and standardized protocols and APIs for interacting with directories. These types of customized identity stores must be avoided and if in place should be retired as part of a Zero Trust initiative.

LDAP

Lightweight Directory Access Protocol (LDAP) is a protocol specification, defining a set of messages (effectively an API) for interacting with directory services across a network. LDAP is a well-established standard, outlined in a series of RFCs from the

Internet Engineering Task Force (IETF).[3] LDAP v3, initially published in 1997, has been a very successful standard, in the sense that many directory providers (both open source and commercial) support the protocol, and components from different vendors can successfully interoperate.

LDAP provides a straightforward API for operations against the set of entities in the directory, and is also very commonly used to authenticate users' credentials (passwords). LDAP is very widely deployed and supported today, with broad support across identity, security, application, and infrastructure vendors. For example, Microsoft's Active Directory—arguably the most widely deployed directory in the industry—supports an LDAP API.

While we anticipate that LDAP-enabled directories and applications will be running successfully for a very long time, we do believe that newer, standards-based authentication and authorization protocols will supplant LDAP over time. In particular, LDAP requires direct API calls to the directory, while modern protocols support indirect token-based mechanisms that are better suited to today's distributed environment. Having said that, it's likely that your enterprise will continue to have one or more LDAP-based directories in place, and your Zero Trust platform must be able to interact with these services without requiring them to change. There's nothing inherently wrong with continuing to use LDAP, as long as it meets your functional needs.

Identity-as-a-Service

The shift to cloud-based services has of course included identity management vendors, resulting in a successful and rapidly growing industry segment known as Identity-as-a-Service (IDaaS). These vendors provide cloud-based directories, which relieve organizations from having to operate on-premises directory servers, provide a modern web-based UI, and deliver end-user-friendly features such as Single Sign On (SSO) and, increasingly, passwordless authentication.

These services typically provide both newer APIs such as SAML and older APIs such as LDAP and RADIUS. These services are well positioned for continued growth, as the acceptance and maturity of cloud-based security services grow. Note that in many cases, these vendors provide on-premises software (agents) to perform specific functions, including federation or data replication, and integration with legacy directories and authentication schemes.

---

[3]See https://tools.ietf.org/html/rfc4510 for the IETF's "roadmap" overview document.

Ultimately, every organization will have one (and often multiple) identity stores. Zero Trust systems must integrate with them, and embrace the reality of organizations needing a way to standardize and normalize across multiple disparate identity stores. This is especially true when securing access for third parties, with their own identity stores. We'll explore this further when we discuss *Authentication* within the *Access Management* section of this chapter. Before that, we want to talk about the identity lifecycle, another important part of IAM.

Identity Lifecycle

Every identity has a lifecycle, whether it's explicitly and formally defined, or not. Identities are created, they exist for a period of time, they potentially have different roles over time, and eventually they are destroyed. Organizations need to have technical tools and business/IT processes to manage and control identity lifecycles. These areas within IAM, known as Lifecycle Management and Identity Governance, are indirectly part of a Zero Trust initiative.

Lifecycle Management

When we talk about human users, we typically refer to the identity lifecycle as being made up of "Joiners, Movers, and Leavers."[4] A human entity (user) typically goes through the lifecycle depicted in Figure 5-2. This includes provisioning of "birthright" privileges, which provides the access that's automatically assigned when every user (*Joiner*) is first added to the corporate directory. Of course, users typically receive access rights beyond these, which should be assigned based on role. Organizations do need to be cautious about assigning overly broad permissions to users, especially making the mistake of using an existing user's rights as a template for new users (the "make Sally look like Jimmy" problem). This will result in users with more access than necessary, potentially creating security and compliance issues. A well-run identity management program will avoid this problem through roles and identity governance, as we discuss shortly.

---

[4]It's generally preferable to refer to employees as "joining" and "leaving," rather than being "created" and "destroyed."

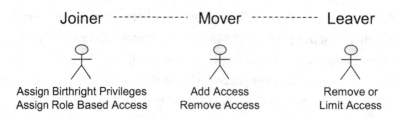

Figure 5-2. *The User Identity Lifecycle*

As a user moves (*Mover)* through an organization, either laterally or hierarchically, their access will change, as they are granted additional access as part of their new role. Adding access is straightforward—there are obvious triggers for this, as the user will require (and demand) access in order to do their new job. Removing access is more subtle, especially since there is typically a transition period where a user needs both new and old access. Because this period may span weeks or months, there need to be business processes in place to track and manage this (this is typically part of an identity governance program).

Users in the final lifecycle phase are known as *Leavers*. This phase can be initiated for a number of reasons, including planned voluntary departure (leaving for another job or retiring) or involuntary departure (immediate termination). In many cases, users will exist in an identity management system for a period of time, for example, so managers can access the departed employee's email. In some cases, departed users may exist in systems and retain certain access for extended periods of time (e.g., to be able to access personal payroll, insurance, or tax records), or even indefinitely (such as a *student* transitioning to an *alumnus* of an educational institution).

An identity management system needs to manage, and ideally automate, the assignment, provisioning, and deprovisioning of user access based on these lifecycle events. Most organizations do a good job at HR and payroll onboarding and offboarding. However, the associated IT processes often lag behind in maturity and effectiveness. For example, anecdotally, it's uncommon for people to continue to be paid after they depart an organization. However, it's quite common for users to retain access to IT systems (especially for SaaS applications) after they depart.

Managing non-human accounts (service accounts) requires a slightly different type of diligence, as these systems are typically disconnected from any obvious external or HR-driven triggers, such as hiring or firing. Service accounts are simply accounts that are created for servers or infrastructure code to use, rather than for human users.[5] These non-human access mechanisms can include not only accounts but other access control mechanisms such as API keys or certificates.

Like regular user accounts, these accounts have privileges and roles associated with them, which must be actively managed. Also like user accounts, these accounts must have only the minimal set of privileges associated with them. This is often more of a challenge for service accounts, since they are often performing system-level activities, and there may not be a robust model in place to limit their privileges in the target system. Too often, these accounts are granted full admin rights, either by necessity or by the need to solve a problem quickly ("Don't worry...we'll fix it later"). And these account credentials are often shared, stored in clear text, and typically not rotated. The clear conclusion is that service accounts must be included in identity governance processes, just as user accounts are, and that Zero Trust systems should be used to enforce access policies for these accounts. Note that Privileged Access Management (PAM) solutions often do have service account vaults and services that can help solve some of these problems. We'll be covering PAM in a later chapter.

Identity Governance

The policies (or, if you will, rules) that determine "who should get access to what" as part of the identity lifecycle discussed previously is termed *identity governance*, and is another part of the typical scope of IAM programs. Governance is commonly driven by both compliance and security requirements, often with a heavier compliance driver. In many cases, these compliance requirements are centered on financial applications and controls, especially for publicly traded companies.

Vendors in this market have created identity governance products to assist with meeting these compliance requirements, and enterprises typically deploy these solutions as part of their identity governance initiatives. Of course, not all organizations have formal identity governance programs—smaller or unregulated enterprises may not need them. But *all* organizations make decisions about "who should have access to what"—either implicitly or explicitly—as part of the identity lifecycle processes. Ultimately, these decisions will get rendered as changes to underlying software systems—such as changes to user attributes or group memberships in directories, or the creation, deletion, or authorization changes to user accounts within applications.

---

[5]Reusing user credentials for service accounts or in scripts is an exceptionally bad idea.

These access control decisions may be automated by a provisioning system, or may be implemented through manual IT and business processes. In either case, the identity governance policies need to be aligned with Zero Trust policies. We'll explore this topic, and the relationship between these layers in the following text, when we discuss authorization.

Access Management

Access management is at the heart of identity management, and consists of two major components: first, the means by which entities prove that they are who they claim to be, *authentication*, and, second, the model for defining and expressing the set of actions that a given entity is permitted to perform, *authorization*. Let's look at each of these in turn.

Authentication

In this section, we provide a brief introduction to common authentication protocols, mechanisms, standards, and trends. We're doing so in order to explore their relevance within Zero Trust deployments. Let's start with some basic definitions, included for clarity:

- Username/password: Simple authentication, in use for decades. This is the principle of validating *something you know*.

- Multi-Factor Authentication (MFA): The use of more than one authentication factor as part of an authentication process. This often uses a physical token, smartphone app, or biometric mechanism to validate *something you have, or something you are*.

- Step-up authentication: The process of prompting a user for an additional form of authentication, after some event or trigger has taken place. For example, this may be triggered by an already-authenticated user attempting to access a high-value resource. This often uses a form of MFA, since it's predicated on the user already having been authenticated.

- Passwordless authentication: This is a general principle, of using factors other than passwords for initial authentication. We welcome and encourage this change, as it eliminates the well-known risks associated with weak password, password theft, and password reuse. These solutions often use the kinds of mechanisms listed previously under MFA.

Now, let's look at several authentication protocols and mechanisms that are currently in use.

LDAP

We introduced LDAP previously, as it's an API that can be used both as a means of interacting with directories and for authenticating users. From an authentication perspective, the LDAP API includes native support for username and password-based authentication, which is what's commonly used. The LDAP API does include an extension mechanism by which other authentication types can be added, via a challenge-response mechanism. These are frequently used, but are implementation-dependent (non-standardized).

RADIUS

RADIUS is another older authentication protocol—its age clearly shows in its very name; it's an acronym for *Remote Authentication Dial-In User Service*. It was initially created to provide Authentication, Authorization, and Accounting (AAA), essentially precursors to today's Identity Management. While the term AAA isn't in as widespread use today, those themes are clearly part of today's mainstream Identity and Security initiatives.

Despite its age, RADIUS is still widely used in practice today. As part of several official IETF standards (RFCs), it's supported by many vendors, and offers reasonable interoperability between inter-vendor components. Like LDAP, RADIUS has a simple model whereby a RADIUS client (typically called a "network access server") interacts directly with a RADIUS server, to perform authentication on behalf of a principal (usually a user). RADIUS will only return an *accept* or *reject* (potentially after an additional *challenge*, which enables MFA). RADIUS can be used to provide identity context via protocol extension, although we haven't seen this in broad use.

However, RADIUS does support standards-based authentication mechanisms beyond just username and password, and its ability to do so has certainly extended its lifespan. In fact, many modern identity providers offer RADIUS APIs or Gateways, permitting older applications or infrastructure to be integrated into these newer platforms. With this approach, older systems can use the newer MFA or passwordless authentication approaches supported on modern identity platforms, which can be invoked by RADIUS.

SAML

The Security Assertion Markup Language (SAML) grew from a desire and a need within the industry to have a reliable, trusted, and interoperable way to enable Single Sign On (SSO) for users into web applications, especially for web apps from different providers. More formally, SAML defines an XML representation and an HTTP-based protocol, with which web applications ("service providers," in SAML parlance) can consume user authentication and attribute information from a separate Identity Provider (IdP). That is, in addition to authenticating the user, the SAML response data (known as *assertions*) can contain additional information about the user, requested by the web app and supplied by the identity provider.

As a standard, SAML has been a terrific success—with broad acceptance among both identity providers and SaaS and private web apps, enabling a rich marketplace for SSO from Identity-as-a-Service providers. As a straightforward and reliable standard enabling an easily configured trust relationship between web apps and IdPs, it's a great example of a *network effect*, where the value of supporting the standard increases with each additional supporting player. With a wide set of open source toolkits and plug-ins, there's no excuse for web apps not to support SAML. Likewise, Zero Trust solutions must embrace the broad adoption of SAML-enabled identity providers, and support SAML as an authentication mechanism.

SAML provides the ability to support attributes, group memberships, and roles as "claims" within a SAML response. This further enhances the value of using it in conjunction with a Zero Trust environment, as these claims are clearly a primary source of identity context for consumption by Zero Trust policies (essentially, input into RBAC and ABAC access control models).

OAuth2

OAuth2, a standard defined by the IETF,[6] is designed as a mechanism for developers to create authorization protocols so that a third-party application can access a limited set of functions or resources within a web application, on behalf of a user. For example, a user could grant a photo-printing service access to their private photos on a photo-sharing site, without having to share their username and password. More formally, OAuth2 is a

---

[6]OAuth2 is defined in RFC 6749 and 6750.

way for a client to obtain a security token from a trusted token service (typically an IdP), and transmit that token to a relying party for use. Note that fundamentally, this is based on permission granted by the user.

Technically, OAuth2 is an authorization protocol, and not an authentication protocol. OpenID Connect, which we discuss next, is an example of an authentication protocol built on top of OAuth2.

OpenID Connect (OIDC)

OIDC is built on OAuth2 using a JSON Web Token (JWT)[7] as its token. It's designed to add authentication on top of OAuth authorization and is most frequently used by web apps to provide authentication and authorization utilizing the underlying OAuth framework, based on an interoperable REST format. An OIDC token contains trusted claims about the user, for use within the target application (relying party).

Certificate-Based Authentication

From an enterprise identity management perspective, certificates (and their supporting systems) are often used to validate user and device identity—the possession of a valid certificate can positively identify an entity. In practice, for user devices, what this means is that a given user's device has a valid and current certificate installed on it, that this certificate was issued by the organization's own Certificate Authority (part of its Public Key Infrastructure), and that the user can log into the desktop or mobile OS in such a way that the certificate—secured in the OS's local key management system—is accessible to the user's account. Non-user devices, such as servers, or IoT devices, each have their own mechanism by which the owning enterprise can install certificates, and use them for identification and authentication. Finally, some physical identification cards contain enterprise-issued certificates, which are accessed by a user entering a PIN, and utilized as a form of multifactor authentication. Common examples of this are the CAC (Common Access Card) and PIV Card (Personal Identity Verification) used in the US Government and Defense sectors.

---

[7]JWT is an open standard framework defined by RFC 7519 to define claims securely between two parties.

FIDO2

FIDO2 is an emerging standard that is bringing the "passwordless" experience to the end-user community through FIDO Universal Authentication Framework (UAF) and two variants of the Client-to-Authenticator-Protocols (CTAP1 and CTAP2). Through these protocols, which are based on PKI, FIDO2 supports browsers, mobile devices, and hardware fobs as means of authentication.

Mobile and Biometrics

While not authentication standards of course, modern authentication methods increasingly leverage user-friendly and/or mobile device-based technologies for user authentication. End users are comfortable with technology such as fingerprint recognition or facial recognition on their mobile devices, and mobile apps for One Time Password (OTP) generation have generally replaced their hardware token-based variants.

MFA is a big part of Zero Trust, and mobile devices are a reliable and user-friendly way of enforcing a second factor. In fact, given the incredible ease-of-use that consumer-facing applications now provide (such as contactless payment), end users expect the same level of convenience in their enterprise IT systems.

Unfortunately, it's not always easy or simple to achieve this, because enterprise IT is solving a more complex problem than authentication and authorization of a simple, one-time credit card transaction. Enterprise security systems are typically authenticating users, and authorizing access into business or technical applications, for minutes or hours. Enterprise IT is also typically hampered by a more complex network topology, with many constraints. Having said that, these standards and technologies do work well, and we are beginning to see broader acceptance and prioritization of using newer authentication means, and moving away from passwords. Zero Trust security architectures, with their inherently dynamic and holistic scope, and their rich integration capabilities, are helping accelerate this.

Authorization

Authorization is the end goal of access management, which after all is ultimately responsible for mapping from some policy model (technical or business policy) to enforcement points. Done properly, identity management systems provide authoritative characteristics—roles and attributes—that are associated with entities, and have governance policies and processes in place to ensure that these are correct.

Of course, these attributes are only meaningful if there are runtime IT components that can actually enforce these policies correctly. For example, just because Sally is in a directory group named "Astronauts" doesn't mean that she's actually an Astronaut.[8] Likewise, Sally's membership in directory group "ABC123" has no inherent meaning. In both cases, what matters is how the rest of the IT, application, and security system interpret this information, and how it affects Sally's set of accounts and access. In practice, authorization occurs at multiple levels, as depicted in Figure 5-3.

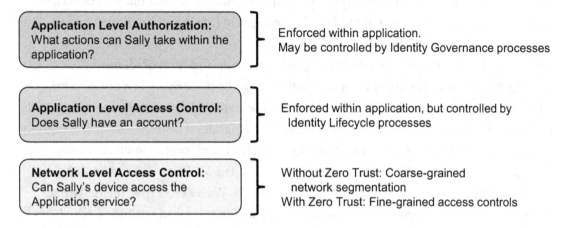

Figure 5-3. *Access Control Levels*

At the top is the application level *authorization* model, controlling what actions our user (Sally, in this case) can perform within the application. This is typically enforced directly within the application,[9] based on the roles or permissions associated with Sally's account. Note that while it's perhaps simplest to think about the "application" as a business application, such as a financial management system, this model is equally applicable if the application in question is more technical, such as a source code repository or database system, or even a completely different type of service, such as an

---

[8]However, we encourage you to try this yourself in your enterprise directory. Please let us know if this works, as we'd be keenly interested in replicating the results.

[9]There are a relatively small number of applications that externalize their authorization model. Even with standards such as XACML, this approach has not gained significant market traction within traditional application architectures. Interestingly, one of the key elements that Zero Trust provides is effectively the externalization of the **network** authorization model. Network infrastructure has a very impoverished authorization model compared to applications, and Zero Trust is a way to replace that with a much richer policy model. We'll be covering this in depth later in the book.

SSH login into a server. In any case, more mature organizations will have a set of identity governance processes, with associated tools, to validate and enforce application level authorization. Less mature organizations will typically do this in a more ad hoc manner based on simple or predefined application roles.

The middle layer can be thought of as the application *account* level—basically controlling application access by the presence or absence of a given user's application account. This layer requires the user to present valid credentials in order to access the application. That is, access is enforced via authentication. Note that many access control solutions operate at this layer, including Single Sign On (SSO) and Privileged Access Management (PAM) solutions.

These first two layers represent the traditional scope and limit of identity management, with a generally clear separation from the underlying layer of *network-level* access control. Without Zero Trust, security or networking teams typically have only been able to enforce access control in a static, coarse-grained fashion—such as assigning users to an entire Virtual LAN (VLAN) comprising hundreds or thousands of hosts, remotely connecting entire networks with WANs such as MPLS or site-to-site VPNs, or giving remote users full network access via user VPNs. With Zero Trust, the network layer can enforce fine-grained access controls, based on roles and attributes, which, in traditional security systems, are only available and effective at the application layer.

As we close out our *IAM in Review* section and transition to talking about Zero Trust and IAM, we want to briefly discuss Role-Based Access Control (RBAC) and Attribute-Based Access Control (ABAC). These are terms that describe the general approach of basing access control on attributes associated with an identity, typically obtained from an identity management system. (Technically, a role can just be considered as a particular kind of attribute, and thus ABAC can be thought of as subsuming RBAC). The "control" part of ABAC refers to the ability of an organization to define access policies which can express logical conditions under which an identity is permitted to access a given resource.

If this sounds familiar, it should—attribute-based policies are exactly what Zero Trust enforces. In fact, we'd argue that Zero Trust architectures are the most effective way to achieve attribute-based access control. Ultimately, ABAC is just a concept which needs to be expressed in a concrete architecture, on a platform which gives organizations a rich vocabulary with which to express these access control policies. It's this policy model—its scope, capability, and effectiveness—that should be at the center of any Zero Trust initiative. We discuss this more next.

Zero Trust and IAM

Now that we have reviewed IAM and its components, we want to examine the why and how of IAM's importance to Zero Trust. Recall that IAM systems are used by the Zero Trust PDP to authenticate entities, and as a source of context (roles and attributes) for making policy decisions. As we discussed previously, we're fortunate that people in our industry have created a variety of standardized authentication APIs and protocols. These have achieved widespread adoption, so much so that we can rely on our identity provider and Zero Trust platform to be able to interoperate. Zero Trust platforms, in addition to using enterprises' existing IAM systems for user authentication, must be able to obtain identity context from them so that PDPs can make access decisions. One again, this underscores why support for standard protocols (LDAP and SAML, in particular) is a requirement for Zero Trust systems.

Note that these principles are true, independent of the Zero Trust deployment model (or models) chosen. In all cases, Zero Trust systems must be integrated with identity systems—this is at the heart of what makes this approach to security so much more effective than traditional approaches. Let's briefly contrast Zero Trust with traditional approaches, which we believe will illustrate not only identity integration and Zero Trust but the overall value of Zero Trust in a nutshell.

Authentication, Authorization, and Zero Trust Integration

Figure 5-4 depicts three scenarios, where a user is accessing some application. In all cases, the user has an account with the application, must authenticate, and has a certain set of privileges that they can perform within the application. For example, if this is a website content management system (CMS), the user may have the ability to edit pages, but not be able to push edited pages into production. However, what's interesting are the differences between the three scenarios from a security and integration perspective.

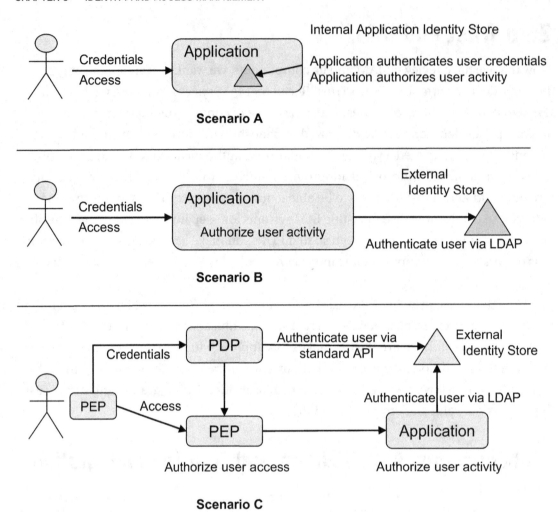

Figure 5-4. *Authentication, Authorization, and Zero Trust*

Scenario A shows a classic, self-contained application, with its own internal identity and credential store. Users authenticate directly within the application, which also enforces user permissions. While this certainly works, and there are countless applications built this way, it suffers from a number of shortcomings. As a standalone and self-contained identity system, it's the definition of a "silo." Not only does custom code such as this often exhibit security vulnerabilities that could be exploited, it also risks being omitted from mover or leaver lifecycle events, resulting in accounts that are still active but unused ("orphaned"). It also may not be using an encrypted network protocol, and may not support MFA.

The application in Scenario B is definitely improved in some ways. Because it uses an external, LDAP-based identity system, it avoids being a silo and will automatically piggyback on the organization's centralized identity governance and lifecycle processes. The LDAP system may also support MFA, improving authentication strength. However, like Scenario A, this application may use an unencrypted network protocol. And, also like Scenario A, this application (and other services running on the same host) is very likely visible to any user on the network. As a high-value application, our web CMS represents an appealing target for an adversary—imagine being able to inject malicious code into an organization's official website!

Scenario C depicts the application within a Zero Trust security framework. While the application still authenticates users against LDAP, network access to the application is now protected by a PEP. This ensures that only authorized users can access that host across the network, making it much more difficult for the adversary to attack. In addition, not only can authorized users access the application remotely, network traffic is encrypted between the user's device and the PEP protecting the application. It's likely that the Zero Trust system can enforce MFA as needed, based on policy and user context. And, depending on the capabilities of the identity and Zero Trust systems, users may even be able to be automatically authenticated into the application via SSO.

Enhancing Legacy System Authentication

One of the interesting and unique aspects of a Zero Trust system is the way in which it can extend the reach and value of authentication systems, which typically have limited scope. Because Zero Trust systems are integrated with identity systems and can enforce policies at the network layer, they enable new ways in which authentication systems can be applied. For example, consider the "legacy" application depicted in Figure 5-5.

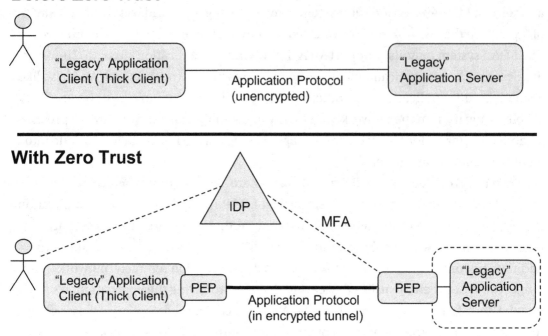

Figure 5-5. *Before and After—Legacy Application Authentication*

In the "before" state, users access this core business application via a thick client, which uses an unencrypted application-specific protocol. Although this traffic is transiting a standard TCP/IP network, and originating from a standard enterprise-managed device, this application traffic is not using modern application protocols (such as HTTPS), and therefore is inaccessible to modern tools and security systems, such as those relying on HTTP headers. And yet, despite being "closed" to security tools, the application sends sensitive business data unencrypted. In addition, this organization is unable to modify this application to make it web- or SAML-friendly.[10] All these factors make it challenging for them to meet their security and compliance requirements of imposing MFA and encrypting network traffic.

In the "with Zero Trust" state, the organization has put in place a modern authentication system. This system acts as the authoritative identity source for both initial user logins and enforcing MFA. While this legacy application isn't connected

---

[10]There may be a number of sensible reasons for this, such as it being a closed-source application not under the organization's control, an internally-built application leveraging using older technologies, or an application which the organization no longer has the expertise to modify.

to the from an identity or primary authentication perspective, the Zero Trust PEP can intercept the user's access to the application, and call out to the IDP to enforce MFA prior to permitting the user's access to proceed. This approach has several significant benefits for the organizations: First, they meet their MFA and encryption requirements. Second, they use the same IDP consistently across the enterprise, thereby providing a simpler user experience and reducing operational complexity. And, the Zero Trust solution allows them to achieve all these goals without making any modifications to the application server or client.

The preceding example, while simple, does illustrate one way in which Zero Trust principles and benefits can be obtained, even with in-place elements of an IT infrastructure that cannot be changed. In particular, as an overlay onto existing networks, Zero Trust architectures are uniquely positioned to bring this kind of value while minimizing disruptive changes. While on the topic of change, let's discuss how Zero Trust systems may be able to help organizations advance their IAM programs.

Zero Trust as Catalyst for Improving IAM

Zero Trust projects are an excellent opportunity for organizations to incrementally improve or significantly transform their identity systems. When approached properly, Zero Trust projects allow organizations to simplify and smooth out their in-place identity systems, or to migrate to more modern and more effective systems.

For example, many larger organizations have multiple incompatible directories in place for authentication and user attributes. These systems may have grown independently over time, perhaps initiated by separate departments with unique requirements for various projects, or perhaps inherited as the result of an acquisition. These may not be limited to directories within a single infrastructure, but could include directories in the cloud, customer identity systems, or even business partner identities. An identity practitioner may want to consolidate all of these directories into a "one Directory to rule them all"; this may be a project to undertake, but should not be a gating factor prior to beginning a Zero Trust project, for two reasons.

First, in many cases, these disparate identity systems have different and in some cases conflicting sets of requirements, so that it's often impossible for a single identity system to satisfy them all. These differences may appear as technical platform or integration requirements, support for specific regulatory or compliance guidelines (such as data residency), or even something as simple (yet important) as local language support.

Second, organizations need to look at the Zero Trust project as not just a catalyst for replacing certain outdated technologies (which we'll spend considerable time examining in later chapters), but also as a mechanism for normalizing disparate systems. When done properly, Zero Trust can simplify security and operations, by acting as a homogenizing layer which masks the underlying complexity—almost like a blanket of snow which smooths out a complex landscape.

That's not to say, however, that Zero Trust programs can compensate for (or magically fix) identity systems that are fundamentally broken. However, most organizations' identity teams are run by smart and focused people, struggling with a complex mixture of tools and a large volume of work. When done properly, Zero Trust can help simplify and streamline identity operations, and reduce complexity of the overall identity program, without requiring wholesale or disruptive changes.

Summary

Identity management systems have a broad scope, which we've introduced throughout this chapter. They tend to be complex—inherently dynamic and often messy, handling Joiner, Mover, and Leaver processes every day, exceptions and all. Realistically, this complexity is unavoidable—identity systems are essentially serving as a software and process model of the organization, its people, and their roles. Viewed from this perspective, it shouldn't be surprising that enterprises create specialized teams to operate these systems and that there's a vendor and consultant ecosystem around them.

The identity lifecycle (including identity governance) is ultimately responsible for determining "who should have access to what" (i.e., authorization), but is typically reliant on manual or automated IT systems for provisioning of accounts,[11] which is how application level access control is enforced. Zero Trust systems add network level enforcement of access control, and in order to accomplish this, the Zero Trust system must be able to retrieve identity attributes for input into its policy model, at time of identity authentication as well as periodically thereafter.

---

[11]Automating the provisioning process is an inherently "messy" part of IAM—typically requiring adapters or custom database work in order to onboard applications with a provisioning engine. The industry has made some advances in this area in recent years, with the IETF standard SCIM—the System for Cross-domain Identity Management. See https://tools.ietf.org/wg/scim/ and http://www.simplecloud.info/.

Zero Trust teams need to be deliberately—and by this, we mean via *organizational design*—closely aligned with identity management teams. Zero Trust systems enforce access rules (some of which will originate from the identity team), based on data from the identity systems. As with any inter-system integration, this will rely on documented and stable APIs, database schema, versioning, and change management. Yes, this is work, but it shouldn't be looked at as a daunting task. IAM processes *have to* exist within organizations—every day, people join, move, and leave—and it's incumbent on security teams to efficiently support these processes, enabling user productivity while maximizing security.

Identity is at the heart of Zero Trust, and there are a broad set of mature and emerging standards that can be leveraged to integrate these elements very effectively. Getting an understanding of how your organization's IAM systems work will be a natural part of every Zero Trust initiative, since you'll be using them for authentication and identity attributes. Somewhat surprisingly, identity management programs (technology, people, and processes) can be valuable for your Zero Trust initiative, even if they are relatively immature—your IAM environment doesn't have to be perfect (but it cannot be "broken," either). Ultimately, organizations can and should embrace Zero Trust regardless of their IAM platforms' starting point.

CHAPTER 6

Network Infrastructure

Networks, and the hardware and software infrastructures that make them up, are clearly going to be impacted by an organization's move to Zero Trust. In fact, a large part of the strength and value that Zero Trust brings is its ability to enforce identity and context-aware policies at a network level, bridging these normally separate worlds. As a result, enterprise network infrastructure, operations, and potentially network topology will be affected by a shift to Zero Trust. Security and network architects need to be aware of this, and be able to plan for these changes. Few enterprises will be starting from a completely blank sheet of paper, and security architects planning for Zero Trust need to collaborate with their IT counterparts to understand their current environment. Existing infrastructure components must inform and influence an enterprise's Zero Trust architecture and requirements while at the same time not imposing too many constraints. That is, networks and their teams, operations, and processes *will* be required to change as a result of adopting Zero Trust. These changes must be embraced, rather than fought. We know, this is easier said than done, and sometimes changes are more difficult culturally than technically.

Even changes that may be fairly straightforward and can be deployed as "like for like," such as replacing a VPN with a Zero Trust remote access solution, can be organizationally or politically challenging. We'll be exploring some of the nontechnical aspects of Zero Trust deployments later, in Chapter 19, while in this chapter, we'll be focusing on the impact that Zero Trust has on primary network infrastructure components: firewalls, DNS, and Wide Area Networks. We also briefly touch on some secondary areas—Web Application Firewalls, API Gateways, and Load Balancers/Application Delivery Controllers. We have a lot more to say about other network elements, such as NAC and VPN, and we'll be addressing these in dedicated chapters. Finally, note that with the exception of our discussion of NAC in Chapter 7, we're largely omitting discussion of network hardware and switching or routing.

© Jason Garbis and Jerry W. Chapman 2021
J. Garbis and J. W. Chapman, *Zero Trust Security*, https://doi.org/10.1007/978-1-4842-6702-8_6

Network Firewalls

Network firewalls, of course, have historically provided the foundation of network security infrastructure, serving as the original network "policy enforcement points." Firewalls will definitely continue to exist in a Zero Trust network, although their role will change. We believe that there will be one of two outcomes, as depicted in Figure 6-1.

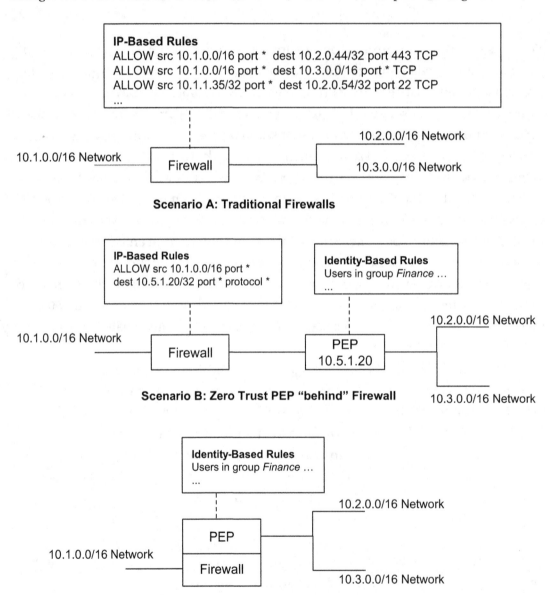

Figure 6-1. *Firewalls and Zero Trust*

Scenario A in Figure 6-1 shows a simplified view of a traditional firewall, enforcing IP-centric access rules. Traditional firewalls have only a very limited vocabulary with which to express their rules, using the classic firewall 5-tuple: source IP, source port, destination IP, destination port, and protocol. This limited (we should say, *impoverished*) vocabulary only permits the definition of access rules based on (local) IP addresses, not on identities or context, and typically leads to overprivileged network access. This is, of course, due to the fact that IP addresses are not identities, and are not unique. Unless the originating device and the firewall are on the same network, it's likely that the incoming IP address will not be unique. Most commonly, IP addresses get translated (remapped and shared) across network or subnet boundaries, making it impossible for the firewall to make any kind of identity or context-aware decisions about access controls.

Zero Trust, of course, is designed to solve this problem, by enabling identity and context-aware policy enforcement points on the network. This will result in one of two outcomes. The first case, as depicted in Scenario B, is that the firewall's rules will become far simpler, as it effectively cedes all control to the PEP. Because the PEP is typically terminating an encrypted tunnel, it has knowledge of the entity at the origin point of the tunnel, and can enforce identity-centric rules.

The alternative is shown in Scenario C, where the PEP is merged with the traditional firewall. This scenario is likely when the Zero Trust vendor is also your (next-gen) firewall vendor. On the surface, scenarios B and C will provide essentially the same functional outcomes. The differences will arise as you evaluate specific vendors' capabilities in terms of policy models, operations, and manageability. Scenario C is often the approach taken by Next-Generation Firewall (NGFW) vendors, who in some cases have added Zero Trust PEP capabilities to their firewall stacks (we'll be covering NGFWs in an upcoming chapter).

Ultimately, Zero Trust PEPs need to act as firewalls—after all, they are network enforcement points. A Zero Trust system will result in simplified firewall configurations with fewer rules, and reduced ongoing workload for their management and maintenance. In some cases, organizations can reduce the size, complexity, and cost of their firewalls, since they've shifted the enforcement work from the firewall to the PEP. That is, the access controls that organizations have traditionally attempted to perform with firewalls can be achieved more easily and more effectively via Zero Trust policies enforced in PEPs.

The Domain Name System

The Domain Name System (DNS) is an incredibly important part of our network infrastructure, as well as a common headache (and a widespread meme[1]). DNS is, of course, the system that translates domain names and hostnames to IP addresses, which is ultimately how computers communicate with one another. Standard DNS does not provide any encryption or privacy, and has some interesting complexities associated with it when users are remote.

Public DNS Servers

Public DNS works in a straightforward hierarchical manner, with devices' standard network settings generally configured to query a DNS server on their local area network. This typically acts as a recursive server which relays uncached queries to a set of external recursive, root, top level domain, and authoritative servers.[2] Public DNS servers do have some security woes, including confidentiality issues (discussed later in this chapter), and issues with security of the DNS infrastructure (not in scope for our discussion, but there are some promising standards in progress with the IETF). Finally, note that public DNS records are (by definition) intended to be publicly available on the internet, to any unauthenticated user.

Private DNS Servers

Private DNS, on the other hand, is a very different beast, and is the source of much frustration and many memes as noted earlier. The fundamental reason is that these DNS servers and their contents are intended to be private—only available to a limited audience. Part of this privacy is achieved implicitly by making the private DNS server only available from a local network, therefore restricting access to only those users physically present on that network. Another aspect of this privacy is that generally, private DNS queries return private (non-Internet-routable) IP addresses, which are only accessible from that private network.

---

[1] Just search for "it's always DNS" if you need a chuckle.

[2] For technical introductions, see `www.digitalocean.com/community/tutorials/ an-introduction-to-dns-terminology-components-and-concepts` or `https://aws.amazon. com/route53/what-is-dns/`.

Local devices are typically assigned a local (private) DNS server as their initial starting point for hostname resolution requests. To resolve public DNS entries, the server will either return a cached response or recursively query its configured external public DNS server, which returns the publicly routable IP address. To resolve private DNS entries (e.g., server1234.internal.company.com), it simply references its local database, and returns the private IP address for the server.

Most organizations have complex domains and networks, and DNS complexity quickly escalates. For example, an organization with three internal domains connected via LAN must make sure that either the DNS servers replicate their contents or that all DNS servers are reachable for devices to issue DNS requests to. Obviously, the internal IP addresses returned by the private DNS servers must also be accessible on the network.

So far, we've only discussed local users, and things get even more complicated when users are remote from the target servers. This is, of course, a common occurrence, with the combination of IaaS-based private resources and many users working from home. In these situations, IT and security teams are challenged by the requirement for users to access private servers that reside in disparate and isolated domains, such as geographically distributed locations, or spread across IaaS environments.

Traditional remote access solutions (read: VPNs) have limited capabilities, often supporting either full tunneling of all DNS traffic to an internal server or split tunneling based on domain names (search domains). In the former case, all DNS queries are sent to the remote DNS server; in the latter case, some DNS traffic is directed to the local (LAN) DNS server. Zero Trust solutions must, of course, also solve this problem, and different platforms approach it in different ways. Some Zero Trust platforms require that internal servers have records published into public DNS, which will direct external users to external (or externally facing) proxies for the applications. This is often an approach taken by cloud-routed Zero Trust systems, and tends to be more static. Other Zero Trust models may take a more sophisticated approach, and, for example, transmit client DNS requests to private DNS servers via a PEP based on search domains. This eliminates the need to have public DNS entries for private servers, and permits dynamic resolution of hosts, which can be essential for virtual or cloud environments.

This is a very complex topic, and there isn't a standard way that Zero Trust solutions approach this—it's highly dependent on the platform architecture. But it is an important question that you should pose to your potential providers, to ensure it aligns with your network architecture. From our perspective, Zero Trust security platforms should provide the ability to automatically resolve (and make available) services running on private hosts, based on policy. Because so many environments today are dynamic, with services being continually created, updated, and destroyed, a Zero Trust solution must support these agile, DevOps-style initiatives, and not impose friction upon them.

Monitoring DNS for Security

Monitoring DNS traffic is a widely used security function, and should likewise be part of your Zero Trust system. DNS requests to resolve known bad domains are a clear sign of malicious activity, and should be quickly detected and responded to by an appropriate enforcement point—this is a high-value and low-risk component of a Zero Trust platform. The simple conclusion is that your Zero Trust architecture must include DNS monitoring, should likewise include DNS filtering or blocking, and would ideally be able to rapidly react to known bad DNS requests by adjusting user access. If your Zero Trust solution sends DNS traffic through an encrypted tunnel, be aware of how and where your enterprise is monitoring this traffic, and how it may be impacted by this.

Before we conclude our discussion on DNS, we'd like to introduce a brief sidebar on its use of encryption. Standard DNS is an unencrypted protocol utilizing UDP—both requests and responses are transmitted in cleartext and therefore visible to observers (both malicious and benign) on local or intermediate networks. However, infrastructure security continues to evolve—there are in-progress specifications (as well as some open source approaches) that introduce encryption into DNS in various ways. The IETF is leading this effort with several RFCs that address different aspects of DNS security, including proposed standards that specify DNS over TLS/DTLS (DoT), and DNS over HTTPS[3] (DoH), both of which do encrypt DNS traffic. These approaches vary in terms of how they work, although the latter (DNS over HTTPS) is somewhat controversial in the industry, and for good reason.[4]

What's important for security architects to understand is how their security systems are using DNS query monitoring or filtering, and to understand the ways in which a shift to encrypted DNS can impact their visibility and control. Organizations should consider adopting DoT, since it provides security benefits and can work within existing enterprise DNS setups nondisruptively (although it may impact DNS monitoring as just discussed).

---

[3]DNS over TLS is in RFC 8310, and DNS over HTTPs is in RFC 8484. These are both available at `www.ietf.org/`.

[4]We encourage you to read about some of the ways in which DNS over HTTPS negatively impacts enterprise security, and may not meet its goals of improving security. See Appendix A for links to relevant articles.

Some Zero Trust systems will by design improve the security of DNS—for example, it may support sending DNS requests through an encrypted tunnel as discussed previously, driven by a Zero Trust policy. This would provide the benefits of encrypted DNS combined with the ability to perform DNS monitoring and filtering. Based on today's standards, security and IT should avoid having users utilize DNS over HTTPS, since it bypasses enterprise DNS controls in ways that can be harmful.

Wide Area Networks

Wide Area Networks (WANs) have been a mainstay of enterprise networks since the 1980s, connecting geographically distributed enterprise sites and networks well before the Internet was widespread and reliable enough to use, with underlying technologies gradually shifting from circuit-switched to packet-switched networks. WANs are primarily centered on delivering reliable and efficient network connectivity, rather than security. What this means in practice, is that WAN traffic is generally privately routed over carriers or network providers, but without additional encryption. That is, the traffic isn't publicly visible in transit, but it is accessible to the network service providers as well as to any other intermediary actor with legal (or illegal) access to the network.[5] The takeaway is that network traffic encryption is typically not provided by the WAN itself.

Likewise, access control is simply not in scope for the WAN—they are designed to connect distributed enterprise networks, and not to provide a model for controlling access based on firewall rules or policies. Enterprises using WANs will of course need to deploy and configure network firewalls at the edges, immediately behind their service provider WAN router. They also need to decide whether and how to encrypt traffic traversing the WAN, either via an encrypted application protocol or through some other means.

Over the past decade or so, Software-Defined Wide Area Networks (SD-WANs) have emerged, based on the premise that basic Internet Service Provider (ISP) connectivity has sufficient bandwidth, reliability, and low latency to be used as a basis for enterprise WANs. SD-WANs can definitely deliver reduced costs, as traditional WANs can be quite expensive (as well as slow to be provisioned by ISPs). SD-WANs typically utilize an encrypted tunnel overlay such as IPSec between remote nodes, ensuring data privacy and integrity. They also often provide multiple routes (network pathways) between their

---

[5]Of course, this is also the case for traffic transiting the Internet today.

nodes in order to ensure network quality of service, which has some implications when combined with Zero Trust, which we discuss later. Like traditional WANs, SD-WANs provide network connectivity between distributed locations, and do not provide a built-in security model or enforce access policies.

As enterprises design and deploy Zero Trust systems, they may naturally find themselves with less reliance on WANs (and more reliance on encrypted connections initiated from user devices). This isn't to say that WANs will disappear, it's just that there are two factors both contributing to a reduction in their importance. First, Zero Trust systems "don't care" about the underlying network—they presume it's insecure and encrypt all traffic. And second, in today's world, Internet connectivity is mostly ubiquitous, inexpensive, and generally fast and reliable enough to be used for business-critical enterprise communications.[6]

While most Zero Trust deployments probably won't result in immediate changes to WAN infrastructure, it will at least open the door to reducing or replacing them, which is a conversation that the network, IT, and security teams should definitely have. Of course, change often brings complexity, and Zero Trust is no exception. Specifically, recall that Zero Trust systems typically establish an encrypted overlay tunnel across intermediary networks, most often between the user agent PEP, and the PEP in front of the protected resources. This tunnel is, by design, opaque to network intermediaries. While this brings with it the benefits of data privacy and integrity, it can also negatively impact the ability of legitimate network intermediaries to perform their tasks (this will be a common theme throughout this book). SD-WANs often rely on network traffic metadata such as port and protocol in order to make network routing and prioritization decisions (traffic shaping), in order to meet quality-of-service goals. This can usually be partially compensated for, but will require coordination between the Zero Trust and networking teams.

In summary, adoption of Zero Trust will very likely impact enterprise usage of WANs, often beneficially by reducing the costs or bandwidth consumption, and in some cases, they can even be eliminated. However, because Zero Trust network traffic is typically overlaid on top of existing WANs, you'll need to pay attention to how your WAN may be using network traffic metadata, and how that might be impacted.

---

[6]The growing deployment and adoption of wireless cellular communications, including 5G, will only, accelerate this trend.

Load Balancers, Application Delivery Controllers, and API Gateways

Load Balancers, Application Delivery Controllers (ADCs), and API Gateways are widely deployed components of networking and IT infrastructure. Together, they are used to provide better performance and higher scalability and resiliency for applications, and also enable a layer of abstraction between providers of a service and consumers of that service. They can be complex, and often can achieve their goals through several technical approaches. For example, even simple load balancers may use one or more techniques (such as round-robin, random, or load-based) to assign workloads to servers. ADCs and API Gateways reduce server workload by performing certain network, content optimization, and API consolidation functions in front of their back-end servers. This can include capabilities such as SSL termination, content caching, connection multiplexing, traffic shaping, and microservices abstraction or consolidation. In general, note that these systems provide network and application functions and, other than helping with *availability*, are not typically considered as security appliances.

The functions provided by these systems are valuable, and will continue to exist in Zero Trust systems, largely unchanged. However, one thing to be aware of (like with SD-WANs as discussed previously) is the potential impact of network topology changes and new use of tunneled encrypted traffic within the Zero Trust system. This traffic will likely become opaque to intermediary components such as these—it all depends on where the PEPs are, and how the PEPs enforce policies. In general, if load balancers, ADCs, or API Gateways are behind a PEP, they should work well with the enclave-based and cloud-routed deployment models. Resource-based and microsegmentation models could possibly interfere with these components, because they may conflict with the need to have an active network intermediary.

The key here is to be aware of how your organization is using these systems, and to engage with your peers across networking, application, IT, and security teams. Keep in mind that not all applications and services must necessarily be included in a Zero Trust system. It may well be that a web application server (including load balancer and ADC) is in place to provide a publicly available application, which is by design intended to be visible to and accessible by unauthenticated and anonymous users. For example, an organization's website or a SaaS application could fall into this category.

Conversely, an API service might need to be accessible from across the Internet, but could benefit from being protected by a Zero Trust PEP. It depends on the access model, and the type of client systems authorized to access the API.

In conclusion, we'd like to call out one more important point. Even though there may well be services that are intended for use by public and unauthenticated users (such as the website example), there will likely be *other services running on the same host* which require authentication and authorization, and should be included in your Zero Trust scope. For example, a public-facing web server (or load balancer hardware) will have a management interface, such as SSH. Access to this interface *must* be restricted to authorized users, and hidden from unauthorized users—a problem for which Zero Trust is a perfect solution.

Web Application Firewalls

Web Application Firewalls (WAFs) are security components which sit in front of web servers, protecting them by parsing, monitoring, and securing HTTP traffic. The term WAF is perhaps a bit misleading, as they are less of a *network firewall* and more of a *security proxy*. In fact, technically, these systems are reverse proxies, examining incoming HTTP traffic to detect and prevent attacks such as SQL injection and Cross-Site Scripting.

WAFs are frequently deployed to protect public-facing web servers, which of course, are almost certainly going to be probed, scanned, and attacked on a regular basis. Clearly, such resources warrant investment in security solutions such as WAFs. Interestingly, though, WAFs are also deployed to protect *internal* applications which are only accessible to internal users. In this case, they're protecting against malicious insiders and compromised devices on the internal network. From a Zero Trust perspective, we applaud the additional security even for internal applications, and the presumption of compromise which likely motivated it.

Zero Trust systems can't eliminate attacks, of course, but they can reduce the surface area which a compromised machine can attack. So, for a hypothetical internal web application, a proper Zero Trust system will limit access to only those users with legitimate business needs and an account in the web app. If 10% of the user population uses this application, the Zero Trust system will eliminate the ability of the remaining 90% of devices to even attempt to attack it. In terms of WAFs, there's definitely still a place for them internally with Zero Trust, since the 10% of users may well be hosting malicious software which can attempt to attack the application.

Summary

It should be clear that some elements of your network infrastructure will most certainly be impacted by the adoption of Zero Trust. Even though your journey won't affect everything on the network, at the very least, all network elements will require some thoughtful analysis and discussion. That is, as a Zero Trust architect and leader, you need to proactively obtain an understanding of your enterprise network, and how various security, connectivity, availability, and reliability components are deployed.

Zero Trust systems, because they act as an encrypted overlay on top of underlying networks, will require this type of coordination, cooperation, and understanding. That's not to say that Zero Trust projects are necessarily going to be disruptive, and we don't want to discourage you from starting on this journey. In fact, there definitely are use cases and scenarios where Zero Trust can be incrementally and easily deployed. But an enterprise Zero Trust architecture will impact much of the network and networked applications, and will require a broad analysis of infrastructure elements. This chapter, and the remaining ones throughout Part II, will provide you with the context and understanding to do this successfully.

CHAPTER 7

Network Access Control

We're addressing Network Access Control (NAC) solutions separately from the Firewall, DNS, and Load Balancer solutions we covered in Chapter 6 for two reasons: First, to give vendors credit—NAC solutions represent early (and ongoing) attempts at achieving some of the principles of Zero Trust—specifically, the ability to enforce identity-centric access policies at the network level. Second, NAC deployments are generally going to be impacted as organizations deploy a modern Zero Trust architecture—the value and importance of NAC (as an established category) is going to be diminished, replaced by the more effective ability of Zero Trust to serve as a broader and more capable network access control solution.

Introduction to Network Access Control

What the industry today refers to as NAC is a category which consists of several functions and network protocols related to identifying and validating user devices, authenticating users, and enforcing policies that specify which network resources users are permitted to access. Commercial NAC solutions often perform device discovery, and can validate device posture checks such as antivirus protection level, system patch level, and device configuration. This enables these systems to enforce policies such as quarantining failed devices into remediation-only network segments. Once the policy is met, the computer is able to access network resources and the Internet, within the policies defined by the NAC system.

NAC's goals are laudable, and the functions described do in fact represent a subset of our Zero Trust principles. So why are we critical of NAC, and believe its future is limited? The issue with NAC isn't its goals, but the way in which NAC systems are architected. Specifically, their approach (and the network protocol they use, 802.1x) typically requires that a single organization own and operate the network hardware infrastructure that's in

© Jason Garbis and Jerry W. Chapman 2021
J. Garbis and J. W. Chapman, *Zero Trust Security*, https://doi.org/10.1007/978-1-4842-6702-8_7

place for all users and all servers. Therefore, NAC solutions are of no use for remote users whose devices are connected to a personal or third-party network, or who are accessing resources running in the cloud. Because NAC systems operate at network Layer 2, they are hardware-based and simply do not work in cloud environments or for remote users.

When used for appropriate scenarios—on-premises users accessing on-premises resources—NAC can be useful, although in practice, they tend to provide only coarse-grained user assignment to virtual LANs (VLANs), which themselves typically have many dozens (if not hundreds) of services available. This is not well aligned with Zero Trust goals. And, it's important to note—NAC solutions do not provide network traffic encryption or remote access.[1] There is one additional aspect common to NAC solutions, which merits its own discussion—guest network access. We'll discuss that later in this chapter, but first, let's examine 802.1x (verbally referred to as "eight-oh-two-one-ex"), the protocol that all traditional NAC solutions use.

802.1x, which is an open protocol defined through a combination of IEEE and IETF papers, specifies a network authentication mechanism for authenticating and authorizing devices for connection to a LAN. In short, a NAC system is responsible for authorizing a device's access to a network, and allowing (or preventing) it to obtain an IP address in that LAN. This works in conjunction with network hardware (switches), as shown in Figure 7-1.

---

[1]Although, to be fair, many NAC vendors also have products with those capabilities in their portfolio, with varying degrees of integration.

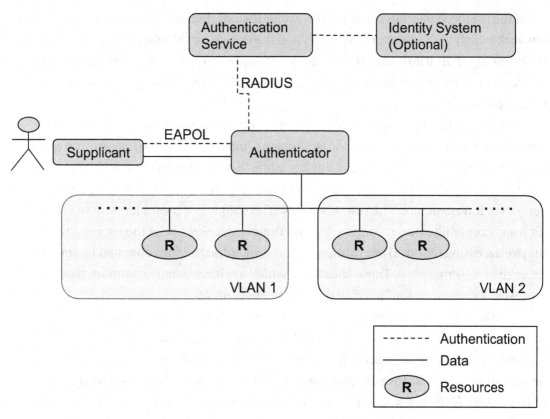

Figure 7-1. *802.1x Authentication*

As the diagram shows, the user's device (termed the *supplicant*) uses the Extensible Authentication Protocol (EAP) on LAN (EAPOL) to communicate credentials or certificate information to the Authenticator. When the supplicant first connects to the network switch, it's set as "unauthorized," and only allows EAP traffic—UDP, TCP, and ICMP are not permitted.[2] EAP is, by design,[3] a very basic protocol which operates at layer 2, after the IP layer. As such, it's literally a *local network* protocol accessible only on the local subnet (broadcast domain) with no ability to be routed.[4] The Authenticator validates the user's credentials with the Authentication Service, typically using the RADIUS protocol. Products built on 802.1x may support either user credentials validated against an identity system or certificate-based authentication.

---

[2]In fact, at this point in the authorization sequence, the supplicant doesn't even have an IP address assigned if using DHCP.

[3]See https://tools.ietf.org/html/rfc3748, Section 1.3, Applicability.

[4]Some NAC-as-a-Service vendors effectively route this traffic by capturing it via a local agent, which in turn communicates it up to a cloud-based authenticator.

If the user's credentials are valid, the Authenticator then sets the supplicant's network switch to the "authorized" state, and the device can obtain an IP address and start sending UDP, ICMP, and TCP traffic. Most importantly, the Authenticator assigns the device to a network segment (a virtual LAN, or VLAN) by making a configuration setting on the network switch.

The implication of this protocol is that the supplicant and authenticator must be located on the same network broadcast domain—that is, both using the same physical network media (Ethernet or Wi-Fi). Furthermore, they must use network hardware owned and operated by the enterprise, and this hardware must be ubiquitously deployed across the infrastructure. The result is that NAC is simply not useful for remote users, or for users accessing cloud resources. In both these scenarios, either the user or the service they're accessing (or both) are running on network infrastructure operated by someone other than the enterprise. These situations, which are increasingly common, therefore represent a significant limitation in the effectiveness of NAC.

Once a user's device is assigned to a VLAN, many NAC solutions have no further involvement in terms of access control (other than a periodic reauthentication). Controlling user or device access within the VLAN is then the responsibility of the organization's firewalls (or next-gen firewalls), which of course have their own access policy model. Note that some advanced NAC vendors do have additional capabilities (outside the scope of 802.1x) and do support integration with other security components.

Finally, 802.1x only supports coarse-grained assignment of users to virtual LAN segments (VLANs), commonly with dozens if not hundreds or more services or peer devices visible on the network. And, because each device can only be assigned to a single VLAN at a time, NACs perpetuate the problems of overly broad network access. While it's true that NACs can be augmented by the use of firewall ACLs, those tend to be static and IP-centric, and as such are poorly aligned with our Zero Trust goals.

Zero Trust and Network Access Control

The coarse-grained assignment of devices to networks, which in practice grants users broad network access to all ports and protocols across an entire VLAN, is simply not compatible with the principle-of-least-privilege tenet of Zero Trust. This is not to say that a NAC solution can't be *part of* a Zero Trust enterprise—in fact, we'll explore a few such scenarios later, and we previously explained NAC's role in the BeyondCorp infrastructure. However, we'd caution you to look carefully at NAC vendor solutions and how they map to your Zero Trust requirements, before deciding how to include them in your Zero Trust architecture. NAC vendors are certainly aware of the limitations of 802.1x, and some NAC vendors have added capabilities beyond the 802.1x protocol to their product portfolios to overcome these limits. For example, some NAC vendors also have endpoint inspection capabilities and remote access features or even deliver NAC as a cloud-based service.

Note also that enterprise networks typically have a nontrivial percentage of devices that do not support 802.1x, such as printers, VOIP phones, or IoT Devices. NAC solutions generally do provide VLAN assignment for these, typically based on MAC addresses, but these approaches are limited to local network access controls, and are often a hassle to manage. We'll discuss how these devices are approached in Zero Trust environments later, in Chapter 16.

In any case, there are NAC capabilities which make may sense to retain even with a Zero Trust architecture, especially if they're already in place—specifically guest network access and device discovery. Let's take a look at them.

Unmanaged Guest Network Access

Guest network access is an area which, in some ways, can become less of an issue in a Zero Trust network. Let's first define this, so we have a common understanding for our analysis:

> *Guest networking is the process and control of providing Internet access for non-employee users with unmanaged devices.*

The guest network provides Internet access, and may include a few additional devices accessible to guests, such as wireless conference room A/V systems or a guest printer, but these users and devices must be isolated from the enterprise's employee network.

Note that nowadays, guest networks are almost exclusively wireless (Wi-Fi) based, rather than wired—and our discussion is therefore aimed just at these types of networks. Many (perhaps even most) guest networks are protected by a static Wi-Fi password and typically are made up of a single flat network segment, so all devices on the network have peer access to all other devices. In some environments, this is sufficient security—it's a reasonable approach when, for example, the guest network Wireless Access Point (WAP) is isolated from the corporate network, and there's not a great deal of concern about access to sensitive assets or malicious behavior by guests.

Enterprises may choose to operate this guest network with little or no monitoring or management, or may choose to invest in these capabilities. The key point to note here is that for this approach, by definition, there is no user or device authentication—all users are treated identically, and there is no attempt to distinguish among users or device types. We explore the implications of this approach later, in the section "Managed vs. Unmanaged Guest Networks: A Debate." Finally, note that unmanaged guest network access as described previously, a common feature of WAP hardware, does not use the 802.1x protocol.

Managed Guest Network Access

Managed guest network access is a capability that's common to many commercial NAC solutions, and generally consists of the following types of features:

- Access registration portal, typically with email or SMS verification

- Basic workflow of employee (sponsor) request for guest access, with temporary network access provisioning

The primary distinction between unmanaged and managed guest network access is that the latter approach requires user self-identification with authentication, and typically only grants access for a limited period of time. Generally, these systems require registration—either self-service by the guest or by a sponsor employee—via a simple portal, and only grant access for a limited period of time (typically 24 hours or less). Time-limiting access provides an additional layer of security, beyond the inherently proximity-based nature of short-range Wi-Fi. This managed guest network portal and workflow is a common feature of commercial NAC solutions.

Managed vs. Unmanaged Guest Networks: A Debate

While not quite in the realm of the Lincoln-Douglas debates, there are different perspectives and approaches to security for guest networks, with no clear right or wrong answer—organizations need to make their own decisions based on what's right for their environment and their risk profile. There are multiple capabilities that can be associated with a network which organizations need to consider, which can be roughly put onto a spectrum from less secure to more secure, as shown in Table 7-1. These are interesting trade-offs, and remain relevant even on Zero Trust networks. Note that under all circumstances, a guest network must be separate from the employee or corporate LAN.

Table 7-1. Network Security Attributes

Network Security	Attributes
Open Wi-Fi: No Password	No network traffic encryption. No user authentication or identification.
Password-Protected Wi-Fi	Network traffic encryption.[5] No user authentication or identification. Captive portal for accepting Terms of Use (optional).
User Registration	Time-limited network access. User self-identification and authentication (typically email-based, not validated against a directory). Form for accepting Terms of Use.
Employee Sponsorship	Time-limited network access. Validated employee workflow required to enable access. User identification and authentication. Form for accepting Terms of Use.
Device Isolation	Some Wi-Fi networks support the ability to isolate devices from one another via router firewall rules, even though these devices are connected to the same Wireless Access Point. This is a good practice, to prevent curious users (or malware) from performing network and port scans on the local network.[6]
Network Monitoring	These can include services that are commonly used on enterprise networks, including DNS filtering, or IDS/IPS.

---

[5]Note that while typical Wi-Fi standards in use—WPA and WPA2 with pre-shared keys—do encrypt the traffic so that users without the password cannot view it, the encryption does **not** provide privacy from other authorized users on the network. This has been addressed in WPA3, but—as always—Zero Trust requires the use of encrypted application protocols on top of any L1 or L2 network-level encryption.

[6]Occasionally, this curiosity can result in improved security, as Jason notes: Once, while at the dentist's office waiting for my daughter, I connected to their guest Wi-Fi and ran a network scan. Sadly, I discovered all their office computers and printers were visible on the network, with open ports. Fortunately, the dentist was a neighbor of ours, so I contacted her, strongly encouraging her to demand that their IT service fix this. At my next visit, approximately six month later, the office devices were properly inaccessible. White hat achievement unlocked!

Each organization and security team needs to make their own decisions about this, but from our perspective, a password-protected Wi-Fi guest network is likely sufficient for most enterprise environments, as long as it's separated from the corporate network. WPA3 is preferred over WPA2, if available, and device isolation is a nice benefit but can be considered optional.

Enterprises with Zero Trust networks should continue to provide guest Wi-Fi, of course, with the combination of network security attributes that are appropriate for their environment. A Zero Trust network doesn't affect the need for a guest network, and doesn't change the considerations previously discussed.

One interesting aside: Your enterprise guest network will likely be at least as secure as public Wi-Fi networks, such as airports and coffee shops. And—as we've discussed throughout this book—your Zero Trust system must permit your users to access enterprise resources from those networks. So, there's no reason your general employee population can't also use the guest network, just as if they were remote. Of course, as a counterpoint, enterprises often do frequently have additional security or compliance controls, or more bandwidth, for their employee networks. As a result, they may prefer that employees use the employee network rather than the guest network on a regular basis.

Employee BYOD

Many organizations permit employees to use personal devices to access enterprise networks and enterprise-managed resources. This may include the use of a personal smartphone or tablet, or a user's preference for a particular type of laptop device or specific operating system. Organizations may take a hands-off approach—permitting user access from any device—or may require some degree of enterprise footprint on the device, such as the installation of enterprise-issued certificates or device management software.[7]

---

[7]The latter can be controversial, as it's right at the intersection of user productivity, privacy, and security. Many employees object to giving their employer's security team the ability to manipulate their personal smartphone—with (legitimate) concerns about corporate access to private information such as photos or browsing history. This leads some people to choose a dreaded "two-phone" existence.

Security teams must decide whether and how to permit employees from using BYODs to access enterprise resources. With traditional NACs, this may or may not be achievable, depending on how stringently network access is controlled, and to what degree the security team requires installation of certificates or management software on user devices. We've summarized different approaches in Table 7-2. Note that this is generally uniform for both laptop and mobile devices, although of course there may be some minor differences across OSs and security platforms.

Table 7-2. *BYOD Configuration Comparison*

Device Configuration	With NAC	With Zero Trust
"Pure" BYOD— nothing installed or configured	Guest network with Internet access. Coarse-grained (full-network) access controls via Wi-Fi password security. Applies to on-premises users only.	Guest network with Internet access. Access to secure resources with "clientless" Zero Trust access possible. Applies to on-premises and remote users equally.
BYOD with corporate certificate installation	Employee network (VLAN) access via built-in 802.1x supplicant. Provides coarse-grained access controls. Applies to on-premises users only.	Same as "pure BYOD." Generally, access to the device certificate store requires installation of client-side software.
BYOD with software installed and configured (corporate certificate optional)	Employee network (VLAN) access via 802.1x (either built-in or installed). Can include device posture checks via installed management software.	Granular network access control with Zero Trust client installation. Can use certificate and device posture checks for conditional access. Applies to on-premises and remote users equally.

Device Posture Checks

Ultimately, this set of requirements—to block all access by unauthorized users and/ or devices, to quarantine/limit access by authorized but non-compliant devices, and to permit limited access by authorized users on validated devices—is common to both NAC and Zero Trust solutions, and in fact are important goals for security, regardless of the underlying implementation. Throughout this chapter, we've tried to explain the ways in which 802.1x-based NAC solutions work, and highlight their shortcomings in terms of their alignment with Zero Trust principles. Next, we're examining the topic of device configuration analysis. Note that this capability is outside the scope of the 802.1x standard, but commonly included in NAC products.

NAC solutions often provide the capability to perform user device configuration checks—commonly referred to as posture checks. This combines the retrieval of device information—such as OS patch level or presence of an up-to-date antivirus solution— with the ability to define and enforce a policy that determines which network resources (if any) a device should be able to access given its device profile. A common example is: If a device is not "up to date" with security or A/V patches, quarantine it to an "IT Remediation" VLAN that can only access the IT helpdesk portal/self-service portal.

This is a worthy goal—in fact device attributes must be included as part of any Zero Trust policy and enforcement model. Of course, this requires the ability to obtain device information for use within the policy—with the different ways to approach this shown in Table 7-3.

Table 7-3. *Device Posture Approaches with NAC*

Approach	Implications
Native 802.1x Supplicant	Device attributes are not part of the 802.1x standard, and may not be provided by built-in OS capabilities.
Product-specific 802.1x Supplicant	Many NAC products include a client agent (802.1x. supplicant) with additional capabilities to retrieve client device attributes.
Additional device agent (e.g., MDM)	Enterprise device management solutions include the ability to retrieve device posture information, for use by a network access policy enforcement point. This approach generally requires integration between the NAC authentication server and an EDM server via API call.

Ultimately, the ability to obtain device attributes is only part of the equation—and, we'd argue, a less-important part. The ability to create and enforce a dynamic policy model to control network access based on these attributes is what's most important. We'll be talking about a Zero Trust policy model in depth later, in Chapter 17.

Device Discovery and Access Controls

Shifting our focus back to the network, there's one final capability that NACs typically provide, device discovery and visibility. Clearly, the ability to discover and report on what devices are operating on an enterprise's network is a core requirement for network and security teams, and there are many different types of products which can help with this, not just NACs. NACs provide this because they are part of the network infrastructure, and detect new devices at the infrastructure layer when they connect to the network. This discovery is a direct byproduct of how they work, and is necessary to perform any authentication and VLAN assignment.

Understanding what's in place on a network (including users, devices, and workloads) is of course a prerequisite for applying a policy model and enforcing access controls. A key part of any Zero Trust model is that entities need to be authenticated and that the system uses a variety of attributes in order to make contextual access decisions. NAC solutions can be *part of* a Zero Trust solution (for both coarse-grained network assignment like in BeyondCorp and device discovery information) but cannot provide the dynamic, fine-grained, and universal access controls for all users and all resources.

In terms of what security and network teams need to accomplish on enterprise (non-guest) networks, we've summarized this and compared NAC with Zero Trust approaches in Table 7-4.

Table 7-4. Device Security Approaches on Enterprise Networks

Device Type	With NAC	With Zero Trust
Unauthorized Devices	Block from all network access: no VLAN, no IP address assigned.	Block from accessing any protected resources. May block from Internet access. Device is on network, but unable to access anything.
Authorized but unmanaged or non-802.1x Devices	VLAN assignment (typically by MAC address grouping).	Access controls based on device type (e.g., MAC address grouping). Finer-grained than VLAN.
Authorized and managed or 802.1x-enabled Devices	Authenticate devices and assign to VLAN (may be based on identity groups).	Authenticate, and apply fine-grained and identity-specific access controls.

One additional comment—using device MAC addresses for access controls is, of course, a "not great but better than nothing" approach, and any use of this needs to be done with a clear understanding of the associated risks and threat model. It's trivial for a malicious actor with physical access to a network to change their MAC address and masquerade as an authorized device in order to get access. Knowing this, it's important to go through the thought experiment, and ensure that if this were to happen, the device would only have very limited access (e.g., to a printer or VOIP VLAN).

Summary

In this chapter, we introduced the functional area of Network Access Control, and explained how the 802.1x protocol works. We then looked at NAC solutions from the perspective of Zero Trust, exploring how NAC solutions approach guest network access, which is still a required use case even in Zero Trust networks. Finally, we considered a few other aspects of NAC, including BYOD, device profiles, and device discovery.

NAC solutions can be part of a Zero Trust environment, especially if they provide needed capabilities around guest network access controls, but 802.1x-based NAC functions are not suitable to use as the core part of any Zero Trust environment. Some NAC vendors have innovated beyond 802.1x and added Zero Trust capabilities, although enterprises considering them must evaluate them carefully against their network and architectural requirements.

CHAPTER 8

Intrusion Detection and Prevention Systems

Enterprise security platforms clearly need the ability to prevent and detect intrusions—which we'll succinctly define here as *unwanted software execution or unwanted human activity on an enterprise device or network.* Intrusion Detection Systems (IDS) provide the ability to *detect, log,* and *alert* on suspicious activity, and Intrusion Prevention Systems (IPS) add the ability to *respond,* by blocking or terminating the activity in some way. Intrusion Detection and Prevention Systems (IDPS[1]) typically rely on signatures (pattern matching) and/or anomaly-detection mechanisms (often using statistical analysis or machine learning) to identify unwanted activity. They also often integrate with threat intelligence systems, in order to obtain updated data to inform their algorithms. These solutions are commonly available as both standalone solutions, as well as within many Next-Generation Firewalls (NGFWs[2]).

IDPS have traditionally been most effective in environments where they can be placed into well-defined network "chokepoints," obtain visibility into traffic, and ideally perform deep packet inspection. In a Zero Trust architecture, PEPs are a natural place for these functions to be performed. In fact, we believe that modern IDPS, when integrated into a Zero Trust system, effectively can become a PEP. Like other elements in our security ecosystem, IDPS will magnify their value and effectiveness when they can consume and enforce Zero Trust policies, and act as a source of events to the PDP, which will in turn trigger other PEPs to take action and, for example, initiate changes in user risk levels or access.

---

[1]Throughout this chapter, we'll refer to the overall category as IDPS. If we're discussing one of the areas in particular, we'll use either the IDS or IPS acronym.

[2]In fact, as we'll note in Chapter 10, the addition of IDPS into traditional firewalls was one of the key capabilities that enabled those vendors to credibly position their products as "next generation."

© Jason Garbis and Jerry W. Chapman 2021
J. Garbis and J. W. Chapman, *Zero Trust Security*, https://doi.org/10.1007/978-1-4842-6702-8_8

One final introductory note for context—so far, we've just discussed network-based IDPS; there's another category of *host-based* IDPS. We'll compare them next, to see what they do and how they're impacted by the shift to Zero Trust.

Types of IDPS

There are two general approaches to commercial IDPS, *host-based* and *network-based*, which differ in where and how they're deployed, as shown in Table 8-1. Note that in general, *prevention* systems must include at least some of the *detection* functions; in order for them to take action, they must of course first detect unwanted (or at least unexpected) activity.

Table 8-1. *Typical Intrusion Detection and Prevention Functions, by Deployment Model*

Function Type	Detection	Prevention
Host-Based	File integrity monitoring	Process whitelisting
	Process behavior analysis	Process termination
	Network metadata analysis	Prevention of software download or
	Local log and event analysis	installation
	Log and event forwarding	Network connection termination
	Device or user behavior monitoring	
	Software installation or download monitoring	
	Privilege escalation or rootkit detection	
Network-Based	DNS monitoring	DNS filtering
	Network metadata analysis	Network content blocking
	Network traffic inspection (deep packet inspection)	Network connection termination
		Sandbox "detonation" of suspicious content

It should be clear from Table 8-1 that there are a very wide variety of potential functions and mechanisms by which security solutions can detect and respond to unexpected activities. This degree of complexity is one of the reasons that modern IT and information security can be so challenging—there are many ways in which malicious activities can be expressed, and there are many potential approaches to defending against them. Some of these actions, such as network connection termination, are clearly well within the scope of a Zero Trust system. Others, such as host-based process termination, or sandbox payload "detonation," are likely outside the scope of a Zero Trust system. Nevertheless, those systems can add value by acting as a source of data or events for a Zero Trust platform.

Now that we have some context, let's look at the two IDPS deployment models and discuss the implications of each as an organization moves to a Zero Trust architecture.

Host-Based Systems

Host-based intrusion detection and prevention systems utilize a software agent running on either user devices or servers (resources). Host-based systems have the advantage of being able to deeply examine everything occurring in the OS, including process and network activity, and to take local actions. Local presence on the host is advantageous in many Zero Trust deployments, which typically utilize encrypted traffic tunnels across networks (we explore this further later in this chapter).

One disadvantage is that these types of systems require installation and management of software on potentially large numbers of devices, and typically requires elevated privileges to run. These agents also have the potential to reduce mobile device battery life, to interfere with legitimate user activity, and reduce device performance on all platforms. This latter factor is potentially a concern, in terms of how it may impact end-user experience.

Having said that, we do recommend that organizations generally deploy some sort of agent onto devices which are accessing protected resources, for a variety of reasons, as discussed previously in Chapter 3. However, one challenge that IT teams often face is that of agent proliferation (and functional overlap between agents), especially on end-user devices. This is an unsolved problem, since these agents are typically distributed as binaries with their own unique deployment footprint, dependencies, and configuration. Agent consolidation and release coordination among vendors are unlikely to occur, and enterprises shouldn't realistically count on this. Instead, security teams must accept reality, and take a thoughtful approach to agent deployment. Fortunately, modern devices and OSs generally provide enough memory and processing capacity to support operation of multiple agents without significant issue.[3]

---

[3]Note that Internet of Things (IoT) and some types of unmanaged devices generally don't support the installation of software agents. Network-based IDPS can be used with these devices, of course. We'll explore IoT devices and "things" from a Zero Trust perspective later in chapter 16.

Network-Based Systems

Network-based IDS and IPS are deployed into an organization's network, where they have the ability to monitor (and potentially modify) network traffic. Modern networks are distributed and segmented, of course, and the scope and capability of any network-based IDS/IPS system is entirely dependent on where the system nodes are deployed, and which type of network traffic they have access to. For example, an IDS deployed within an employee LAN subnet can potentially examine traffic among devices on that one subnet, or traffic between those devices and remote resources. An IDS on a WAN link connecting distributed data centers may be able to examine the inter-data center traffic, but cannot see any local LAN traffic within a given data center or network.

Network IDPS can be deployed via a network tap or span port (passively observing traffic) or in-line (observing traffic as it transits through the node). The latter approach has the advantage of being able to more reliably terminate connections in response to a detected threat. The in-line approach is one reason that NGFWs, which include intrusion detection and prevention as a function, are a popular and still-growing market area.

One could argue that ideally, an organization should deploy network-based IDPS with nodes "everywhere," so that the system in aggregate can monitor "all" network traffic. However, our counter-argument is that

- Organizations may be limited by capital and operational budgets, and not be able to deploy network-based IDPS across the entire network.

- In today's environment, many users and resources operate on third-party networks, outside the control of the enterprise—with users working from home or on hotel networks, accessing resources that may be running in a cloud environment (especially IaaS). Traditional IDPS may not be able to operate in these environments.

- Finally, the prevalent use of encrypted network protocols makes it more difficult for network-based IDPS to be as effective as they have in the past.

Zero Trust environments make this last bullet point even more relevant, and often makes network-based IDS more challenging to deploy, since the encrypted tunnels commonly in use by Zero Trust systems make traffic largely opaque to network intermediaries. The impact that encrypted network protocols have on network-based security systems is an interesting topic, which we'll look at next.

Network Traffic Analysis and Encryption

Clearly, a Zero Trust system changes an enterprise's security architecture and network. It will change the ways in which different IT and security components interact with one another, and also change the network—potentially from a topological perspective, but definitely by changing network segmentation and imposing additional layers of encryption. That last change is particularly important to understand, especially for organizations with network-based IDS systems.

Modern application protocols utilize encryption (most commonly TLS), as they should, since it ensures message integrity and confidentiality from network peers or intermediaries. This implies, of course, that the contents of encrypted traffic are opaque even to authorized network intermediaries attempting to perform security functions. The solution to this is the well-established practice of having the intermediary be an active participant in the conversation, terminating one encrypted link and initiating the other in order to perform traffic inspection.[4]

This is typically enabled through the distribution of an enterprise PKI-generated certificate, based upon a root of trust that's common to both ends of the encrypted TLS connection—essentially a legitimate Man-In-The-Middle (MITM) attack.

We mentioned that this approach is well established, and in fact, it's in use by many security products as a way of examining encrypted traffic. However, it's based on a simple usage model—that of one-way authentication with a static set of certificates, whereby the client authenticates the server's certificate as part of establishing the TLS connection, but the server performs no validation of the client at the network level. This is very useful for models where the server *should* legitimately accept a connection from any client, and where it performs client authentication later in the process, at the application level. The simplicity of this model is also what makes it possible for an intermediate network security component to perform TLS termination, since it only requires the sharing of a single, static server certificate.

However, this model may not be applicable in Zero Trust environments. Many Zero Trust implementations use mutual TLS (*mTLS*, also known as *two-way TLS*) for communications between the user agent PEP and the network PEP. With this method,

---

[4]Although technically straightforward, this is nonetheless a complex area that balances security with privacy and regulation. For example, in many countries, employers are often legally required to **not** decrypt certain types of traffic, such as employee access to personal healthcare sites.

both PEPs validate one another's certificate. This results in increased security, since a malicious actor cannot perform an MITM attack with only a single stolen certificate—it requires possession of both components' certificates, a much less likely scenario. Some Zero Trust systems go further, and use short-lived certificates for these communications. The consequence of this improved security is that a standard network IDPS running "between" PEPs will not be able to access encrypted portions of network traffic. That is, even if the IDPS has access to the certificates used to encrypt the *application protocol*, it won't have access to the certificates used to encrypt the *Zero Trust tunnel.*

We discuss this in depth in the next section, but first, one additional note on TLS. The industry is in transition to TLS v1.3 (finalized in August 2018), which changes certain security aspects of the TLS connection and makes things more difficult for network security solutions. Specifically, additional portions of the TLS handshake are now encrypted, reducing the ability of a passive network observer to detect malicious activity. If you're interested in deeper analysis, we recommend this thoughtful and well-written IETF document, *Impact of TLS 1.3 to Operational Network Security Practices.*[5] The bottom line is that the movement to TLS 1.3 is in progress, and must be embraced rather than fought.[6]

Zero Trust and IDPS

Modern security infrastructure requires IDPS—defined in its broadest sense—as a general set of functions across an organization's platforms. This will continue to be important, even as organizations move toward a Zero Trust security architecture. But, the *how* of IDS/IPS will likely change with the deployment of a Zero Trust approach. Organizations need to be aware of this, and be willing to make changes. For example, Zero Trust will bring changes to network segmentation and network traffic encryption patterns. This may require organizations to increase their use of host-based IDS/IPS, or to invest more in network-based IDPS that are part of a Zero Trust system. This is depicted in Figure 8-1.

---

[5]This whitepaper is available here: `https://datatracker.ietf.org/doc/draft-ietf-opsec-ns-impact/`.

[6]This will require a shift away from passive network traffic monitoring (even by in-line devices) and a shift toward active man-in-the-middle TLS decryption, or host-based IDPS. The implications of this may be a reduction in network performance, and the need for increased investment in network infrastructure hardware and/or host-based IDPS solution.

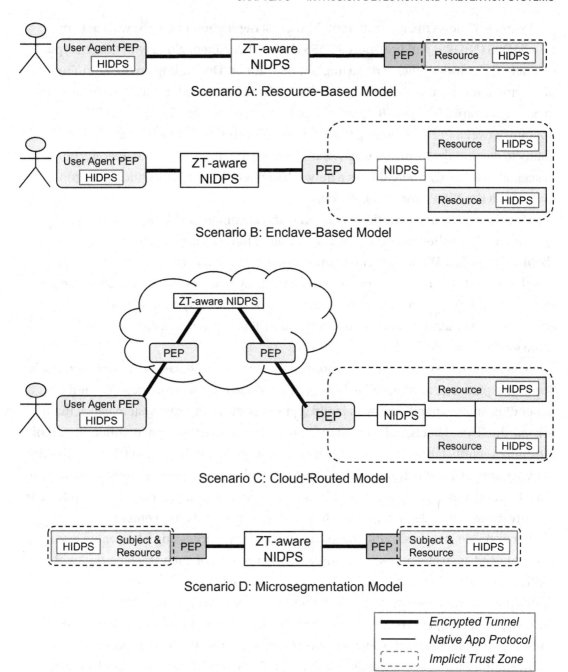

Figure 8-1. *IDPS and Zero Trust Deployment Models*

Figure 8-1 shows the four different Zero Trust deployment models, with network-based IDPS (NIDPS) and host-based IDPS (HIDPS) depicted, along with the encrypted (tunneled) network traffic, and the implicit trust zones. Depending on the Zero Trust deployment model, the NIDPS may be blinded by the tunneled traffic. You can see this in all the scenarios in Figure 8-1, where a NIDPS must be "Zero Trust-aware" if it's to operate between PEPs—meaning that it's part of the Zero Trust system, and has the ability to decrypt the tunneled traffic. Standard NIDPS *can* continue to operate, but only in scenarios B and C, where there's a network segment within the implicit trust zone onto which the NIDPS can be deployed.

Host-based IDPS will continue to operate largely unaffected by the encrypted network traffic, as they run on hosts, and therefore have access to network traffic "behind" the PEPs. While they can operate unchanged in a Zero Trust environment, host-based systems in fact can provide more value by being even just loosely integrated into the Zero Trust environment. For example, a host-based system on a server may adjust its level of scrutiny and alerting if the Zero Trust system indicates a higher risk score for the host's network.

In general, IDPS capabilities are more likely going to be "baked in" to an enterprise's Zero Trust platform, as opposed to being a standalone tool. To some degree—and depending on its capabilities—you could argue that the Zero Trust system will actually *become* the IDPS. That is, IDPS becomes not a separate function, but an inherent part of the entire security fabric. They may be achieved by PEPs which contain IDPS capabilities, or by separate IDPS which sit "behind" the PEPs with some degree of integration into the Zero Trust environment. They should be able to consume policies, resource metadata, or identity context, in order to adjust the level of inspection and enforcement.

For example, network traffic transiting an IDPS that's accessing a low-value resource may not need as stringent (read: resource-intensive) level of analysis compared with traffic for a high-value resource. Or, access from a local user on a corporate-managed device may warrant less scrutiny than a remote user accessing from a BYOD device. These types of integrations can reduce the infrastructure required to support the IDPS, and can also reduce the set of alerts (false positives), which IDPS are prone to.

Integration with Zero Trust also enables the IDPS to take a broader set of actions in response to detected intrusions. While IDS can just notify, and IPS can block the attempted network access, Zero Trust systems have broader reach, and can take actions globally. For example, they can prompt users for step-up authentication, or quarantine user devices across all networks.

Let's examine another area—client-side security products (often comprising both antivirus and IDPS in a single program) are a valuable element of a Zero Trust security architecture. But these solutions can deliver better security (and more value) when integrated with a Zero Trust policy model that can act as a network enforcement point. For example, organizations may want to define an access policy that requires up-to-date antivirus signatures on client devices before permitting access to enterprise-managed resources. The client profile data can be provided by either the client slide or by a central antivirus management system. In either case, the Zero Trust system—acting as a network-based Policy Enforcement Point—can ensure that non-compliant devices are unable to access resources and, for example, only permit access to an IT helpdesk or self-service system for updating antivirus signatures. Because Zero Trust controls all network access to all company resources, this policy can be enforced regardless of the location of the user or the type and location of resources they are accessing.

These are examples of what we believe are really the right way to look at these types of capabilities—not just as IDS or IPS functions but as sources of data (input) into Zero Trust systems, as potential catalysts for action by a Zero Trust system, and as mechanisms for the enforcement of policies. Approaching things this way can improve both security and efficiency, for example, by aligning policy enforcement throughout the network and removing unnecessary or redundant enforcement points.

There is no single way or single correct answer about how to deploy these capabilities—it's entirely dependent on each enterprise's security infrastructure, ecosystem, and approach to Zero Trust. And this is a hard problem, with many divergent products and few standardized ways to tie them together. The good news is that the industry is making progress in this area. For example, the threat intelligence community has been developing and promoting standardized and structured ways to represent and transmit threat intelligence information, through the STIX and TAXII specifications.[7]

Imagine a standards-based threat intelligence feed, which notifies a Zero Trust system about newly detected malware that uses a vulnerability in a specific desktop client OS version, and targets specific application types. This information can be used to increase the scrutiny that an IDPS places on the targeted applications, and trigger the Zero Trust PEP to enforce the installation of a client OS patch before any access is granted.

---

[7]STIX is the Structured Threat Intelligence eXchange, and TAXII is the Trusted Automated eXchange of Intelligence Information. See https://oasis-open.github.io/cti-documentation/ for more information.

We're optimistic about the kinds of integrations that these types of specifications will enable, helping organizations get more value out of their existing IT and security infrastructures, and to better progress on their journeys to Zero Trust.

Summary

In this chapter, we introduced the concepts behind Intrusion Detection and Prevention Systems, including the set of functions these systems typically perform. We also compared the two primary types, host-based and network-based IDPS, and discussed the impact of encrypted network protocols on IDPS. Finally, we looked at IDPS from the perspective of the Zero Trust deployment models, and discussed the potential for their role as a Zero Trust Policy Enforcement Point.

CHAPTER 9

Virtual Private Networks

Virtual Private Networks (VPNs) were first created and deployed in the mid-1990s, as a response to the increasing adoption of enterprise networks, combined with increasingly broad home usage of PCs (either "portable" or desktop PCs deployed in people's homes). Underlying network protocols have evolved and become more standardized (and more secure) over time, of course, but the core concept has remained unchanged: An encrypted network tunnel is established between remote nodes, permitting application traffic to be securely transmitted through this tunnel, across an untrusted intermediary network.

Today, the term "VPN" is actually overloaded, referring to three general types of solutions, as depicted in Figure 9-1.

- Consumer VPN: Shielding end-user Internet-bound traffic from intermediaries, for privacy and security. Often used to ensure privacy or bypass restrictions imposed by ISPs or governments.

- Enterprise VPN: Connecting remote users to an enterprise network. This is our focus, and the type of VPN most impacted by Zero Trust.

- Site-to-site VPN: This is one of the ways by which enterprises can create WANs.

© Jason Garbis and Jerry W. Chapman 2021
J. Garbis and J. W. Chapman, *Zero Trust Security*, https://doi.org/10.1007/978-1-4842-6702-8_9

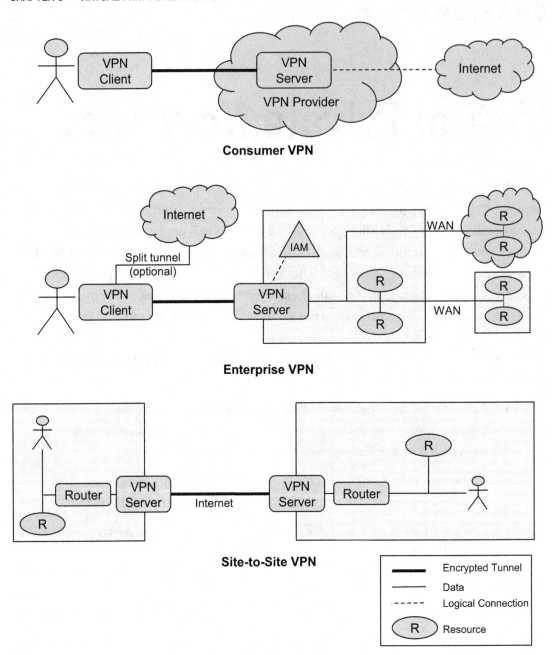

Figure 9-1. *VPN Types*

VPNs require two cooperating components which rely on a shared secret and/or a shared root of trust[1] in order to establish a secure encrypted tunnel. User-centered and enterprise VPNs establish this tunnel between a user's service running a VPN client and the VPN Server (sometimes referred to as the *VPN Concentrator* or *VPN Gateway*). Note that the VPN client in this case may be separately installed software, included in the user's OS, or even run within a browser.

For both of these first two scenarios, some or all user traffic is sent through the encrypted tunnel, in order to maintain privacy and integrity across the untrusted intermediary networks. Once the traffic reaches the VPN server, it's removed from the encapsulating tunnel, and forwarded to its intended destination. For Consumer VPNs, traffic is sent to a destination on the Internet, while for Enterprise VPNs, it's routed to a destination somewhere on the internal corporate network. Note that many enterprise VPNs support "split tunneling," in which only traffic bound for the enterprise network is sent across the tunnel; other traffic proceeds directly from the user's device. The alternative (full tunnel) sends all the user's traffic into the enterprise. This adds latency (and bandwidth costs), but enables the enterprise to perform security functions on all of the user's traffic.

Site-to-site VPNs work slightly differently, providing a secure encrypted WAN tunnel between two fixed locations, effectively turning them into a single logical LAN. In this case, users and devices on those LANs will have some of their traffic routed over the VPN link in order to reach the remote destination. This is all transparent to users; they're not running any VPN software, and their traffic just reaches its destination.

Enterprise VPNs and Security

Let's now examine the Enterprise VPN scenario, beginning with the positive aspects of what they provide. First, of course, they provide an encrypted tunnel for user traffic, between the user's device and the enterprise network. And, they are typically configured to use the enterprise's identity management system (IAM) for user authentication, often via the LDAP or RADIUS protocols.

---

[1]Different types of VPNs approach this differently, e.g., TLS vs. IPSec. The distinction isn't relevant for our discussion.

They can also use basic IAM attributes (such as group memberships) to map users into VPN access control groups. Some VPNs can enforce MFA at the time of initial connection, and some provide host posture checks as additional context to achieve a level of dynamic access control.

All of those features sound positive, and in fact are capabilities which must also be present in a Zero Trust solution. So why are we negative about enterprise VPNs, and insistent that they must be replaced?

We'll be examining VPNs from a Zero Trust perspective in the next section, but even from a traditional point of view, enterprise VPNs have a number of shortcomings. For example, even though their rules can be set up to manage access for individual IP addresses and ports, in general practice, they are not. It's far simpler for network and security teams to assign access to a VLAN or full subnet—which in practice is likely the same broad access that users obtain when they are on premises.[2]

Now, to be fair, it is entirely possible to use VPNs to grant limited and focused access to a minimal set of enterprise resources. This works best for users or user groups who are well defined, and who only need access to a known, fixed set of applications. For example, consider a group of remote workers who are using an internal application to analyze insurance claims. These users might only need access to that one application to do their job. Or consider a third-party contractor who needs access to only a single application. In both these cases, if the applications they need have static IP addresses, a VPN can be used to grant limited network access. However, even if this is the case (which is typically not true for most users), VPNs still exhibit five other flaws.

First, while VPNs can and do use enterprise IAM for authentication and group membership, access control policies are typically very basic from an identity perspective. For example, access will very often be the same for a given set of user credentials, regardless of the device from which the user is connecting. This makes it harder for security teams to restrict access from personal devices, or to prevent the abuse of stolen credentials.

Second, VPNs' access control models are very static from a *resource* perspective— they're configured to grant access to a fixed subnet or set of IP addresses or hostnames. They are simply not designed to dynamically resolve target resources, and adjust user access. Today's IT environments tend to be dynamic, especially for organizations using virtualized resources, or using a DevOps model. This leads organizations to grant too-broad network access, in order to keep users productive.

---

[2]We find it bitterly ironic that the too-permissive network access granted to on-premises users can be used as a justification, however misguided, to grant remote users the same broad access.

Third, as depicted in Figure 9-1, VPNs impose a particular network model on organizations—they only support a single entry point onto the enterprise network. This perpetuates a perimeter-based network model, in which all enterprise resources must be connected via an internal network (LAN or WAN). As we've discussed throughout the book, this represents a security risk, and is also often technically difficult or impossible to achieve in today's distributed and cloud-based world. The implications of this are that either the organization's network is unnecessarily open, or users are forced to continually disconnect and reconnect to a different VPN server in order to access specific resources. The latter will definitely frustrate and impede end users.[3]

Fourth, in order for users to connect, VPN servers *must* expose an open port on the Internet. This makes them an inviting target for attackers worldwide. Unfortunately, there have been many, many recent and widely publicized VPN vulnerabilities, in which unauthorized remote users can compromise a VPN server and obtain entry into the enterprise network. From our perspective, in today's threat landscape, it's unconscionable to expose the "front door" of your enterprise network in this fashion.

And fifth, VPNs are ultimately only a remote access tool—and as such, are a silo. They cannot be used to enforce access controls for on-premises users. Organizations are required to deploy and manage a separate set of network and security tools for on-premises users. This results in duplicated expenses, duplicated work, and inconsistent access controls across toolsets (which will again likely result in too-broad network access, in order to avoid impeding user productivity).

VPNs clearly exhibit many security shortcomings, in addition to a generally poor end-user experience, limited bandwidth, dropped connections, and application conflicts. These are the reasons we're so vehement about their elimination. Let's now contrast them with a Zero Trust approach.

Zero Trust and VPNs

From a Zero Trust perspective, VPNs should really be considered to be *remote access* tools, and not *security* tools. We acknowledge that this is a controversial stance and that organizations can and have achieved some measure of success with their VPNs, but we

---

[3]The split tunneling capabilities of enterprise VPNs don't help here—they only separate enterprise-bound traffic (sent through the single tunnel) from Internet-bound traffic (not tunneled).

believe that VPNs exhibit too many flaws to justify their continued usage. That is, even a well-configured VPN will suffer from limitations that a proper Zero Trust solution shouldn't exhibit. Let's examine how and why this is the case.

A Zero Trust solution should dynamically adjust user access based on contextual information about the user, device, network, system, and target resources. All of this should be driven by the centralized PDP. The solution should also support step-up authentication, based on context and user activity. The Zero Trust solution should also support the ability for remote identities to have multiple concurrent entry points into the enterprise network. This eliminates the requirement to have all distributed resources accessible from that single entry point (the traditional perimeter-based security model). The Zero Trust model inherently supports distributed PEPs, each protecting a logically or physically related set of resources, as depicted in Figure 9-2. Because users access

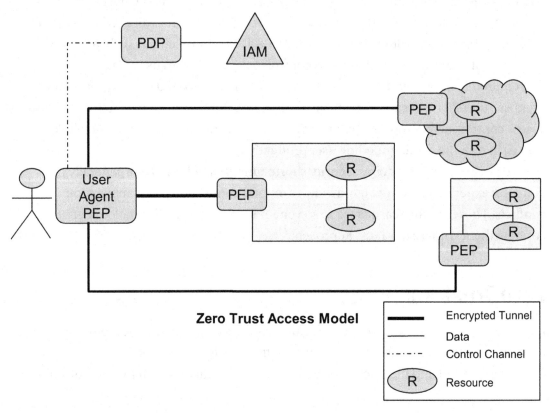

Figure 9-2. *Zero Trust Access Model*

these PEPs directly, there is no need for the enterprise to maintain WAN connections between each of the distributed locations.

Let's now emphasize the two final ways in which Zero Trust systems are superior to VPNs. First, Zero Trust systems should hide the enterprise network entry point from unauthorized users. That is, following the principle of least privilege, remote entities who do not have permission to access any enterprise resources should not be able to see or connect to the network entry point. This, in and of itself, is a huge step forward in terms of security. Note that this can be achieved in two ways—either by cloaking the network entry point in the way that the Software-Defined Perimeter does it[4] or by moving the entry point from the enterprise network to a vendor's cloud-hosted platform (like in the cloud-routed model).

Finally, and perhaps most importantly, Zero Trust provides (by design) a single access control model for on-premises and remote users. VPNs are *only* remote access silos, and as such are just prolonging the headaches and inefficiencies associated with being a standalone solution. Zero Trust's unified access control model simplifies operations, giving organizations one centralized platform within which to define and enforce access control policies across all environments.

Before we close out this chapter, we'd like to briefly discuss how the different Zero Trust deployment models approach remote access, because they can be different. The enclave-based and cloud-routed models both inherently provide remote access capabilities as part of their architectures, and as such will fully replace VPNs. The other two Zero Trust deployment models, resource-based and microsegmentation, however, may not provide built-in remote access capabilities. As you're evaluating potential vendors and architectures, it's important to have a clear grasp of these requirements and potential differences, and to be armed with an appropriate set of questions to distinguish and evaluate the different offerings.

Summary

VPNs provide an outdated and frankly insecure approach to remote access, and must be retired or replaced as organizations move to Zero Trust. As we explained in this chapter, VPNs are flawed solutions, so much so that even well-deployed and well-managed VPN implementations suffer from some significant shortcomings. It's time for organizations

---

[4]Using Single-Packet Authorization, as discussed in Chapter 4.

to move forward, and utilize a richer and more effective set of tools with which to build their access control models.

With the adoption of Zero Trust, your enterprise network and security infrastructure shouldn't contain a remote access solution (enterprise VPN). It should just *be* an *access* solution, which is deployed so that it enforces access control for both remote and on-premises users, based on a unified platform and policy model. And, unlike VPNs, it embraces rather than fights the distributed nature of resources that users are accessing.

CHAPTER 10

Next-Generation Firewalls

In this chapter, we're largely going to be examining the place of Next-Generation Firewalls (NGFWs) within a Zero Trust landscape. We've actually already discussed most of the primary functions that are part of NGFW products, including core firewalling, IDS/IPS, and VPN, in previous chapters. As such, this chapter will discuss the role that NGFW capabilities and platforms should play in a Zero Trust world, rather than a direct analysis of their functionality.

Our goal is to help you understand where and how NGFW solutions should be part of your Zero Trust architecture, and how to ensure that they can be well-integrated into the rest of your enterprise components. In order to do that, we'll first examine the market category.

History and Evolution

Enterprise network firewalls began by providing a very focused set of basic network functions—the classic 5-tuple firewall rule introduced in Chapter 6. These traditional firewalls—especially when viewed from today's perspective—were clearly more focused on *networking* (allowing or disallowing network packets) with no concept of *identity*. Over time, successful firewall vendors innovated, and eventually the market settled on the "Next-Generation" moniker.

Today, essentially, all enterprise firewalls are "next generation" and typically include IDS/IPS, traffic analysis and malware detection for threat detection, URL filtering, and some degree of application awareness/control. Like the NAC market segment, vendors in this area began a journey to identity-centric security around the same time that Zero Trust ideas began percolating through the industry. Today, many NGFW vendors offer Zero Trust capabilities, with varying degrees of success in meeting the principles we've outlined prior. Let's look at them from this perspective.

© Jason Garbis and Jerry W. Chapman 2021
J. Garbis and J. W. Chapman, *Zero Trust Security*, https://doi.org/10.1007/978-1-4842-6702-8_10

Zero Trust and NGFWs

We believe that it's fair and reasonable to give some NGFW providers credit for being pioneers in enabling and enforcing some Zero Trust principles for on-premises enterprise networks. Their NGFW products provide a degree of identity centricity and fine-grained policies, but fall short of meeting our Zero Trust principles. Most notably, NGFW are still firewalls, in the sense that their scope of control is limited. Most notably, they are not platforms that can provide security for "all users for all resources regardless of location"—this is simply not a design goal. They don't provide fine-grained remote access, generally don't have user authentication, encryption, or device isolation (no user agent PEP), and are typically hardware-based.

Of course, NGFW vendors have built on and expanded their platforms, via acquisition and organic feature development, adding in remote access and other capabilities as we've covered in earlier chapters. While this has been a successful market space, for certain, and there are NGFW vendors with credible Zero Trust offerings, we don't believe that it'd be quite accurate to state the NGFW space has morphed into Zero Trust. There are many credible Zero Trust providers who didn't begin from a NGFW perspective, and whose platforms have different architectures.

It's important to understand that we're not attempting to analyze specific vendor offerings or architectures here—as we discussed in our introduction, that's a rapidly moving target, and such an assessment would be neither accurate nor fair. What we are attempting to do is provide an explanation and framework so you can understand the functional components that typically make up an NGFW, and assess them from the perspective of a Zero Trust architecture.

A Zero Trust architecture may or may not include products that are categorized as NGFWs. But it will certainly include those capabilities that historically have been part of NGFWs—such as IDS/IPS and an identity and application-aware policy enforcement model. As such, it's important to talk about the role of NGFWs in a Zero Trust architecture. There are two aspects of this that we want to cover: first, the implications of having network traffic encrypted between components on the network, and second, the overall network topology NGFW-based solutions may impose.

Network Traffic Encryption: Implications

One important implication of Zero Trust principles is that network traffic must be encrypted, either within its native application protocol (e.g., HTTPS) or as a result of being routed through an encrypted tunnel. While the former is suitable for some scenarios (e.g., SaaS applications), most Zero Trust implementations rely on an encrypted tunnel into a PEP, for a variety of reasons that we discussed in Chapter 3. The implications of this are that the traffic between user agents and the network PEPs becomes opaque to any intermediate network component. We touched on this topic in our chapter on IDS/IPS, and want to revisit it here from a slightly different perspective.

Network traffic that's encrypted between the user's device and a PEP has several implications, as depicted in Figure 10-1.[1] In all cases, intermediate network components (middleboxes) can continue to perform core firewall functions, which operate at a network header level and do not need access to any encrypted payload data. All functions that require access to payloads can be deployed "behind" the PEP, when the network traffic has been extracted from the encrypted tunnel, and is being transmitted with its native application protocol. Note that by definition, this is occurring within the implicit trust zone, as shown in Figure 10-1, Scenario A.

---

[1]Note that this diagram depicts the enclave-based deployment model. Similar arguments apply with the other Zero Trust deployment models.

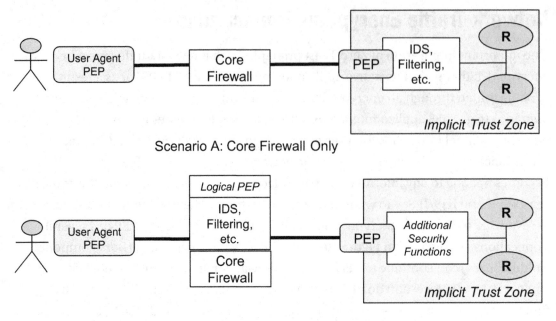

Scenario A: Core Firewall Only

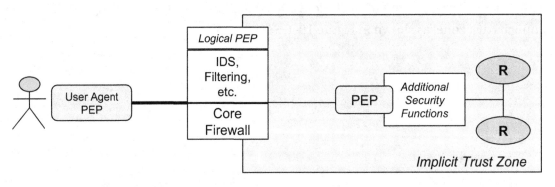

Scenario B: Logical PEP with re-encryption

Scenario C: Logical PEP with expanded implicit trust zone

Figure 10-1. *Next-Generation Firewall Deployment Scenarios*

If the networked component is intended to perform analysis or take action based on the payload, it has no choice but to decrypt the payload as depicted in Scenario B. This implies that the NGFW is a logical Zero Trust PEP—from our perspective, if it has access to the encryption key, it must be considered part of the Zero Trust platform. This logical PEP performs one or more security functions (such IDS or URL filtering), which may also require performing application traffic proxying. Scenario B depicts the situation where this component re-encrypts the network traffic, sending it toward the second PEP and into the implicit trust zone through another tunnel. This scenario requires a substantial amount of processing by the NGFW, which will add network latency and may require a heftier (and more expensive) appliance with the necessary horsepower.[2]

Alternatively, the NGFW can send the application traffic to the second PEP without re-encrypting it, as shown in Scenario C. This reduces (somewhat) the workload on the NGFW, but also results in an expanded implicit trust zone, so you need to understand the implications of this in your environment and network. In both scenarios B and C, the existing PEP (or components behind it) can perform additional security enforcement functions.

It's very important to be aware of any potential misalignment of policies that are being enforced by the NGFW as a logical PEP and the second PEP. This is especially important if these security components are provided by separate vendors, or have different policy models. None of this is intended to imply that Zero Trust platforms from the NGFW vendors are inherently better or more effective than alternatives—in fact, as we'll see next, there are additional trade-offs and considerations that warrant attention.

Network Architectures

In any Zero Trust architecture, it's critical that your team has a solid understanding of any solution's overall network topology, and how it aligns with your enterprise network architecture. Such architectures are in some ways continually evolving—such as through the adoption of cloud-based resources—and in some ways very static or unchanging, for example, WAN links that may have been in place for years.

We're examining this topic here, because some NGFW-based solutions may require certain network architectures, or impose certain constraints which may limit the ability to smoothly proceed on your journey to Zero Trust. Let's look at two examples of Zero Trust network architectures, depicted in Figure 10-2.

---

[2]To be interpreted as RAM, CPU speed, etc.

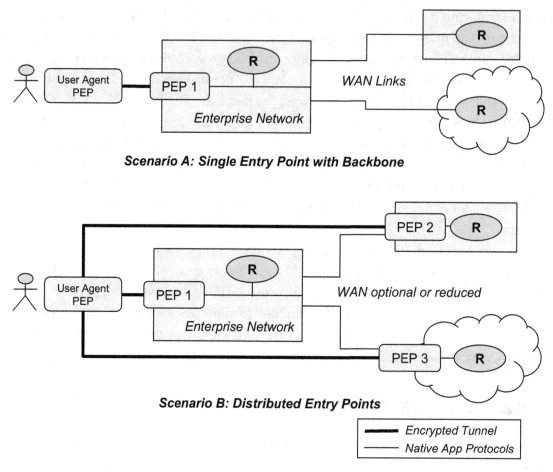

Figure 10-2. *Zero Trust Network Architectures*

Scenario A shows an architecture that may be imposed by NGFW-based Zero Trust platforms, with a single entry point into the enterprise network for remote users. Distributed resources (which all modern enterprises are using today) require a Wide Area Network or backbone. The WAN will have simple firewalls in place at the ingress points of the remote networks, enforcing basic network Access Control Lists (ACL).

The overarching issue with this approach is that it perpetuates the notion of a hard perimeter with a soft internal network. Because PEP1 is the only point where Zero Trust tenets are being enforced, this architecture falls short of our goals. There are also two other issues with this approach.

First, the WAN itself imposes additional network latency, essentially requiring backhaul of all user traffic to the PEP 1 ingress point. And of course, WAN bandwidth has a cost to the organization. Second, this approach can impose a loss of fidelity in terms of policies—PEP1 is so "far away" from the resources in the remote locations that it's difficult for it to be very effective in terms of enforcing fine-grained or dynamic access policies.

Let's contrast this with Scenario B, which has distributed entry points—users connect directly to their authorized PEPs. This eliminates the need to backhaul user traffic to PEP1, reducing latency and WAN costs. Organizations can significantly reduce their WAN usage, and can often eliminate it completely, replacing it with simple Internet connectivity. This also has the advantage of retaining complete fidelity—all PEPs have their full ability to enforce fine-grained, identity-centric, dynamic policies against their local resources. Also, because PEP 2 and PEP 3 are full Zero Trust enforcement nodes, they have the ability to make API calls and discover attributes about their protected environments and resources.

Be sure to keep in mind that actual architectures may differ from this—many vendors will support a blended or hybrid model, and your enterprise will no doubt have unique aspects to it. We encourage you to ask good questions, and make sure you invest the time and energy to understand your current and planned network topology from the perspectives discussed here.

Summary

To recap, we believe that the adoption of Zero Trust will have a significant impact on the NGFW market, continuing to blur its lines as a previously well-defined and standalone segment. Just like the "enterprise firewall" market matured, so that today essentially every enterprise firewall has features that previously were considered "next-gen," we're seeing NGFW vendors add Zero Trust capabilities.

We think that moving forward, enterprises will increasingly deploy network security solutions that embrace Zero Trust principles, which by definition require a broader perspective and a broader policy model. This is a good thing—organizations are consistently looking to deploy fewer solutions that cover a broader area; they recognize that siloed security solutions are antithetical to a Zero Trust approach. As a result, they should ensure that their chosen security components support rich APIs and the ability to be easily integrated (one of our extended Zero Trust principles).

In our minds, the key decisions about a Zero Trust architecture are the sources of identity and context available to the PDP, and how broadly the policy model can be applied via PEPs distributed across enterprise assets. There isn't a single commercially available platform today with a policy model and set of PEPs that can be applied universally across your users, infrastructure, and use cases. This is one of the reasons that Zero Trust is a journey.

This underscores the importance of choosing wisely—ensuring that your chosen platforms and tools align well with your initial use cases and that they have the ability to be integrated with the rest of your environment and PEPs. You might choose to use an NGFW vendor's platform as a core part of your Zero Trust architecture, and that may well be a sensible decision. Just make sure to be aware of the limits (boundaries) of the platform, ask some hard questions about how it can be integrated into your broader ecosystem, and be aware of any architectural constraints. You will have PEPs that are outside the vendor's platform, yet which need to be integrated. Make sure your chosen platform will efficiently and effectively support this in your environment.

CHAPTER 11

Security Operations

Many enterprises have invested in creating a Security Operations Center (SOC) as a physical or virtual organization, compiling a set of focused people, processes, and technologies to address threats, vulnerabilities, and incident response. This chapter examines two primary tools in use in SOCs—Security Information and Event Management (SIEM) and Security Orchestration, Automation, and Response (SOAR). We'll be looking at these tools from the perspective of Zero Trust, exploring how together they can improve the effectiveness and efficiency of daily operations in the SOC. But before we can tie these systems together, let's discuss some of the reasons that SIEM and SOAR tools exist.

Modern IT systems generate immense volumes of log data, in wildly different formats, locations, and schema. These logs serve multiple purposes, such as, periodic IT access for troubleshooting or diagnostics, ongoing anomaly detection, and longer-term archives for forensic or audit purposes. These logs not only provide a broad picture of infrastructure elements and their interactions, but also allow SOC analysts and tools to review and synthesize events across the entire IT environment. SIEM tools have grown to handle the large volumes and wide diversity of log data, and have become an indispensable part of modern SOCs.

Of course, security analysts do much more than examine logs—they spend a lot of time and effort on incident response and event management. Fortunately, SOAR tools provide automated (or at least semi-automated) workflows that can be quickly integrated to support the necessary incident response requirements across the breadth of tools in the SOC. As SOC operations are core to an organization's security program, the growing capabilities of SOAR tools will help transform how SOC teams utilize the immense amount of data and number of security events to become more effective.

In practice, SIEMs and SOARs are increasingly becoming two inseparable parts of a SOC. The value of SIEMs and SOARs will in fact only continue to grow as organizations adopt Zero Trust architectures, and in this chapter, we explain how and why these tools benefit from being well-integrated into a Zero Trust architecture, as identity context becomes more prevalent throughout the security ecosystem.

143

© Jason Garbis and Jerry W. Chapman 2021
J. Garbis and J. W. Chapman, *Zero Trust Security*, https://doi.org/10.1007/978-1-4842-6702-8_11

Security Information and Event Management

SIEM tools provide mechanisms for collecting, aggregating, and normalizing log data for detection and evaluation of security events within an organization. IT organizations have been utilizing logs and aggregating log management systems for decades, and the security-specific market area, which we now refer to as SIEM, emerged around 2005. SIEM vendors innovated beyond basic log management, and developed a set of security-focused capabilities for unifying, normalizing, aggregating, correlating, and analyzing log data, turning it into security information and (ideally) actionable events. This log data is typically ingested from not only IT infrastructure (servers, firewalls, etc.) but also from security systems such as IDS/IPS, endpoint management, authentication systems, and others.[1]

These types of enterprise systems and networks generate large volumes of log data, which are often overwhelming for analysts. SIEMs help sort this out and provide analytics, filters, visualizations, and other tools, for example, to reduce the number of false positives.

Historically, SIEM providers have been deployed in an on-premises model, but recently have shifted toward a cloud-based model. There are advantages and disadvantages of the two SIEM deployment models (on-prem vs. cloud), but from a Zero Trust perspective, these differences are largely irrelevant—the integration scenarios, requirements, and benefits we discuss later are identical. That is, regardless of your SIEM location, you can obtain substantial value by integrating it into your Zero Trust architecture.

In addition to aggregating logs, SIEMs can help map an organization's network infrastructure by synthesizing this raw data. This can benefit security and IT teams, as it provides useful context about where events are happening in a network. This is interesting because it starts to provide information about high-value (or at least, highly utilized) assets in the organization, which can help organizations better define and plan their Zero Trust strategy and architecture, for example, by influencing policy definitions or deployment locations for PEPs.

---

[1]We've noted some of the systems that provide data to the SIEM; others include antivirus systems, Endpoint Detection and Response, User and Entity Behavior Analytics (UEBA), Mobile Device Management (MDM), and Unified Endpoint Management (UEM). In short, any enterprise IT system log can be fed into a SIEM.

SIEMs by themselves have proven quite useful, providing data aggregation and aiding in decision-making for security analysts, and a natural extension for these platforms has been to provide structured and event-driven ways to automate responses and actions to detected events. These capabilities have coalesced into a set of offerings that we refer to as SOAR.

Security Orchestration, Automation, and Response

SOARs are often used in conjunction with SIEMs; in fact, sometimes, they're provided by the same vendor as part of an integrated platform. A SOAR will consume information (and detected events, or threshold alerts) reported from a SIEM and provide a model and mechanism for automating a series of response actions, often guided by machine learning.

This is helpful, because as SOARs sift through the large number of events emitted by a SIEM, they provide a common context for events, and ultimately automate processes or workflow in response to the event. This integrated automation helps reduce the number of false positives in an environment, so that true incidents can be reviewed by security engineers.

SOAR's value is not just automation but also the modeling of the logical analysis and response flows. These workflows contain information about enterprises networks, systems, dependencies, and how to work with them—which is too frequently just "tribal knowledge" that solely exists in senior analysts' heads. With a SOAR, this knowledge can be built into an automated, repeatable, and reliable platform, which never needs to take a day off work. This codified knowledge can (and should) elevate a SOC into a seamless integration of people, process, and technology. From a Zero Trust perspective, achieving these principles requires more than standalone technologies—it requires integration and coordination, as well as "reach" to effect changes across the enterprise security infrastructure—something that a SOAR is well suited to achieve when connected with a Zero Trust platform. In particular, SOARs help SOCs achieve their mission, by providing automation of repeatable, predictable processes. Most SOARs will recognize decision patterns and help manage the entire incident response lifecycle while also actively gathering threat intelligence, and reacting and providing context to data. Additionally, vulnerability management[2] and threat intelligence are core responsibilities in a SOC—with the SOAR providing a good workflow and incident response pattern to support these, and their results contributing to the continued growth and learning of the SOAR solution.

The analysis and actions that SIEM and SOAR provide are very important components of an effective Zero Trust system—as additional context into and catalysts for decisions to be made by the PDP, which we'll explore further in the next section.

Zero Trust in the Security Operations Center

SIEMs and SOARs will remain key parts of enterprise security, and in fact, their value and importance will be increased as organizations adopt Zero Trust. That is, as enterprises proceed on their journey to Zero Trust, they should expect (and demand) improved breadth, depth, and overall effectiveness of their SIEM/SOAR. Additionally, the automated learning achieved by a Zero Trust-integrated SOAR will only improve decisions made by the PDP to support the overall environment. Let's now explore the ways this occurs.

Enriched Log Data

One of the key features of SIEMs is their ability to correlate data from siloed systems—such as the assignment of a dynamic IP address to a user, and network activities later performed by that IP address. However, SIEMs are limited to the set of data provided by their source systems, and are often stymied by underlying technical limitations and siloed infrastructure elements. For example, network access often traverses network boundaries where Network Address Translation (NAT) occurs, which can make it difficult or impossible to attribute actions on an IP address to a specific user. Also, in many cases, logs are generated by systems that utilize siloed or disconnected identity management systems, making it difficult for SIEMs and security analysts to consolidate or disambiguate user IDs across disparate log sources.

---

[2]Vulnerability management is interpreted in many ways, but at the end of the day, it's about ensuring your network and devices are secured through proper techniques, and providing visibility into these devices' status.

Zero Trust systems not only eliminate many of these technical limitations, they also significantly increase the richness of data ingested by SIEMs and therefore increase their ability to correlate and detect security-related events. Specifically—because it's fundamentally identity-centric, a Zero Trust system will be able to log detailed identity-enriched data into a SIEM. This enriched log data will be more meaningful to the SIEM and to SOC engineers, enhancing their ability to effectively respond. Put another way—a Zero Trust system should be able to log all network access by all users, and to enrich this log data with information about their identity, devices, and overall context. This should be true regardless of where a user is located, how many intermediate network boundaries are crossed, what network protocol is used, or how a given application's identity system may refer to a specific user.

Orchestration and Automation (Triggers and Events)

Enterprise Zero Trust systems require a high degree of automation, and must have the ability to detect and respond to various triggers and events at scale. As we've discussed throughout, the *dynamic* aspect of the Zero Trust policy model is a significant contributor to its value. SOAR systems, because they are broader in scope than Zero Trust, can enhance and improve the effectiveness of a Zero Trust system. In fact, combining SOAR and Zero Trust through a set of coordinated events, orchestrated API calls, and triggers will benefit both systems.

The details of which component is performing which function will be dependent on your specific architecture and platforms, but in general, workflows that are coordinated between a PDP and a SOC security analyst will inform and execute on real-time decisions and actions. We'll be exploring a few examples in the following sections. Of course, this integration requires a set of bidirectional APIs,[3] to perform actions such as exchanging updated data, triggering a policy evaluation refresh, or programmatically creating new policies or virtual infrastructure components.

---

[3]Strictly speaking, this integration could occur via APIs, messaging, consuming configuration files such as YAML, or other means. They may also be synchronous or asynchronous. Good Zero Trust and SOAR platforms will support multiple integration means. We're depicting these integrations here as synchronous API calls for simplicity, but evaluate your specific platforms' capabilities and choose the most appropriate mechanism for the use case at hand.

We'll be covering these in more depth later, in Chapter 17, but we wanted to provide an overview here since it's relevant to this discussion. From the perspective of a Zero Trust system, there are four primary types of triggers, which are natural ways to interface with external systems such as SIEMS and SOARs. Three of these are initiated by the Zero Trust system, with the fourth initiated by an external system.

Authentication Trigger

For users, this typically occurs just once or a few times per day. For services (non-person entities), this can be much less frequent. This trigger of course initiates a policy evaluation by the PDP, and is a natural time for the PDP to make queries to a SIEM/SOAR to obtain additional user or environmental context.

Resource Access Trigger

Identities, of course, access resources many, many times throughout each day, via a PEP. It is often appropriate for a PEP to make occasional calls to a SIEM/SOAR to obtain up-to-date context, especially for attributes that may have changed in the time period since authentication, such as device risk level based on observed activity. PEPs shouldn't be re-evaluating things on every access, so look at how your Zero Trust system models this trigger.

Periodic (Session Expiration) Trigger

Many Zero Trust systems have a concept of an identity session, which naturally has a limited lifespan (such as several hours). Upon session expiration, Zero Trust systems often perform a refresh on the identity's assigned policies, and this is also a natural time for the PDP to make calls to the SIEM/SOAR, similar to authentication time, to obtain additional context.

External Trigger

Finally, many Zero Trust systems support inbound APIs by which external components can trigger events and update contextual information.

Of course, your SIEM/SOAR must support a corresponding set of both inbound and outbound APIs, in order to obtain maximum benefit from a Zero Trust system. As you're evaluating Zero Trust systems, look for one that provides a rich set of actions, in order to support a wide variety of integrations. Let's dive into three examples of integrations between Zero Trust and SIEM/SOAR, to make this concrete.

Zero Trust Querying for Additional Context (Authentication Trigger)

In our first scenario, a Zero Trust system is making API calls into a SIEM[4] as depicted in Figure 11-1, at the time of user authentication. This integration is designed to provide the PDP with additional information for better decision-making.

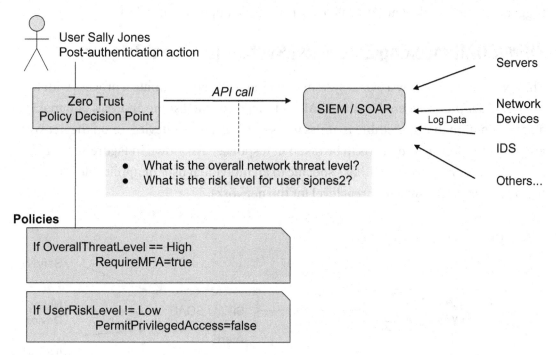

Figure 11-1. *Zero Trust System Making Decision Based on SIEM/SOAR*

In this example, the Zero Trust system is taking the immediate next step after Sally has successfully authenticated, and therefore performing its role as a PDP—evaluating policies and making decisions about which resources Sally should be permitted to access at this point in time, based on relevant contextual information. In our example, the Zero Trust system uses two attributes that it obtains from the SIEM system via API call—the overall threat level on the network and the risk level associated with Sally.

The policies shown evaluate these attributes, and use them within the Zero Trust system's means of enforcement. The first policy requires MFA if the SIEM has indicated that the overall network threat level is High. The second policy prevents access to

---

[4]Note that this is distinct from the baseline capabilities of feeding Zero Trust log data into the SIEM, which we discussed previously.

resources categorized as requiring privileged access if the user in question has been flagged as not currently having a low risk level—perhaps based on device posture or observed network behavior.

The previous example shows the PDP querying the SIEM/SOAR in response to the authentication trigger. The Zero Trust system will also benefit from being able to perform a similar query based on the session expiration trigger, as well as the resource access trigger. Let's now look at an API call occurring in the opposite direction.

SIEM/SOAR Invoking Zero Trust System (External Trigger)

This example shows how a SOAR system makes an API call to initiate a process with the PDP. This action is triggered by the SOAR system performing some analysis, and making a determination that something is amiss in a server, in a user's device, or on the network and that therefore action needs to be taken in response.[5] As shown in Figure 11-2, this call may contain information that's specific to an individual user or applicable more broadly (such as the overall threat level for the network).

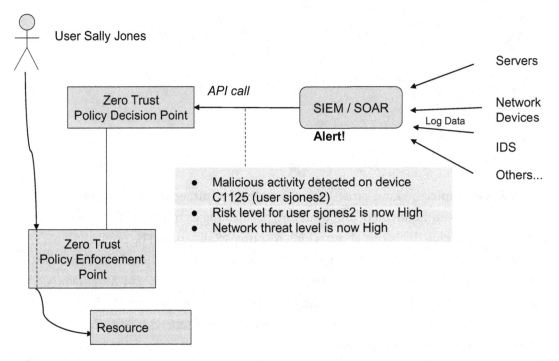

Figure 11-2. *SOAR Initiating Workflow/Response*

---

[5]This may be triggered by a SIEM analyst in the Security Operations Center, or be the automated response of a SOAR.

In this scenario, of course, the Zero Trust system must be able to respond appropriately to the API call from the SOAR, based on policies. For example, given an observation of anomalous behavior on Sally's device, the Zero Trust system could take actions that might include

- Prompting Sally to re-authenticate on that device[6]

- Prompting Sally for some sort of MFA

- Immediately restricting Sally's device access, such as by quarantining it on the network

- Warning Sally

Indirect Integration (External Trigger)

One final note on the interaction between the SIEM and the Zero Trust system. The previous example, while simple in its interaction, is actually complex behind the scenes—it requires that the SIEM/SOAR be configured to be aware of which data the Zero Trust needs in order to evaluate its policies. This adds complexity and operational overhead to the system, because now there's a bidirectional dependency on data between these two systems. If a policy in the Zero Trust system is configured to start using a new attribute from the SIEM/SOAR, now the SIEM/SOAR will also need to be changed to include that attribute in its API calls into the Zero Trust system. This requires coordinated changes on both sides, adding complexity. An alternative, and simpler, approach is to have the Zero Trust system ask the SIEM/SOAR for the data it needs. This way, changes to a Zero Trust policy won't require any changes to the SIEM—as long as it contains the data it's being asked for, it can provide it. This model is depicted in Figure 11-3.

---

[6]Security teams should put some thought into their threat model and desired user experience when designing these responses. If the premise is that there is malware actively running on Sally's device, it's reasonable to assume that it could be recording keystrokes and screen captures. Therefore, prompting Sally to enter her credentials or an OTP on that infected device may be a poor choice, which can further compromise security. Far better would be to prompt for MFA on a separate device (e.g., smartphone), or simply quarantine the device. The severity of response must depend on the level of confidence in the malicious activity and the team's experience with false positives from their SIEM and SOC.

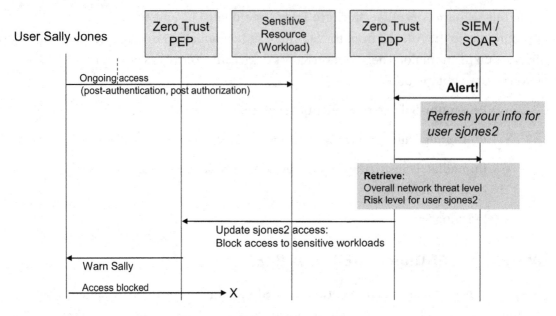

Figure 11-3. *Swimlane of SOAR and PEP Interaction*

In this diagram—depicted as a swimlane for simplicity—Sally has already authenticated and been authorized to access a sensitive workload. Then, the SOAR system notices anomalous activity associated with Sally or her device and makes a simple API call into the Zero Trust PDP, telling it that something has changed and that the Zero Trust system needs to update its information for Sally (user sjones2). Based on that API call, the Zero Trust system then reacts—likely by re-evaluating the entire set of policies for Sally, which includes retrieving updated information about her from multiple systems, including the SOAR. Notice that it's the Zero Trust system, not the SOAR, which is deciding which information it needs—this means that there is no need for the SOAR to be aware of what data elements the PDP needs to evaluate its policies. Based on this updated information, the PDP makes the decision that Sally should no longer have access to the sensitive resource, and it informs the PEP of this change. In our example, the security team has also chosen to warn Sally, perhaps via a pop-up message, or an SMS.

Summary

SIEM and SOAR tools have become indispensable elements of modern SOCs, providing invaluable analysis, visualization, and response capabilities for security analysts. In a Zero Trust architecture, the SIEM or SOAR can (and should) become instrumental in bringing solutions together for immediate and near-real-time analysis and response. The integration scenarios we discussed here illustrate how these systems can be brought together at different times, based on different triggers, to improve security and response efficiency and effectiveness. These examples are far from exhaustive—there are many other ways in which Zero Trust systems and SIEM/SOAR can integrate to perform valuable and interesting functions. Look at how your SOC team operates with the tools they have in place, and educate them on the kind of identity and context-enriched data your Zero Trust system can feed into their platforms. It's very likely that together you'll think of a myriad of ways in which these integrations can help your organization. And, having the SOC team on board can only help accelerate your Zero Trust journey.

CHAPTER 12

Privileged Access Management

Privileged Access Management (PAM) is a sector of the IT security industry, with vendor offerings that control, manage, and report on how privileged users (system admins) access systems or resources, via a set of security functions and processes. PAM can be used to control access to *any* system, but is generally just applied to high-value resources such as domain controllers and production servers. Zero Trust security, of course, is based on the premise that it should be used to protect *all* systems, but high-value systems—the ones typically also protected by PAM—are good candidates for initial Zero Trust projects or scope.

PAM solutions have evolved and expanded as the market has matured and today provide features centered on password vaulting, secrets sharing, and session management. While PAM typically does authenticate users with enterprise identity providers, and can often use group membership to control access, we believe it makes sense to categorize these solutions as identity-aware, rather than identity-centric. This distinction is necessary to understand because a PAM solution may look in some ways like a Zero Trust system, and it may even provide some PEP-like capabilities, but cannot be considered a Zero Trust solution on its own. We'll return to this topic at the conclusion of this chapter, but first let's take a look at the three core functions typically provided by PAM.

Password Vaulting

PAM solutions began by offering the simple concept of a *password vault*—instead of relying on admin users to individually maintain passwords for privileged accounts, these credentials are instead stored in a secure repository. The vault provides secure storage and access management for passwords, and also automates their lifecycle, including expiration

155

and rotation. These systems implement the required business processes, including access request and approval processes for "checking out" passwords for use (historically, password vaults acted like a library for passwords, and users "checked out" passwords in the same way that patrons check a book out of a library). In practice today, credentials are actually often ephemeral, and are typically rotated after the designated period expires. Sometimes users never even see the password; they're authenticated automatically, with the PAM system signing them into the target system behind the scenes.

Today, password vaulting has evolved from a simple process of storing passwords for privileged accounts, to providing passwords through APIs to support service accounts, as well as password management for these accounts. These API capabilities help applications, scripts, and service accounts avoid storing passwords in clear text, or in locations that are vulnerable to compromise.

In the context of PAM, password vaulting is valuable because it's a means to achieve several goals. First, it provides a least privileged model around access to credentials, which is obviously a component of Zero Trust environments. Second, it helps enforce business processes around obtaining access to sensitive resources. Last, it ensures that access to privileged systems is logged and auditable, which is important in many regulated environments.

Secrets Management

Over time, PAM solutions expanded from storing and managing relatively simple user passwords to supporting a broader set of *secrets management* capabilities. Secrets are not limited to passwords, they can include any type of information necessary to directly or indirectly secure systems. The following are examples of elements other than passwords that may be stored in a secret sharing solution:

- Hashes

- Certificates

- Cloud tenant information

- API keys

- Database storage information

- Personal Information

- SSH connection information

What these all have in common is a need to reliably store this sensitive information in a way that's only accessible to authenticated and authorized identities and maintains its data integrity (i.e., cannot be tampered with). Secrets management systems must support both user and system access in ways that are secure and auditable.

In addition to the technical benefits of secrets management, there are some business- and process-oriented benefits as well—specifically, the workflows and processes put in place to both store and obtain these secrets. The simple fact that there's a (controlled) location and secure storage provides organizations with the ability to ensure they avoid ad hoc storage of credentials, reducing the risk that they get stolen or lost.

And as a last note, as mentioned previously, non-person entities accessing the secrets management location via API mechanisms can be used to automate the retrieval of secrets in an application or server during the bootstrapping of that environment.

Privileged Session Management

Privileged Session Management (PSM) is one of the most important aspects of PAM— especially since it's not typically a native part of a Zero Trust solution. Often, compliance requirements and audit issues will be the drivers that prompt organizations to budget and deploy a PSM solution, rather than a strict security driver. PSM solutions essentially intercept or proxy system administrator access to target systems, providing a mechanism to monitor, record, and constrain admin access through protocols such as Remote Desktop Protocol (RDP) and Secure Shell (SSH) access.

PSM solutions typically provide two main functions for enterprises. First, they can provide keylogging or session recording of admin access, ensuring that all such activities are logged for audit, compliance, and forensic purposes. Second, they can also provide "supervised" admin access, where a second individual can view an admin's session in real time, as a way to ensure oversight of high-risk activities.

PSM is also often used to enforce role-based access on a privileged system, by providing users with just enough permissions to support necessary tasks. This can take the form of restricting permissions granted to the admin's account, as well as by actually blocking certain commands from being executed on the target device. For example, imagine that a Windows developer needs to deploy code and then restart a specific site within an IIS server, but should be prevented from issuing an IISRESET command. The PSM can ensure that their granted role only has the minimal necessary permissions. Another example for a Linux system would be having the session management system prevent users from attempting to move laterally via the *ssh* command.

Summarizing our introduction to PAM, Figure 12-1 shows one way in which a PAM solution may be deployed, with a central PAM policy server and a distributed set of PAM agents running on production servers (the protected resources). In this example, the organization may have chosen to use their PAM solution as an alternative to other approaches, such as jump boxes.

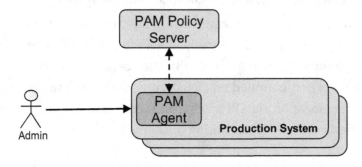

Figure 12-1. *PAM Providing Access Control Through Session Management*

In this example, the agent receives information from the policy server, which defines what permissions a given user can perform on the target system. That is, while the user has direct access to the server, the agent controls who can log in, and may also provide RBAC controls as well as control of admin actions. Note that we're deliberately portraying the PAM components using terminology that's consistent with Zero Trust, since there are in some ways commonality between them. There are also some important differences, which we'll explore in the next section.

Finally, looking forward (and looking more broadly than just Zero Trust), the growing adoption of serverless computing and DevOps-style "immutable infrastructure" is changing the ways in which admins perform privileged actions, and making traditional PSM (and to some degree password vaulting as well) less relevant. As organizations make this philosophical change, they shift so that admins *never* actually have to log into a production system to perform a manual task. Done properly, this results in faster and more reliable outcomes, where more is driven "as code" and less performed via manual tasks. Note that we'll talk about this later in the DevOps scenario in Chapter 18.

Zero Trust and PAM

Now that we've looked at PAM from the perspective of traditional IT and security, let's talk about how the elements of PAM exist within a Zero Trust environment. Keep in mind that while PAM functions (vaulting, secrets, session recording) will continue to have an important role to play in security architectures, there may be some changes (and potential diminishment) within a Zero Trust environment.

As we mentioned previously, many PAM solutions do already have a built-in policy and access model, and are able to integrate with identity providers for user authentication, role-based access control, and attribute-based access control. In this way, they are to some degree acting like policy enforcement points. But let's first address the "800-pound gorilla" of PAM—password vaulting. The entire premise of password vaulting is based on the non-Zero Trust approach of a too-open network, where every user has ongoing network access to every server, and therefore a vault with server password obfuscation and rotation is required. This premise is no longer true with Zero Trust! In theory, in a Zero Trust network, you could actually do away with passwords for privileged access to servers, and instead rely on the PEPs to enforce Zero Trust policies, tied to context and business processes. Now, we're not suggesting you actually do this, but it is an important perspective, and does illustrate the way in which a Zero Trust network can alter the value proposition of a password vault. We don't recommend actively decommissioning PAM vaults, but you should consider not using PAM vaults for new environments and projects. Do keep in mind that the other functions within PAM—secrets management and session recording—will remain relevant in a Zero Trust world.

Let's continue exploring how PAM relates to Zero Trust. The most straightforward and easily achieved approach is to protect access to the PAM server itself, by putting it behind a PEP, as depicted in Figure 12-2. In this scenario, the PAM solution is a protected resource within the Zero Trust architecture. While straightforward, this is nonetheless sensible and valuable—increasing the security of the PAM solution by preventing unauthorized users or devices from accessing it. This is good security practice—after all, if the PAM server houses the "keys to the kingdom," it's a natural target for malicious actors.

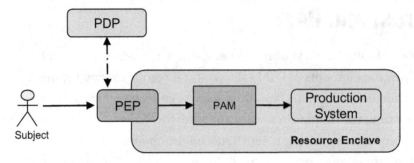

Figure 12-2. *Deploying the PAM Behind a PEP*

Moving beyond this simple scenario, let's explore how PAM could better integrate with a Zero Trust solution, such as by using identity context or helping enforce policies.

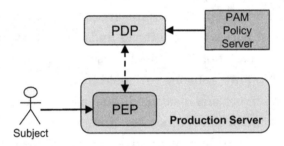

Figure 12-3. *PAM Integration with Zero Trust*

One possible integration is depicted in Figure 12-3, showing how a PDP can be integrated with and able to consume PAM information or policies, for incorporation into the Zero Trust policy model. This integration could be as simple as using the PAM to inform the PDP about which high-value servers require stronger authentication or device posture checks. Or, it could be a more sophisticated integration where the PDP consumes PAM-defined policies about which administrators should be permitted to access which servers, and relays these to the PEP for enforcement.

Another scenario is shown in Figure 12-4, which depicts the PAM consuming information from the PDP, and using this to help better enforce access controls. This could be identity or device attributes that can be used to make better decisions about whether to permit access to the target system. For example, most PAM solutions do not have remote access capabilities built in, while Zero Trust solutions do. A PDP could make the user's geolocation information available to the PAM, which could then use it as a factor in deciding whether to permit access.

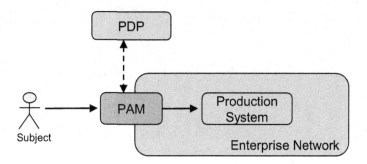

Figure 12-4. *PAM Consuming Zero Trust Context from PDP*

While these last two examples are more forward-looking than scenarios that are in actual practice today, we do believe that as Zero Trust platforms become more widespread, they'll also become more open, and support these kinds of integrations across different security components from different vendors. They may also arise more quickly if PAM vendors expand into the Zero Trust arena.

We think that this also highlights the ways in which PAM solutions today are more identity-aware, rather than identity-centric. While they often use an enterprise identity provider to authenticate users, and can use group membership to determine access policies, this is typically the limit of their scope. The forward-looking scenarios we portrayed in Figures 12-3 and 12-4 are interesting, and will help bring PAM solutions into the dynamic and identity-centric world of Zero Trust.

Summary

PAM clearly provides valuable password and access management functions, and can help meet security, compliance, and audit requirements. While it also helps achieve some aspects of the principle of least privilege, and can use identity attributes to help manage access, it's not a substitute for a full Zero Trust platform. But integrating a PAM with a Zero Trust platform can enhance the value of both systems, and organizations that have a PAM should prioritize protecting the PAM server itself. They may also look at the ways in which these two solutions could exchange information, to make better access decisions together, although this will likely be an advanced or future use case.

CHAPTER 13

Data Protection

Forrester places data at the center of their Zero Trust eXtended (ZTX) framework and for good reason: valuable data exists in every organization, and it must be protected. From our Zero Trust perspective, data, which is often *the* primary target of attackers, is a key enterprise resource that must be secured by PEPs through integration with a PDP, via an identity and metadata-centric policy model.

Data volumes have grown exponentially in most organizations, and high-value data is now regularly stored, accessed, and processed across a wide variety of systems, including on-premises, cloud-based, and mobile devices. The volume and complexity of data will only continue to grow as organizations proceed with cloud migrations and digital transformations. This growth needs to be effectively managed and secured through effective data lifecycle and usage initiatives. Throughout this chapter, we will discuss data lifecycle, data protection and data usage (including tagging and classification), and ultimately how data security should integrate with a Zero Trust strategy.

Data Types and Data Classification

Data can generally be thought of as falling into one of two different types: structured and unstructured. The distinction between these is important, as it affects how security can be applied or how technology can be used to support data security.

Structured data is data that is stored in a database of some sort, and is accessed and created through a specific mechanism (e.g., via Structured Query Language, SQL). The exact process of storing data within a database will be determined by the chosen database technology, but typically, it's stored in a binary format with access control defined within the database system itself. And databases generally use a defined schema, which constrains allowable data types and assigns metadata such as column names. For example, a database table storing employee records could have a set of columns defined,

163

J. Garbis and J. W. Chapman, *Zero Trust Security*, https://doi.org/10.1007/978-1-4842-6702-8_13

such as *date of birth* (date type), *street address* (free-form text), and *employee ID* (integer type). This imposes an implicit level of classification associated with the columns of data stored in that table, which provides guidance about its security requirements, and how it should be treated.

Unstructured data is data that is created through arbitrary means and formatted by the user or the technology storing the data. Most importantly, unstructured data does not fit into any predefined schema and therefore exhibits an inability to automatically define security requirements and classification either holistically or on a per-field basis. That is, the files themselves, because they're unstructured, do not inherently provide information about the data contained within them. Unlike the *date of birth* database column example, a document doesn't explicitly indicate that it contains employee birth date information. In addition, unstructured files have other security differences from data in a database. Files stored on a file share may not be encrypted or obfuscated through any means other than the software that created the file. While the files may be written in a proprietary format, raw access to the files is at the mercy of the controls placed upon the storage location, whether it be a network file share or a SaaS-based service.

Of course, there is a continuum between these classifications since unstructured data may contain some degree of labeling, and have some implicit structure imposed upon it by convention or business process. Likewise, a structured data schema can be inadvertently or maliciously misused, and easily become effectively unstructured; for example, there is little more than convention preventing the use of a "customer account notes" field to store Social Security numbers. Ultimately, the use of a data schema and operating conventions together are what allow us to achieve the enabling feature of data security: classification.

Both structured and unstructured data require a level of classification in order to inform a data security system of how it should be treated. Classification is the process of identifying the level of risk associated with the data, based on its potential impact to the organization. The influential document "Standards for Security Categorization of Federal Information and Information Systems"—FIPS Pub 199[1]—defines the following levels:

---

[1]FIPS Pub 199 is part of the Federal Information Processing Standards series from the US National Institute of Standards and Technology, and provides guidelines for determining the impact of a data breach.

- Low: Loss of confidentiality, integrity, and availability with limited adverse effects on business functions (e.g., marketing or website content)

- Moderate: Loss of confidentiality, integrity, and availability with serious adverse effects on business functions (e.g., customer information, price lists, business plans, or strategy documents)

- High: Loss of confidentiality, integrity, and availability with severe or catastrophic effects on business functions (e.g., source code, banking credentials, or signing credentials)

These classifications, although high level, can be used to influence initial access policies in a Zero Trust environment. We will discuss these classifications and impact to Zero Trust later in this chapter, and once again in the policy model chapter.

Data Lifecycle

Much like an identity, data has a concrete lifecycle. Data's lifecycle begins at data creation, continues through data usage, and finally ends with data destruction. Each of these stages requires different security methods and approaches.

Data Creation

Data can be created in a variety of ways; how it's created determines whether the data is organized as structured or unstructured. As shown in Figure 13-1, data can be created as a file or as a record within a database. Additionally, data is not always created by a person or user—an application or a process can be responsible for creating data, either in a structured or unstructured format. Data also encompasses a wide variety of types, including business files (e.g., documents or spreadsheets), machine-generated data (e.g., sensor data or computed results of analysis), or valuable IP (e.g., source code, equipment designs, or genetic or pharmaceutical data).

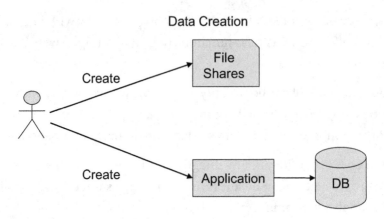

Figure 13-1. *Data Lifecycle—Creating Data*

Regardless of how this data gets created, metadata or tagging is necessary to support classification policies. There are multiple methods to create these classification tags or labels: automated, user-based, or discovery solutions. Automated data classification is where software analyzes and classifies documents through multiple means, including content analysis, document location, user department, or the associated application or business process. This classification is usually executed during data creation. User-based classification requires training and subject matter knowledge of the content of the data. While users can be an effective mechanism to provide tagging and labels, there is a risk of inconsistency as people may apply tags and labels differently, even with training. Finally, discovery tools also classify data, but they differ from automated classification solutions in that they often execute after the data has been created and stored. They provide tagging and labeling based on content, location, and search rules that are applied but, unlike automated classification tools, they may not be aware of the identity, application, or process that created the data.

Data Usage

While all data should be secured, classification enables more effective security within the next phase of the data's lifecycle, when it's actually put to use. There are multiple stages to consider in data usage—data-at-rest, data-in-motion, and data-in-use. These stages all provide both challenges and benefits in data management and security.

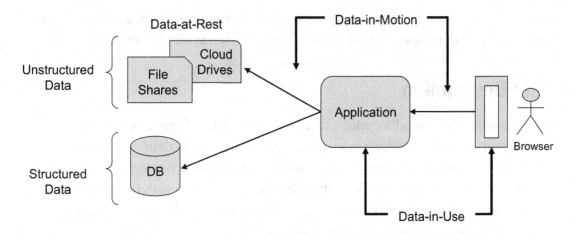

Figure 13-2. *Data Usage*

Figure 13-2 illustrates an example of how data can go through multiple stages when accessed by a user via an application through a web browser. Prior to being accessed, the data is in the *data-at-rest* state. This phase occurs after the data has been created and written to some form of persistent storage. To secure data-at-rest, full-disk or database table encryption (or another holistic approach) provides a level of security, although it is important to understand this does not protect the data as a resource. The process of encrypting the complete disk, or database table encryption, protects against physical or disk-level access to the data, but it is not part of an authorization model.

Continuing with the example depicted in Figure 13-2, when the user accesses the application, there are two occurrences of data-in-motion. The application will make a call to the storage location to retrieve the data; this is the first opportunity to secure data-in-motion via an encrypted network connection between the application and storage. The network between the user device and the application is a second opportunity for securing data-in-motion, which should use HTTPS or another secure TCP channel. Data-in-motion, in many respects, is the simplest phase for which to secure data; it can be solved just by using an encrypted network protocol, and in fact should be applied for all data-in-motion, regardless of its classification.

Finally, data-in-use is when the data is actively held in memory within software such as application clients, browsers, or application servers. This is often the most difficult state of data to secure. As illustrated in Figure 13-2, once the application loads the data in memory, protecting it can be very difficult. There are data security techniques, such as in-memory encryption, data tokenization, or obfuscation, which can be used to protect the data in use. This is highly application and technology dependent. For SaaS applications, solutions such as CASBs can help, while enterprise-built applications will typically rely on developers to utilize proven design patterns and toolkits or libraries.

Data Destruction

The final stage of the data lifecycle is data destruction. Organizations, especially those in regulated industries or which manage sensitive data, need to define and enforce data retention policies, which determine how long data should be stored and remain accessible before it's destroyed. Note that different business verticals have different requirements, which can make managing these "end of life" policies challenging, especially for larger or multi-industry businesses.

Today, there are a growing number of data lifecycle service providers who offer data storage and retention policy enforcement as a service, typically via SaaS. These SaaS platforms can help by providing consistent and simplified enforcement of classification policies, reducing the cost and effort of traditional on-premises storage and management programs.

Data Security

Data security is achieved differently across different stages of the data lifecycle. As stated in the previous section, data can be relatively easily secured for data-at-rest (via full drive encryption) and for data-in-motion (via encrypted transmissions). But the more challenging and interesting phase is definitely data-in-use, which Data Loss Prevention (DLP) solutions can help address.

DLP solutions, which are widely deployed by enterprises, provide a set of technical controls and are typically oriented around the following elements:

- Device control: The means to define how data can be utilized at the device level (e.g., preventing the ability to print or copy-and-paste, or whether USB ports can be utilized on a device).

- Content-aware control: Enforcing and adjusting security controls for data based on the content of the data. This may include data obfuscation.

- Enforced encryption: Ensuring that data-at-rest is encrypted at the drive or physical storage level. Its purpose is to ensure the stored data remains inaccessible even if the device is lost or stolen.

- Data discovery: One of the most important aspects of data security, discovery solutions provide organizations the means to not only find unknown sensitive data but also automate its classification.

DLP solutions have technical means to enforce access control policies, and will remain relevant in a Zero Trust environment. Of course, the actual policies that DLP systems enforce must be defined, validated, and curated by the organization. These activities occur within an area of information security known as Data Access Governance (DAG).

DAG is closely related to the identity governance capability within IAM, and defines where and how data can be accessed, by whom, and ultimately, when they should have access. In a Zero Trust environment, using DAG to define the conditions under which data can be accessed should ideally be tied directly to Zero Trust policies. DAG provides abilities and access rules that govern the data and ultimately how policies are applied throughout the organization.

Through data classification, data governance can effectively provide a mechanism for access policies to be enforced and be further managed through metadata tags. These metadata tags can serve as input into Zero Trust RBAC or ABAC policies.

Digital Rights Management (DRM) is another type of data security measure which provides controls to the owners of proprietary data, data that has a copyright associated, or any other business data that may be valuable intellectual property (IP). DRM imposes technical controls defined by the data owner, and can control how that data can be both used and accessed for short- and long-term purposes. Some DRM solutions can and do tie into Zero Trust platforms, leveraging context such as identity and device attributes.

While DRM is focused on controlling access to the data, other approaches such as traditional data encryption, newer approaches such as data tokenization, and emerging technologies like homomorphic cryptography[2] all obfuscate the data itself, and provide opportunities to support Zero Trust policies in data protection. Integrating Zero Trust into these technologies can enable identity and context-aware data access policies, regardless of the obfuscation method. We'll explore this further in the following section.

---

[2]These algorithms allow arithmetical calculations to be performed on encrypted data without requiring decryption. This effectively eliminates data-in-use and data-in-motion as risk factors for certain use cases.

Zero Trust and Data

In Chapter 3, we introduced several Zero Trust deployment models, each of which ultimately provides ways by which PEPs protect resources. These resources in these scenarios were deliberately portrayed generically—they could be data, applications controlling/modifying data, or transactions. In all cases, the Zero Trust PEP uses policies to protect these resources, and as we've discussed, PDPs must use contextual information to make access decisions. In the case of data, its classification and metadata can be used in Zero Trust policies. So let's examine what a PDP and a PEP look like from the data perspective in a Zero Trust environment.

As stated previously, data classification is achieved via labeling and tagging of data elements in the environment. If possible, this labeling and tagging should be used as elements of Zero Trust policies. These policies grant access based on roles, attributes, or other identity data and should also include access decisions based on data attributes. While these classifications and policies can directly stem from regulatory or compliance standards that are placed upon the organization, the actual controls enforced by the security system need to be based upon the organization's risk model and risk tolerance.

To expand upon this concept, an organization's audit and security team will typically define controls to support regulatory and compliance standards. For example, publicly traded firms in the United States are subject to Sarbanes Oxley (SOX) standards. Since SOX standards focus on data, classification through tagging and labeling will provide support for policies as defined by audit and security teams as it relates to financial data. To implement some of these policies, a data access governance solution can be used to provide these capabilities.

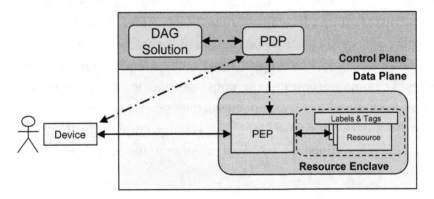

Figure 13-3. *Data Management in the Enclave-Based Model*

Figure 13-3 depicts how a data security solution may be deployed within the enclave-based Zero Trust model. The *resource,* in this model, is the data being protected by the PEP, which uses policies defined by the PDP with input from a DAG solution. In this illustration, the access being protected could be direct access by the user from their device, or an application accessing the data on behalf of the user. For example, if the entire data resource is tagged as "Customer Records," then only identities who are in a given group (Customer Care Team) should be permitted to access this data resource at all. The implication of this policy enforcement is that an application attempting to access this data from outside the resource enclave may be blocked by the PEP. In this situation, the application may have to be an authenticated Zero Trust identity, and provide identity context in order to gain access.

In an effective Zero Trust system, there would be bidirectional integration between the PEP and the data management system or application. The data management tool would provide data attributes to the PDP and PEP, for use within policy decisions and enforcement. And the data management system would be able to consume contextual information from the Zero Trust system to take real-time policy enforcement actions.

Of course, some data may be stored locally on user devices, and yet must still be secured. Zero Trust can work in conjunction with data security solutions in two different ways, depicted in Figures 13-4 and 13-5.

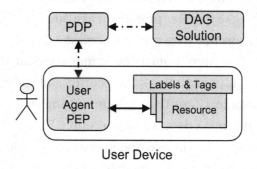

Figure 13-4. *Data Access Governance and Data Protection on a User Device*

Figure 13-4 shows how a Zero Trust system may work with a Data Access Governance solution in conjunction with user agent PEP running on the user's local device. Because DAG solutions define policies rather than actively enforce access controls, the DAG system provides input into the PDP. This additional information should inform the PDP about data policies and help instruct the PEP to locally enforce access controls based on the data's labels and tags. This contrasts with Figure 13-5, which shows how the user's device has a DLP component, which does actively enforce controls.

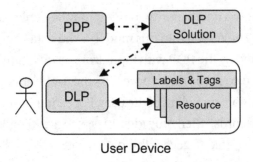

Figure 13-5. *Data Loss Prevention and Data Protection on a User Device*

In this example, the Zero Trust system makes identity and session context information available to the DLP system for use within its internal authorization (access control) model. For instance, a Zero Trust system could provide user geolocation information, enabling the DLP to enforce data residency requirements. Note, this effectively makes the local DLP mechanism into a (mini) Zero Trust PEP.

Summary

Throughout this chapter, we have focused on data as a resource in the Zero Trust environment, which of course requires protection like other resources. From our Zero Trust perspective, this means that data must be accessed through PEPs, which enforce an identity-centric security context. Data lifecycle management, data governance, and DLP are important elements in providing data security, and will continue to exist (and remain effective) even outside a Zero Trust solution. Using an identity-centric security solution will ultimately improve a data security solution. However, this is definitely a more advanced scenario. We recommend that your Zero Trust strategy include context-sensitive data security at some point, although it's typically not the best candidate use case for an early project, and will be dependent on the data security capabilities of your chosen Zero Trust platform.

CHAPTER 14

Infrastructure and Platform as a Service

The adoption of cloud computing has been one of the major and most influential shifts in our industry in the past decade, and shows no sign of abating. The power and ubiquity of Infrastructure as a Service (IaaS) and Platform as a Service (PaaS) offerings have transformed the way that much of our software is built, deployed, and accessed. However, we don't believe that these platforms have yet had a similarly broad and significant impact on security. While these platforms do have sophisticated and powerful access control models, they're largely designed to protect services based within their cloud environments, and not serve as broad enterprise security solutions for all users across multiple heterogeneous environments.

This broad scope—securing access for all users, to all resources—is of course, a fundamental Zero Trust principle. This doesn't mean that these IaaS and PaaS cloud platforms cannot be part (even a significant part) of a Zero Trust security deployment. After all, Google pioneered many of these principles internally and has begun making elements of them commercially available as part of their cloud platform. But in general, the major cloud vendors' security solutions are focused on providing security within their cloud platforms, rather than as general purpose security across the enterprise. The exception to this is Microsoft, which is leveraging its strength in identity, desktop OS, and cloud computing in some innovative and interesting ways.

Recall that our goal is not to evaluate or rank vendors and their offerings—that's a highly dynamic and moving target—our goal is to provide you with a framework and a set of tools so that you can make thoughtful and informed decisions about how to best proceed with your Zero Trust initiative. And in today's enterprises, IaaS and PaaS are so important that any Zero Trust initiative will very likely include them. Let's dive in.

© Jason Garbis and Jerry W. Chapman 2021
J. Garbis and J. W. Chapman, *Zero Trust Security*, https://doi.org/10.1007/978-1-4842-6702-8_14

Definitions

Infrastructure as a Service is well understood and straightforward to define: dynamic provisioning of a full operating system, deployed in a Cloud Service Provider (CSP) environment with a "pay as you go" service model. Enterprise customers are responsible for configuring and maintaining the full OS and its surrounding network, as well as deploying any desired software onto the virtual server. Effectively, the infrastructure that enterprises are using as a service is a virtual "bare metal" machine onto which they deploy and configure an OS image of their choosing.

Platform as a Service, on the other hand, encompasses a wide variety of functions and models across the CSPs, with a potentially bewildering set of capabilities. The term *serverless computing* is also frequently used when discussing PaaS, referring to the ability to deploy custom code which implements functions that you've written, without the need to deploy a full server operating system. Serverless functions are deployed into a PaaS environment, which provides the surrounding infrastructure for accessing, managing, and launching.

We recognize that we're glossing over the very considerable breadth of PaaS capabilities that are available in the major CSPs, such as cloud functions, containerized workloads, service meshes, and everything in between. We'll be exploring some of these later in this chapter as we categorize and examine the ways in which they can be integrated into a Zero Trust environment.

While IaaS and PaaS have considerable differences, they also have some things in common. Primarily, they are both used as means to house and execute custom resources that are designed and deployed by the enterprise. These resources may be custom-code in a function, a full executable program or web application, or even just an enterprise-designed database, for example. In all cases, these are resources (code or data) that the enterprise desires to make accessible to certain identities and which, therefore, need an access control model.

IaaS and PaaS are highly relevant to Zero Trust, as these platforms represent a large proportion of how applications are built and deployed today. Of course, CSPs have sophisticated and robust access control mechanisms, which do provide aspects of Zero Trust. For example, Google's GCP offers the Identity-Aware Proxy which enforces identity-centric remote access policies for GCP resources. However, CSPs' internal security models do impose some complexity when these resources are being accessed by external identities. In particular, remote access is often outside the scope of the CSP, and will require coordination or alignment with another security solution in those places where access crosses boundaries between security domains.

This is where a Zero Trust platform can help, by normalizing security and access controls across system and silo boundaries. Note that integration between Zero Trust and native CSP security is valid and valuable, such as by using cloud metadata tags as input into contextual policies. However, you should be careful not to try to do too much. For example, even though it may be technically achievable, it may not make sense to use your Zero Trust system to manage access control for services which are deployed and invoked entirely within an IaaS or PaaS platform. Deciding where and when to limit the scope of your Zero Trust initiative will be an important factor in determining its success.

Let's continue our discussion of IaaS and PaaS services, and examine the ways in which Zero Trust can and should be used in these environments.

Zero Trust and Cloud Services

The ways in which a Zero Trust security platform fits into an IaaS or PaaS environment is dependent on your Zero Trust deployment model, as well as the types of cloud platform services you've chosen to use. In particular, the Zero Trust enclave-based and cloud-routed deployment models both work well, since in both cases, the PEP is external to the resources they are protecting. That is, they act as a natural architectural component placed at the boundary of the CSP for external access, which allows the Zero Trust system to enforce its identity-centric policies prior to permitting subjects to access resources inside the cloud environment.

In contrast, the resource-based and microsegmentation models require two things that may be a challenge in cloud environments. First, the PEP must be running on the resource itself. This doesn't pose an issue for IaaS resources, but isn't typically compatible with PaaS resources. Second, these two models typically don't provide a mechanism for enforcing access control across network boundaries. That is, they require that subjects have direct network access to the PEPs. This works for services and resources on a local network, but requires a separate access mechanism for remote subjects, which is not an inherent part of these two models. From our perspective, especially for cloud services that are likely accessed from a wide variety of locations, these limitations make it difficult to use these Zero Trust models for IaaS and PaaS resources in many situations. In addition, CSPs have their own internally developed (and usually quite effective) security models for service-to-service access within the PaaS environment. In practice, it's likely better to embrace the CSP's native access control model for internal PaaS services, rather than imposing an external and potentially incompatible one. We explore this later in the chapter where we discuss service meshes.

So far, as we've looked at how we can apply the Zero Trust security model to IaaS and PaaS resources, what we've seen is that the PEP works most effectively as an access control point across the cloud boundary (at the ingress point into the cloud environment). Let's examine how exactly this can work, by looking at the ways in which cloud services are accessed and the corresponding ways in which access can be controlled. Our discussion and diagrams will be based on the enclave-based Zero Trust model for simplicity, although they will work largely the same for a cloud-routed Zero Trust system.

Unlike SaaS services, which we discuss in the following chapter, IaaS and PaaS platforms all have built-in access control methods, which make them universally able to be easily integrated with a Zero Trust PEP. There are multiple technical methods by which cloud platforms enforce this access control; for simplicity here, we'll refer to them generically as an *access gateway*, which provides the ability to perform source IP address filtering as a logical ingress firewall into an IaaS or PaaS environment. This capability, although basic, is all that's necessary for us to achieve our goal: our Zero Trust system (enforced via the PEP) is how we're applying dynamic and identity-centric policies.

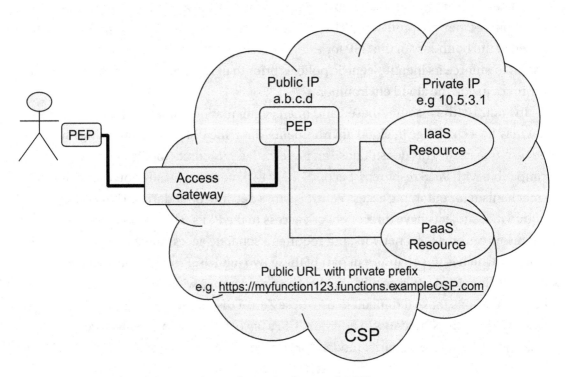

Figure 14-1. *Cloud Access Control via Co-located PEP*

Figure 14-1 depicts the scenario where a PEP running in a CSP platform is used to control access to IaaS or PaaS resources within the same cloud environment. Access controls via this model fall into one of two general categories.[1] IaaS resources are assigned an IP address, and access to that IP address is configured within the CSP's access gateway so that *only* traffic originating on the PEP is permitted to access the resource. Figure 14-1 shows this in the scenario where the IaaS resource has a private IP address of 10.5.3.1 (which of course remote users couldn't route their traffic to anyway). The access gateway is configured to permit remote access to the PEP from any external IP address, such as from a remote user's device. Of course, the PEP (and the PDP, not shown) enforces the Zero Trust policies; the access gateway is used solely to ensure that all resource-bound traffic is routed through the PEP, and therefore subject to its policies.

Note that even if this IaaS resource were assigned a public IP address, the diagram and the end result could be exactly the same. As long as the CSP network is set up so that all resource-bound traffic can only originate from the PEP, the system can ensure that its Zero Trust policies are enforced. Note also that this resource, while depicted as a single object, could actually correspond to a single service (TCP port) running on an IaaS instance. This approach could be useful, for example, for an IaaS instance that is running a publicly accessible HTTPS web server on port 443, but maintains a PEP-protected administrative SSH interface on TCP port 22.

Figure 14-1 also shows a PaaS resource which is accessed via a common pattern used by cloud platforms—a public URL with a private identifier as a prefix to the FQDN. The diagram shows a generic example, `https://myfunction123.functions.exampleCSP.com`, while real-world examples look like `https://abc123def.execute-api.us-east-1.amazonaws.com` for an AWS lambda function, or `https://myapp1.azurewebsites.net/api/myfunction123` for an Azure function.[2] In these examples, there will be a set of public IP addresses that are shared by many, many functions, with the CSP infrastructure performing load balancing and mapping to a given customer's account. These IP addresses, and the compute and network infrastructure that service them, are under control of the CSP and cannot be fronted or interfered with by a given customer. But that's OK; in fact, it doesn't conflict with our Zero Trust security model. This is because,

---

[1]Although of course there are additional variants and capabilities. We can't provide an exhaustive list here due to space and scope limitations.

[2]While these might feel a bit like achieving "security through obscurity," keep in mind that invoking these services typically also requires an API key, in addition to just the URL. Combining them with a PEP is, of course, an even better solution.

even though the IP address and the actual network entry point are public, CSPs provide the ability to restrict the source IP addresses which are permitted to invoke a given function. And, of course, in this example, we'd just configure it to only permit access from the PEP. This is one example of how to leverage some basic functionality in a cloud environment—source IP address restrictions—to open the door to the Zero Trust security model.

Finally, because the PEP is local to the cloud platform, it can make API calls to retrieve metadata about the resources in the local cloud environment, for use when the PEP determines targets (resources) for assigned policies. Likewise, the local PEP can detect newly created service instances across enterprise cloud accounts, and dynamically (and automatically) grant the right remote users the right level of access. As we'll see in our upcoming chapter on policies, detecting new resources and evaluating resource attributes in this fashion is an important capability which PEPs can provide for cloud environments.

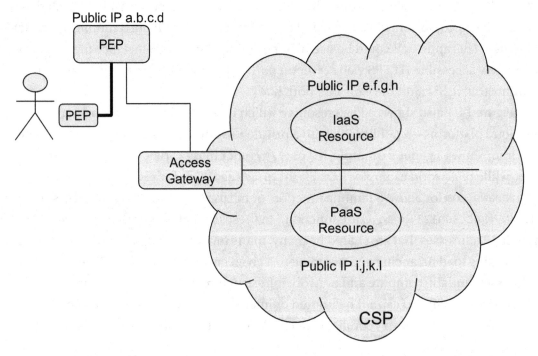

Figure 14-2. *Cloud Access Control via Remote PEP*

Figure 14-2 depicts the use of a remote PEP—running in an arbitrary environment (on-premises or in another cloud environment, it doesn't matter) to enforce access control to CSP-based resources. These resources could be IaaS or PaaS, like in our previous examples, but in either case, they need to have a public IP address associated with them because (of course) they're being accessed remotely. Again, we're using the basic functionality of the CSP to enforce a source IP address restriction, requiring that all traffic for these resources originate from the PEP's public IP address. Like in the previous example, this simple method enables us to apply the identity-centric and dynamic access controls driven by our Zero Trust model to our CSP-based resources. Do note that with this topology, the system uses the native application protocol from the PEP, through the access gateway, and to the Resource, so it's only a suitable choice for encrypted protocols.

Of course, CSPs have many network and security capabilities, which go beyond the generic access gateway that we've discussed here, such as network security groups and IAM policies. At a minimum, these can be combined to impose source IP address restrictions on accessing resources (services), ensuring that they can only be accessed from a Zero Trust PEP. This is the foundational and enabling capability for including cloud resources into a Zero Trust environment.

In our preceding discussion, we have (deliberately) portrayed the network topology in a simplified fashion, to explain the concepts; real-world cloud platforms provide multiple ways by which you can integrate cloud resources into your enterprise networks. For example, CSPs generally provide a "direct connect" model for a site-to-site VPN, which logically extends an on-premises network to a private cloud network via a local telecommunications provider. CSPs also offer more advanced network connection and configuration abilities, with which you can build complex network topologies and equally complex access control mechanisms. However, we recommend that you keep things simple, and externalize the dynamic and identity-centric access controls to your Zero Trust platform. This is what Zero Trust is good at, and it helps you avoid the creation of what will likely turn out to be a new, complex, and CSP-specific security model. The CSP models, while powerful, tend to be network and IP address centric rather than identity centric. And they definitely do not have the ability to define and enforce the types of Zero Trust policies that we need, across our heterogeneous and diverse enterprise environments.

Of course, there are exceptions to every piece of advice, and we acknowledge that it's neither possible nor appropriate to force-fit your Zero Trust system into every part of your environment. In fact, part of a successful Zero Trust journey is to know where to draw boundaries. Ultimately, you have to ensure that you choose the most appropriate and effective security platform, tools, and processes for each part of your environment.

A good example of this is the service mesh, which is a mechanism for deploying and managing containerized workloads in a reliable and scalable way. Service meshes are in some ways essentially a self-contained Zero Trust microsegmentation model and system. Let's take a look at how they work, and how you might tie them into your broader enterprise Zero Trust system.

Service Meshes

Service meshes are a new and rapidly growing approach to deploying containerized workloads at scale. While they're not fundamentally cloud-based (the open source meshes can absolutely be deployed on premises), we have seen them most frequently used in cloud environments. Service meshes, for example *Istio* and *Linkerd*, lend themselves very well to modern DevOps style microservices-based application development.

Service meshes are platforms for operating, controlling, and managing large-scale containerized (microservices) workloads, with an emphasis on managing the communications between microservices. For example, the Istio documentation states "Without requiring changes to the underlying services, Istio provides automated baseline traffic resilience, service metrics collection, distributed tracing, traffic encryption, protocol upgrades, and advanced routing functionality for all service-to-service communication."[3] The Linkerd documentation says

> *It adds observability, reliability, and security to cloud native applications without requiring code changes. For example, Linkerd can monitor and report per-service success rates and latencies, can automatically retry failed requests, and can encrypt and validate connections between services, all without requiring any modification of the application itself.*[4]

What's interesting about these approaches is how they provide a rich set of deployment, communications, and runtime services to microservices through a configuration-based platform. Like the promise of application servers (App Servers) from the late 1990s, this frees developers to focus on business logic rather than infrastructure. Of course, today's technology is considerably different from the 1990s,

---

[3]https://istio.io/latest/faq/general/.
[4]https://linkerd.io/2/faq/#what-is-linkerd.

and the service mesh approach to security has also evolved. Let's now take a look at the internal structure of a service mesh (we've chosen Istio as an example), to see how it is well aligned with the Zero Trust microsegmentation model.

The high-level Istio mesh architecture is shown in Figure 14-3, which we'll look at from a Zero Trust security perspective.

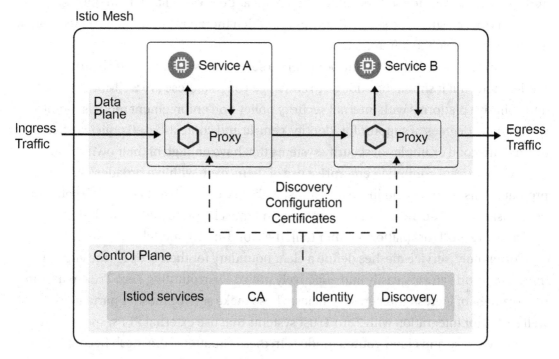

Figure 14-3. *Istio Architecture[5]*

The first thing to note is the familiar separation between the control plane and the data plane, and a set of distributed proxies, one in front of each service. These proxies, unsurprisingly, act as policy enforcement points (PEPs). The istiod services are the policy decision point (PDP) in the control plane, providing core security capabilities, including acting as the system Certificate Authority, service identity management, and storing and evaluating authentication and authorization policies. The proxies ensure that service-to-service communication occurs over an mTLS channel, providing confidentiality as well as service consumer and provider authentication.

---

[5]See https://istio.io/latest/docs/concepts/what-is-istio/ for more information.

The Istio security model is based on a declarative policy mode, which uses service attributes (such as namespaces and labels) as subject criteria to determine which policies apply to which services. The authorization model has the proxy (PEP) evaluate requests based on attributes of the requestor, target service, and the request metadata and header information. Note that within the mesh, requestors and services are addressed by service identifiers, rather than by IP addresses—in fact, in many cases, these services all share the same IP addresses, which therefore ceases to be a meaningful attribute with which to differentiate them.

We've only provided a brief introduction to service meshes and their security models here, but it should be enough to convince you that these are well-thought-out and cohesive platforms with internal security policy and enforcement models (granted, with varying degrees of support for identity-centric and context-based policies). Service meshes are good examples of security systems that have enough of their own "center of gravity" to warrant continued enterprise use of them, even within a broader Zero Trust program. This should stand in clear contrast with services such as IaaS, which generally have basic network-centric security controls, and must be protected through the enterprise's Zero Trust platform rather than the cloud-native model.

Fortunately, service meshes define a clear boundary for their scope—the edge of the mesh—and can very easily and effectively utilize a surrounding Zero Trust platform enforcement of ingress and egress policies. These make service meshes particularly well suited for integration with Zero Trust systems that use external PEPs, specifically the enclave-base and cloud-routed models. In these situations, the mesh becomes the implicit trust zone from the perspective of the Zero Trust system.

What we described (and what is fully achievable today) is essentially an arm's-length deployment of a broad enterprise Zero Trust system side by side with a service mesh. It'll be interesting to see, hopefully in the near future, a Zero Trust solution in which the PEP is able to render policies based on workload attributes within the container environment, controlling external access to containerized workloads. This would only require some basic way to represent the container workload attributes in the Zero Trust policy model and a means of transmitting access control decisions into the mesh for enforcement. Some of this plumbing already exists; for example, it's currently possible to transmit Zero Trust context into Istio via HTTP request headers. This type of integration will be interesting and valuable as organizations proceed into higher levels of maturity with their Zero Trust programs.

Summary

It's clear that IaaS and PaaS will only continue to grow in their importance and impact on enterprise application development and deployment. These platforms have dramatically expanded the breadth and depth of their capabilities, and in fact have even introduced the ability to run certain cloud-managed services on premises. This is largely due to ubiquitous network connectivity and extremely cost-effective compute and memory. This, combined with sophisticated control software, has resulted in an expansion of what we consider to be "as a Service" offerings, even in just the past few years. The notion of deploying service-based (and cloud-managed) compute or sensor nodes directly into an enterprise network is becoming increasingly commonplace, with major CSPs innovating in this area. This trend is somewhat humorously referred to as "fog computing."[6] It'll be very interesting to see how these offerings and architectures evolve from a security perspective—clearly, these distributed compute elements will need distributed security, and there will be an opportunity to integrate them with enterprise and CSP-based Zero Trust platforms.

Enterprise application architectures are moving quickly as well, to take advantage of new IaaS and PaaS capabilities, and security teams need to not just follow but lead and enable this. We believe that a Zero Trust architecture and platform are the best way to accomplish this.

The principles and concepts we've discussed in this chapter should provide you with a clear understanding of how to approach securing IaaS and PaaS deployments within your Zero Trust initiative, and how to support service mesh-based applications. To complete our analysis of Zero Trust and cloud-based systems, the following chapter examines SaaS applications.

---

[6]Because it's a cloud that's very close to you. Don't blame us for the pun, we didn't make it up.

CHAPTER 15

Software as a Service

Cloud-based software delivered as a service (SaaS) is of course a major component of today's IT and business environment, and has had a profound impact on how commercial software is created and consumed. This shift has made it remarkably simpler and easier to utilize sophisticated business software, with businesses now able to sign up, create an account, and begin obtaining value in minutes.

We define SaaS as a publicly accessible web application,[1] in which the service provider (vendor) hosts, manages, and maintains the infrastructure and with which the subscriber performs (and manages) the designated application function across the Internet. SaaS applications are typically multi-tenant for efficiency, with each subscriber restricted to accessing only their private data.

From a Zero Trust security perspective, we can immediately see some important differences between SaaS and the IaaS/PaaS resources we discussed in the previous chapter. First and foremost, SaaS applications are *publicly* accessible by design, with any user on the Internet able to access them over an HTTPS connection. That is, by definition, the entry points into a SaaS system are public, rather than private. And, they are only accessible over an encrypted connection. What this means is that, with SaaS apps, there is no resource hiding needed by a PEP (since it's a non-goal for SaaS), and no need for encryption of the network traffic (since it's already using HTTPS).

This naturally raises the question of whether and how Zero Trust is still relevant to SaaS resources. We believe that using Zero Trust to manage and control access to SaaS applications does provide value, even though we do acknowledge that Zero Trust does fewer things for SaaS resources compared with private resources. Specifically, even for publicly accessible SaaS apps, Zero Trust can enforce identity-centric and context-sensitive access policies. Because the PDP is integrated with identity providers and with other enterprise systems, it can use group membership, as well as identity, device, and overall enterprise system attributes to control access, just like it can for private resources.

---

[1]Many SaaS apps can and do offer non-web interfaces, such as APIs, in addition to a browser UI.

© Jason Garbis and Jerry W. Chapman 2021
J. Garbis and J. W. Chapman, *Zero Trust Security*, https://doi.org/10.1007/978-1-4842-6702-8_15

While many (but not all) SaaS applications certainly can and do integrate with identity providers for authentication, they typically do not yet use device, identity, or system attributes to control access.

Of course, SaaS application security is broader than just access control, and the security industry has built an ecosystem of security offerings aimed at SaaS, including Secure Web Gateways (SWG) and Cloud Access Security Brokers (CASB), among others. Let's take a look at these, and examine how they relate to Zero Trust.

SaaS and Cloud Security

In order to talk about Zero Trust and SaaS, we need to examine the major components of cloud security. We'll begin by looking at native SaaS security controls, and then examining the Secure Web Gateway and Cloud Access Security Broker areas.

Native SaaS Controls

Even though they are publicly available, SaaS providers do recognize and acknowledge the need to have some level of access and network security around their solution. Of course, they have deployed mechanisms to protect their services from Internet-borne attacks such as DDoS, and have in place internal systems to maintain the integrity and availability of their platform. In addition, many SaaS systems provide enterprises with two built-in access control mechanisms. The first is the same foundational network access control capability as IaaS and PaaS platforms—the ability to enforce source IP address restrictions. The second is federated identity management, where the SaaS system delegates user authentication to an external identity provider. Let's discuss each in turn.

In terms of source IP address restrictions, SaaS platforms necessarily implement this slightly differently than IaaS/PaaS, in that they only enforce the source IP address rule for users associated with a given account. For example, any user on the planet can reach the `https://MySaaSApp.com/login` page, but the SaaS platform will only permit users from the mycompany.com domain to log in if their traffic initiates from the designated IP address. This is essentially an authentication access control policy applied to a given customer's tenancy within the SaaS platform. This capability can be used to require access via either a traditional VPN or with a Zero Trust system—both of which route user traffic through an enterprise-controlled network with a known IP address egress point.

Federated identity management is where the application leverages an external identity provider for user *authentication*, through standardized mechanisms such as SAML and OpenID Connect. Effectively, this is another way to enforce identity-centric aspects of Zero Trust access controls, which (interestingly) is independent of network-level security. From a technical perspective, users cannot authenticate directly into the SaaS application—the SaaS app either retrieves a current authentication token from the user's browser or redirects the browser to the identity provider for authentication. This naturally uses whatever authentication factors and contextual controls are configured within the identity provider. Keep in mind that this is generally only connected to authentication. SaaS applications still rely largely on internal *authorization* models, where users are assigned to various roles that control their permissions within the application. Most SaaS applications do not currently have mechanisms to consume external contextual information and make authorization decisions based on this—this is a more advanced and forward-looking use case, which we'll touch on again in this chapter's summary. Finally, note that there's no reason these two approaches cannot be combined—for example, using a federated identity system for authentication combined with a Zero Trust network solution to perform deep device posture checks.

Next, we'll be looking at CASBs and SWGs, two major areas within cloud security which enterprises use to obtain visibility and control of user access to SaaS applications. Interestingly, there's an increasing degree of overlap and convergence between these previously distinct market segments, and in fact this is part of a larger trend toward consolidation of a broad set of network and security functions into an integrated service offering (the Secure Access Service Edge).

Secure Web Gateways

Secure Web Gateways, which may be deployed on-premises or as a cloud-based service, provide enterprises with a way to control which websites their users can access, and to perform some degree of antimalware and threat protection. SWGs generally perform TLS termination, acting as a man-in-the-middle web proxy in order to inspect traffic contents. Some SWGs use endpoint agents to help capture Internet-bound traffic (as well as to provide additional services). On-premises enterprise SWGs are decreasing in popularity, and are generally being replaced by cloud-based SWG services.

The SWG policy model is, in some ways, the inverse of the Zero Trust model—it's intended to block access to prohibited Internet destinations, rather than following the Zero Trust model of only permitting access to explicitly allowed destinations. That is, SWGs typically operate in a "default allow" mode, which makes sense in most cases, given that the volume and breadth of sites on the Internet is nearly infinite.

SWGs are typically integrated with enterprise identity providers for user authentication, and can use attributes such as group memberships to enforce different access control policies. However, SWGs on their own do not provide network security or remote access to private resources—this is simply not in scope for the problem they're designed to solve. Note, as we'll discuss in the following text, some of the cloud-based SWG providers have expanded their service offerings to also include Zero Trust-style access control to private resources.

Cloud Access Security Brokers

CASBs are generally used by enterprises to solve the "Shadow IT" problem, where business teams start using SaaS-based applications outside the visibility and control of IT. CASBs solve this problem by discovering and reporting on SaaS application usage, and by providing a corresponding set of application risk and compliance assessment capabilities. They also provide value by enforcing DLP controls on the SaaS-based data, and can often incorporate some user identity and device-based access policies, typically in conjunction with SAML or OpenID Connect-based identity providers.

It's interesting to think about CASBs acting to enforce adaptive and risk-based authentication and authorization using identity and device attributes. From this perspective, they definitely appear to be acting as Zero Trust policy enforcement points, although, of course, their enforcement model is focused on SaaS applications, so they're not providing network security functions. CASBs are also not designed or implemented to provide access controls for private or on-premises applications, so their policy and enforcement models don't include these types of features. Like the SWG vendors we mentioned previously, vendors who began in the CASB space have also expanded their platform capabilities into other functional areas. We will touch on industry convergence later, after we discuss Zero Trust and SaaS.

Zero Trust and SaaS

It should be apparent that Zero Trust security can be applied to and work well with SaaS applications, whether your chosen security architecture includes a SWG, a CASB, or neither. Zero Trust security systems can provide identity and context-sensitive access control to SaaS applications, as long as the SaaS platform provides source IP address restrictions, and as long as the Zero Trust system is compatible with defining SaaS applications as targets within the policy model, and capturing the traffic bound for them.

SWGs and CASBs will continue to be useful, even in conjunction with a Zero Trust system, although enterprises need to be cognizant of the ways in which these different systems work with and manipulate traffic and network routing. Enterprises could, for example, take the approach of using their Zero Trust system just for controlling access to private resources while using a SWG and/or CASB for their SaaS applications. This is a reasonable approach.

Zero Trust and Edge Services

Currently, there's a trend in the market toward a converged and cloud-based network and security solution that combines many of these functions together. Gartner calls this the *Secure Access Service Edge* (SASE), while Forrester's variant is named the *Zero Trust Edge*. Effectively, these describe how cloud-based security and network providers have combined multiple functional offerings into a single as-a-service platform. Typical functions within this platform include networking (SD-WAN, WAN optimization, QoS, among others) and security (Firewall, IDS/IPS, SWG, CASB, DNS filtering, and Zero Trust Network Access).

Enterprise awareness and interest in SASE and ZTE has without a doubt seen considerable recent growth, and there's been corresponding activity with increased vendor marketing support, innovation, and industry consolidation (acquisition). Taking a step back, these converged platforms offer three main groups of functions:

- Network connectivity

- Security for Internet access (egress access)

- Access to private resource (Zero Trust Network Access, or ingress access)

From our perspective, what's particularly interesting and different is the Zero Trust Network Access (ZTNA) portion of this. This is because even as network management and Internet traffic analysis and security are moved into a cloud environment, ZTNA will continue to require that elements (PEPs) be deployed into enterprise-controlled environments, including on-premises enterprise networks, data centers, and public cloud-based IaaS and PaaS environments. This is due to two reasons. First, TCP/IP networks require a local node to act as one end of the encrypted network tunnel, and to broker or proxy remote connections to private resources on the private network. Second, the local node is required in order to obtain and use context and attributes from local resources as part of access policy decision criteria (we'll be covering this in more depth in Chapter 17, where we focus on policy models).

The requirement for a set of nodes on local private networks—our Zero Trust PEPs—is one reason that we believe ZTNA shouldn't be approached in the same way as the other SASE components. The other reason is that one of our core principles is that the Zero Trust identity and context-sensitive security model must be enforced for all identities' access to all resources, regardless of the location of the identity or resource. Even though organizations make heavy use of SaaS applications, and have shifted many users to work-from-home, they still have on-premises users and on-premises resources. They also need to control on-premises server-to-server access, which cloud-based services often struggle to manage. Taken together, all these reasons are why Gartner, for example, distinguishes "ingress SASE" from "egress SASE", with different sets of requirements.

In any event, this is a rapidly evolving space, and we believe that there is an opportunity for these emerging cloud-based security platforms to integrate with and leverage Zero Trust context, whether provided by their own platform or by integrating with another vendor's offering.

Summary

Let's think about how SaaS and Zero Trust security may look in the not-too-distant future. First (and we acknowledge that this is not exactly a bold prediction), we believe that identity, and, therefore, identity providers, will remain at the center of Zero Trust. However, we think that these providers will not just serve as authoritative directories and authentication points but as "centers of gravity" for user access to web apps, and for access control models. A clear example of this today are the access portals that many IdPs provide, with launchpad icons for accessing SaaS applications. Today, these portals are mostly only providing authentication and access, but we believe there's an opportunity for identity providers to extend the breadth and power of their policy models beyond authentication, and to begin to include authorization.

For example, SaaS applications could start to broadly support account or role provisioning as part of a Just-in-Time (JIT) access initiative, using a standard such as SCIM.[2] SCIM is only a first step, however, and it'll be interesting to see whether and how a standard (whether formal or informal) arises around how to represent authorization.[3] We don't believe that applications will ever fully externalize their authorization, which in fact is one of the reasons that XACML has not achieved widespread industry adoption. However, we do believe that we'll see a commonly accepted way of defining and communicating authenticated (and therefore trusted) identity context to SaaS applications, which they can consume and use in ways that are appropriate for their environment. JIT access provisioning is in fact one narrow example of this.

Without a doubt, this will be an interesting and dynamic space to watch, as we see how Zero Trust-aware SaaS applications can be, and what type of security, operational, and business value this will bring. Over time, we believe that these capabilities will also "trickle down" to non-SaaS applications, but given their sophisticated federation capabilities and investment in their platforms, we anticipate that SaaS providers will lead the way.

---

[2]SCIM is the System for Cross-domain Identity Management. See `https://tools.ietf.org/html/rfc7642`.

[3]Or, for example, if Zero Trust, identity, and SaaS systems begin using existing standards such as XACML, the eXtensible Access Control Modeling Language.

CHAPTER 16

IoT Devices and "Things"

Throughout this book, much of our focus has been on controlling access by authenticated entities—namely, users and servers. What they both have in common are that they're authenticated against an identity system, have attributes or roles for context, and are using modern devices with full-featured operating systems that support the installation of third-party software. This makes these systems well suited for integration into the type of Zero Trust architectures that we've been discussing. Of course, these are not the only types of devices—there are billions of connected devices of entirely different types, running on lower-capability and less extensible hardware and software platforms, often referred to as *Internet of Things* (IoT) devices. These devices often coexist on the same enterprise networks as organizations' most valuable resources. They are also well-known for exhibiting security vulnerabilities and representing an inviting attack surface, and should be included in any Zero Trust security architecture.

These IoT devices span a wide variety of functions, footprints, and capabilities, and we're deliberately including a broad set in our discussion here. We consider this category of IoT Devices and "things" to include newer connected devices as well as more traditional devices which exist on enterprise networks. For example

- Printers
- VOIP phones
- IP cameras
- Badge readers
- "Smart" things, such as blackboards, light bulbs, etc.
- Medical or diagnostic devices on healthcare networks
- HVAC systems

© Jason Garbis and Jerry W. Chapman 2021
J. Garbis and J. W. Chapman, *Zero Trust Security*, https://doi.org/10.1007/978-1-4842-6702-8_16

We also want to consider other types of devices that may be running in widely distributed locations, and located on public or cellular networks, such as

- Environmental sensors

- Remote security cameras

- Machinery or vehicle sensors or actuators

And finally, there are operational technology (OT) systems focused on industrial automation and management, which over the past 10–15 years have shifted to using standardized and interoperable TCP/IP networking, and are more frequently being connected to enterprise IT networks. Zero Trust architectures can be applied to OT environments, although they have some differences and challenges compared to IT environments. However, our focus in this chapter is on IT and enterprise networks.

What all these "things" have in common is that they have an IP address, and need to initiate or receive communications over the network. We're also considering these devices to be relatively closed systems, meaning that enterprises cannot install arbitrary third-party software onto them. This is not true for all IoT devices, of course—there are a growing set of such devices based on full-features OSs, typically a variant of Linux, onto which you can install third-party software. Depending on your environment and architecture, you could treat these as Zero Trust subjects (i.e., computing devices with identities), in which case our standard approach of access control and policy enforcement applies. Or, you can treat them as IoT devices, in which case, the principles and approaches we're discussing in this chapter will apply.

In any case, these devices are frequently designed, manufactured, and deployed without the same degree of concern for security that we expect from enterprise IT products. There are hundreds of examples of flaws in consumer-grade connected products, and these also exist in products targeting the enterprise, especially for specialized vertical products such as medical devices. Common security vulnerabilities in these devices include the use of unencrypted network protocols, hardcoded default passwords, unremovable backdoors, network and OS vulnerabilities, difficulty or impossibility of upgrading firmware, and, for physically accessible devices, the ability for an attacker to use that proximity to gain shell access on the device.

These devices are definitely a ripe vector for attack and data exfiltration, and have served as footholds for malware to perform network reconnaissance and move laterally (not to mention being a favorite weak point for red teams to exploit during pen testing exercises).

Note that some IoT devices are deployed as part of a larger, typically cloud-based modern system—the major cloud service providers each have their own platforms, which utilize both device-installed and cloud-based software that work in conjunction to provide messaging, security, and data management, among other services. These platforms, such as Azure IoT, Google Cloud IoT Core, and AWS Greengrass, each have a well-designed security and communications model, which in some ways will be self-contained with built-in support for secure bidirectional communications (often both synchronous and asynchronous). As such, it may be perfectly acceptable to deploy and operate them separately from your overall enterprise Zero Trust model. This is okay—as we've mentioned throughout the book, not everything needs to be included within the scope of your Zero Trust project. In fact, deliberately excluding certain components of your IT infrastructure will help with your focus, velocity, and success. However, even if you are using a modern IoT platform, it's important to understand its networking and communications architecture, so that you can ensure it coexists with the rest of your network security model.

Of course, most IoT devices sit outside of these cloud-based frameworks, and absolutely should be considered for inclusion in your Zero Trust security architecture. In the remainder of this chapter, we'll first examine some of the security and networking challenges associated with IoT devices, and then look at how Zero Trust systems can be applied to address these problems.

IoT Device Networking and Security Challenges

Unlike user devices or servers, IoT devices often pose some complex management, security, and access challenges when deployed onto enterprise networks, due to their closed nature and often-constrained communications architectures. Figure 16-1 depicts a simplified view of an enterprise network, to illustrate these points. The network is made up of both wired and wireless segments, with a wide variety of device types connected. The wired network in the enterprise has a mixture of user devices and Ethernet-connected things including VOIP phones, IP cameras, printers, and access door badge readers. The wireless network is used by some user devices, printers, and other connected office equipment such as wireless conference room monitors and digital whiteboards.

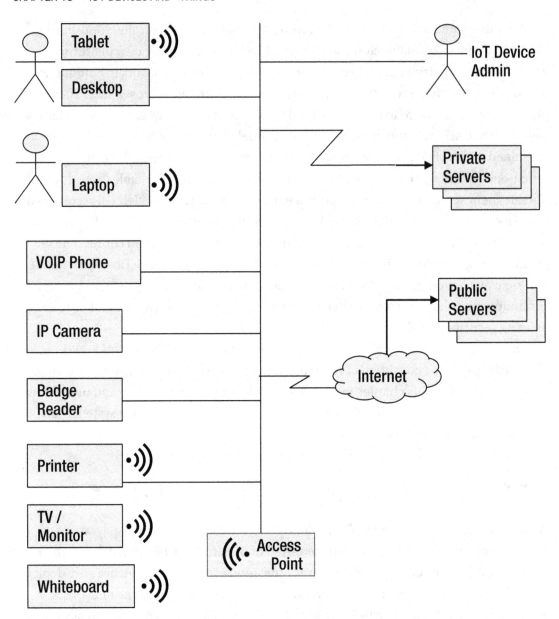

Figure 16-1. *Enterprise IoT Network*

Some of the devices on this network communicate upward to private servers, running on another segment within the enterprise network, while others connect to servers across the Internet. There are also a number of system administrators who periodically need to remotely connect down to these devices, to perform firmware updates or apply configuration changes. These admins may be employees of the enterprise, or may work for a device vendor.

The systems shown in this diagram typically exhibit a number of common security weaknesses, which we touched on in the introduction. First, many of these devices use unencrypted network protocols, making them subject to traffic inspection or Man-In-The-Middle (MITM) attacks that can compromise confidentiality, integrity, and availability. Second, many of these devices have open listening ports. While this is necessary to permit our remote sysadmin to access them, it also allows any other network-connected device to establish a TCP connection to them. Third, these devices often have weak (or hard-coded) authentication mechanisms, and also typically have network stacks that are vulnerable to a variety of attacks. Finally, some of these devices, such as outdoor environmental sensors, remote cameras, or control equipment, may be physically accessible to attackers for long periods of time. As a result, attackers may be able to hijack a wired network connection, or gain access to the device by physically compromising it (e.g., by power-cycling it with a malicious USB stick inserted).

Looking at these devices through our Zero Trust security lens, it should be clear that these systems fall short of meeting our core principles in many ways. Ideally, a Zero Trust system would provide security for these devices in a way that enforces

- Principle of least privilege: Minimize the upstream access that these devices have, in case of device or network compromise.

- Device isolation: Prevent unauthorized subjects on the network from connecting to the devices.

- Traffic encryption: Route native device traffic through a secure and encrypted tunnel.

Of course, some of these devices (such as wall-mounted badge readers) may be in an isolated hard-wired network, and others may be assigned to distinct private VLANs in order to isolate their traffic. Those are good practices, but don't (and can't) apply to all devices, and even when deployed do not make the devices impervious to attacks.

Real-world networks are too often messy, opaque, and heterogeneous, and have often grown organically without a coherent plan. This is typically due to pressure on technical staff to get things working as quickly as possible, and not allocating sufficient time or budget to rework or improve things later. As a result, mixed enterprise networks with these types of devices can exhibit a number of challenges that make them difficult to secure. First, these networks tend to be, in practice, flat and open, with hundreds (or thousands) of diverse sets of devices. This is often due to the difficulty of managing traditional (non-Zero Trust) ACLs across a distributed enterprise, and keeping them up to date and in sync with daily changes. Second, unlike user devices which are typically centrally managed, these IoT devices are typically either managed as standalone devices or via a management software system that applies only to devices of a given type. As such, it's often difficult and labor-intensive to configure or manage these devices at scale. But the biggest challenge with these devices, given the inability to install software onto them, is controlling their network traffic. Specifically, what upstream resources are they allowed to connect to, and what other systems on the network are allowed to connect to them. In a Zero Trust system, this is the role of the PEP, of course—either a network PEP, a user agent PEP, or both. Next, we'll look at how we can bring these worlds together, and some of the technical challenges that often arise.

Zero Trust and IoT Devices

Ideally, IoT devices would be deployed onto an isolated and uniform network, with all north/south network access into the isolated network controlled by a Zero Trust PEP. This idealized logical state is depicted in Figure 16-2.

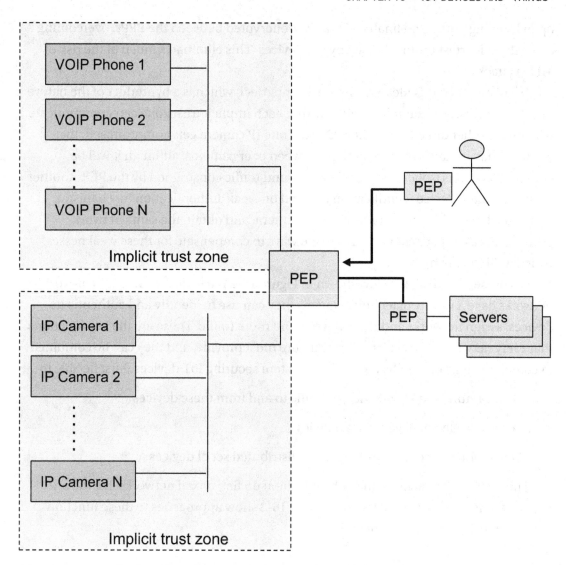

Figure 16-2. *Idealized Zero Trust IoT Network Model*

The benefits of this should be clear, as this model achieves each of the three goals listed previously. First, the principle of least privilege is enforced—all upstream network traffic from each set of devices is controlled by the PEP, meaning that Zero Trust policies are applied and enforced on outbound traffic. This blocks attempts to use a compromised device for data exfiltration, reconnaissance, or DDoS attacks. Second, these devices are isolated within their own uniform implicit trust zone, so that inbound traffic must transit the PEP, which enforces access control policies in front of the devices' open listening ports. And finally, all traffic is encrypted between the PEPs, overcoming any native cleartext protocols used by the devices. This eliminates much of the risk of MITM attacks.

Of course, even this idealized model is imperfect, which is a byproduct of the nature of these devices. For example, devices within each implicit trust zone can communicate with one another directly over the LAN, so if one IP camera gets compromised, that malware may be able to move laterally between peer cameras, although it will be constrained to this isolated zone, with outbound traffic constrained by the PEP. Another example—often device identification is based on weak authentication mechanisms, so an attacker could masquerade as an IP Camera, and obtain the same network permissions as its peer cameras. There are ways to compensate for these weaknesses, which we'll touch on later.

Of course, the idealized view shown in Figure 16-2 is a logical view, and real-world networks have a variety of technical means they can use to identify and authenticate devices, assign networks and IP addresses, and route traffic. These are the key functions that every network and security infrastructure must provide, and they can be combined in complex ways. Ultimately, a Zero Trust system securing IoT devices must be able to

- Capture, route, and encrypt traffic to and from these devices
- Centrally manage access policies
- Enforce access controls across a distributed set of devices

This is difficult to achieve in a robust fashion on flat, mixed networks like the one depicted in Figure 16-1. Tables 16-1 through 16-3 show approaches to these functions, along with the pros and cons of each.

Table 16-1. *How Devices Are Assigned to Networks*

	Pros	**Cons**
Physical Cable/ Switch Port	May be a physically isolated network.	Difficult to change. Isolation may be limited by switch port capacity. Difficult to isolate peer network devices.
Private VLAN	Logical separation within one physical network.	Access granted based on physical network or switch port access.
Wireless Access Point	Usually simpler to reconfigure networks. Built-in device isolation in many Wi-Fi systems.	Not all devices are Wi-Fi enabled Simple password authentication is not strong, and not all devices support WPA-Enterprise.
NAC/802.1x	Dynamic VLAN assignment can isolate devices by type.	Often requires expensive hardware. Difficult to manage large numbers of VLANs. Not all devices support 802.1x.

Table 16-2. *How Devices Are Identified/Authenticated*

	Pros	**Cons**
IP address	Fixed IPs can uniquely identify a device.	Configuration and management overhead. Weak form of identification, easy to spoof.
MAC Address	Supported on all devices. Useful for identifying classes of devices on mixed networks, and assigning to zones (often with 802.1x).	Weak form of identification, easy to spoof.
DHCP Fingerprint	Supported on almost all devices. Reasonably useful for identifying classes of devices on mixed network.	Weak form of identification, easy to spoof.
Certificate via 802.1x	Strong and reliable.	Management and PKI overhead. Many devices cannot use cert-based authentication or identification.

Table 16-3. *How Network Routing Is Assigned*

	Pros	Cons
Default Network Gateway	Assigned automatically via DHCP. Fixed and centralized egress point from LAN is natural policy enforcement point.	DHCP assignment can't always distinguish device types on mixed networks. Configuration separate from DHCP is possible but may be onerous.
Route setting for protected resources by network router	Simple to set up and independent of device configuration.	Secures access to destination resources, but may not filter by source. Does not prevent device access to other resources.
Manually configure devices	Fine-grained control of routes.	Labor-intensive and difficult to maintain as networks change.

The simplest and easiest approach is depicted in Figure 16-3, showing a set of IP cameras deployed onto an isolated and homogeneous network. This could be a physically isolated, wired network, a VLAN assigned by a NAC, or even a camera-only wireless network with an isolated SSID. What's important (and what makes it simple) is that it's homogeneous—all devices on that network are the same type, and therefore have the same set of network access controls applied to them.

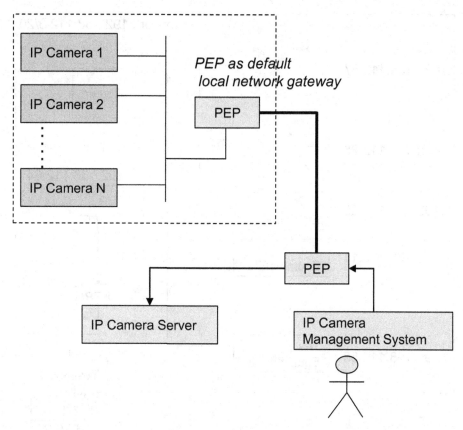

Figure 16-3. *IP Cameras on Isolated, Homogeneous Network*

The key for this scenario is that the IP cameras on the network have the PEP configured as their default network gateway, so that all non-LAN traffic is sent to the PEP, which performs routing and policy enforcement. That is, the PEP is the only egress point from the local zone. The cameras' default network gateway assignment could be performed centrally via the IP camera management system, or via a DHCP server for the camera-only segment.

In any case, it should be clear that is as close to the ideal scenario as possible, making it simple to integrate into a Zero Trust model. Our next scenario, depicted in Figure 16-4, is more typical, and more difficult to control.

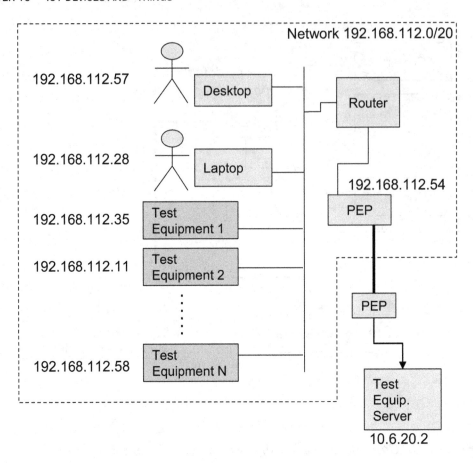

Figure 16-4. *Heterogeneous Enterprise Network*

This diagram shows a mixed (heterogeneous) network segment, 192.168.112.0/20, consisting of hundreds of computers and devices throughout a flat enterprise network in one office building. The devices on this network have essentially random IP addresses assigned to them from the subnet range, via DHCP, and the organization doesn't have an accurate CMDB. This scenario presents a number of challenges to achieving our goals—which are to ensure that only the Test Equipment devices are permitted to access the Test Equipment server, that no other devices can access that server, and that access to the Test Equipment devices is controlled by policy. Unfortunately, in this real-world scenario, we cannot meet all these goals without making changes to the network. This is to be expected in many enterprise scenarios, even outside of IoT devices—but at the very least, you need to be aware of your network's shortcomings and determine how to solve these problems, even if you cannot solve them immediately.

Let's examine what can (and cannot) be achieved here, focusing on securing upstream network access from the Test Equipment. That is, the enterprise needs a way to ensure that Test Equipment-initiated traffic destined for the Test Equipment server (10.6.20.2) on the remote network gets routed to the local PEP for enforcement and forwarding via the secure tunnel. This can be achieved in three possible ways:

- Default gateway configured directly on Test Equipment

- Default gateway assigned to the Test Equipment via DHCP

- Static or dynamic routing on the network

Configuring the default network gateway directly on the Test Equipment may be possible, depending on whether it technically supports this. It also depends on how labor-intensive a process this is. Performing this through a centralized management system is straightforward while requiring individual manual changes across hundreds of devices may be a non-starter. Assigning the PEP as the default network gateway via DHCP, for all devices, may also be a viable approach in some cases. In some cases, the DHCP server may be able to assign different default network gateways for different devices, if the DHCP assignment can accurately distinguish between DHCP requests initiated by the Test Equipment, vs. those issued by other devices,[1] and return different values.

Finally, it's also possible to configure the network router to send network traffic bound for the remote Test Equipment Server (10.6.20.2) to the local PEP (192.168.112.54). This has the advantage of not requiring any other changes to the network, but then requires that the PEP have some ability to distinguish legitimate traffic (initiated by a Test Equipment device) from illegitimate traffic (e.g., initiated by malware on a user's device performing network reconnaissance). This will be difficult to achieve in our scenario, since IP addresses are randomly assigned, and there is no CMDB. It's possible for the PEP to use MAC addresses to distinguish devices, but these are a weak form of identification that can be trivially spoofed, and therefore carries some risk if it's used in this fashion.

---

[1]For example, by examining DHCP fingerprints.

Summary

Like many areas of our real-world networks and systems, IoT devices are often complex and difficult to manage. Zero Trust can help, in many (if not most) situations, but typically cannot provide as robust a level of security as it can with standard enterprise devices (user systems and servers). Zero Trust PEPs can be used to control upstream device access to protected resources, to ensure that network traffic is encrypted, and to control downstream access to IoT devices—with varying degrees of effectiveness, based on the many factors we've discussed in this chapter.

As you look at your enterprise to identify candidate IoT systems for inclusion in your Zero Trust project, there are a few characteristics that you can look for to help you identify well-suited IoT systems. First, understand how these devices' networking is configured, and prefer IoT devices that have a centrally managed mechanism to control these easily at scale. Second, look for areas of your network that are well understood and reasonably well documented. Avoid trying to secure IoT devices on an unmanaged, diverse, and opaque network as an early project—you need to make sure you have some experience and success applying your Zero Trust architecture to IoT systems in simpler and more well-understood environments. And finally, look for some "low hanging fruit" around securing remote third-party user access to internal devices. Zero Trust's ability to require a business process, such as the creation of a service desk ticket, prior to access, can deliver real security value, quickly.

IoT devices are definitely a nascent area for Zero Trust and, as we've explored here, tend to be complex and highly technical and can often be a minefield of older and inflexible technology. But there's a lot of opportunity for improvement, and we've only scratched the surface on this topic—this could be an entire book in its own right. If this is a primary use case for your Zero Trust project, explore carefully and be sure to perform a pilot project in your intended environment to validate the technology's compatibility. Some important questions to ask yourself include

- How complex and mature are your device networks?

- Do you have an accurate and reliable inventory of the devices and their communications patterns?

- How easy or hard is it to capture device network traffic for enforcement by a PEP?

- What network changes will be required, and what impact will they have on other networked devices?

- What network protocols do these devices use? Are they connection-oriented or connectionless protocols? Are they encrypted?

Finally, of course, different Zero Trust implementations will approach this differently, and it's important to clearly understand the capabilities of your chosen Zero Trust solution and deployment model for this use case. Some products and architectures will support these scenarios well, while others will struggle. Having said that, we think Zero Trust systems can bring a great deal of value to often-insecure IoT ecosystems, and we encourage you to investigate whether your organization's environment is a good candidate.

PART III

Putting It All Together

In Part II of this book, we took the Zero Trust principles and architectures from Part I, and used them as our lens to examine a broad set of components across enterprise IT and security architectures. Ranging from on-premises and cloud-based network infrastructure to security and non-security components, this analysis hopefully provided you with a deep understanding of the ways in which Zero Trust can impact your enterprise. This should have armed you with a set of tools, patterns, and perspectives with which you can begin to construct your enterprise's journey to Zero Trust.

Here in Part III, we'll be concluding our journey by building on these foundations. We'll begin with what is in many ways the keystone of Zero Trust—the policy model, in Chapter 17. Recall our architectural premise is that a Zero Trust system is made up of a set of distributed policy enforcement points, and a centralized policy decision point. From this perspective, the policies that get defined, evaluated, and ultimately enforced are arguably the most important part of the system. What this means is that the policy model in your chosen Zero Trust implementation—its language and structure, which will be reflected in that product's deployment models and policy enforcement capabilities—will have a large impact.

After we discuss the policy model, we'll bring things back to more concrete reality in Chapter 18, by looking at seven of the most common Zero Trust use cases, and how your organization should approach them. We'll examine each one from an architectural perspective, discussing considerations and recommendations.

Finally, in Chapter 19, we'll wrap up our journey (and help you begin yours) with discussion and guidance on how you can plan for successful Zero Trust deployments, projects, and initiatives. We'll look at this both from a top-down organizational and program perspective and from a bottom-up tactical project point of view. We'll also look at common roadblocks to Zero Trust initiatives, and how to best overcome them.

Let's dive in, and start our work of bringing all these ideas together into a coherent whole.

CHAPTER 17

A Zero Trust Policy Model

Policies are at the heart of Zero Trust—after all, its primary architectural components are *Policy* Decision Points and *Policy* Enforcement Points. The term *policy* is heavily overloaded in the English language, of course, with meanings at many different levels. In our Zero Trust world, policies are the structures created by organizations to define which identities are permitted to get access to which resources, under which circumstances. Recall that within a Zero Trust environment, access can only be obtained through the evaluation and assignment of a policy to an identity, and that access may be enforced at the network or application levels.

The actual, technical, means by which policies are defined and enforced will be product- and implementation-dependent, but the concepts and components are universal, and should be pervasive in any Zero Trust system. The NIST Zero Trust document states "policy is the set of access rules based on attributes that an organization assigns to a subject, data asset, or application,"[1] and one of the NIST core tenets is that "access to resources is determined by dynamic policy—including the observable state of client identity, application/service, and the requesting asset—and may include other behavioral and environmental attributes."[2] Recall from our working definition in Chapter 2, Zero Trust must "enable the dynamic enforcement of security policies."

As we introduced briefly in Chapter 3, we're adding structure and specificity to the policy discussion, extending some of the concepts within the NIST Zero Trust framework. We're also weaving in and leveraging industry concepts around Attribute-Based Access Control (ABAC), re-interpreting them from the perspective of Zero Trust.

Our goal with this chapter is to provide you with a framework and a structure with which you can think about the scope of your Zero Trust system, and with which to evaluate vendor platforms. Zero Trust systems can be nearly infinite in breadth and depth, and it's important for you to have a strong sense of what should and shouldn't

---

[1]NIST Zero Trust Architecture, page 6
[2]Ibid

© Jason Garbis and Jerry W. Chapman 2021
J. Garbis and J. W. Chapman, *Zero Trust Security*, https://doi.org/10.1007/978-1-4842-6702-8_17

be included, and what's reasonable to include in a policy model. This is required for you to begin to define your policy architecture and lifecycle, and its corresponding set of governance processes. Understanding the capabilities and limits of your intended policy model is also a useful way to set requirements and boundaries for your planned Zero Trust architecture. Let's dive in, starting with an in-depth discussion of the logical components that make up policies.

Policy Components

In this section, we reintroduce the policy structure from Chapter 3, this time providing additional commentary. Table 17-1 depicts the policy structure, which defines the *subject criteria*, *action*, *target*, and *condition* components.

Table 17-1. *Zero Trust Policy Model Components*

Components	Description
Subject Criteria	Subject are the entities performing (initiating) actions. Subjects must be authenticated identities, and policies must contain *subject criteria* which designate the subjects to whom this policy applies.
Action	The activity being performed by the subject. This must contain either a network or an application component, and may possibly contain both.
Target	The object (resource) that the action is being performed upon. This may be statically or dynamically defined within the policy, and may be broad or narrow in scope, although narrow is preferred.
Condition	The circumstances under which the subject is permitted to perform the action upon the target. The Zero Trust system must support the definition of conditions that draw upon multiple types of attributes, including subject, environment, and target attributes.

Note that what we're depicting here is a logical structure, which we believe is a sound way to think about the components of policies. Actual Zero Trust implementations may well structure their policy model differently, but should contain these elements within them. Let's examine each of the policy model components in turn.

Subject Criteria

Ultimately, a subject (an authenticated identity) will be performing the designated action upon the target. Policies are assigned to subjects by the PDP, which evaluates each policy's criteria against the subject in question at various times (we'll be discussing this further in this chapter). Note that policies themselves typically don't reference a specific subject, but instead contain the *criteria* that the PDP uses to determine whether the policy gets assigned to (is applicable to) a given identity. Some policies' criteria can be quite broad ("All employees") or narrow ("Users in group *Marketing*, and assigned to project *Bruin*, who are using Windows devices").

Typical subject criteria include directory group membership, identity-assigned attributes, and relatively static device attributes such as Operating System version and patch level or mobile device jailbreak status. Note that subjects, as we've discussed throughout the book, do not necessarily have to be human users. Servers (or, more logically, the service accounts running within them) may also have identities and therefore be authenticated subjects with policies that are assigned to them, granting them specific access rights.

Note that the approach we're describing here is what the NIST document refers to as the *criteria-based* approach by which the trust algorithm within the PDP makes policy assignment decisions. NIST also discusses a *score-based* approach, which is acceptable as well. We're not endorsing one over the other, although for our discussion here, we believe it's simpler to think about a set of criteria which *all* must be satisfied in order for a policy to be assigned to a given subject.[3]

Finally, note that for now, we're looking at policies and subjects from the perspective of *subject-initiated actions*, which stem from the familiar scenario where a user or a server (which are authenticated subjects) connects to a server via a PEP, to access some resource. Later, we'll explore the more complex scenario where this connection occurs in the reverse direction.

Action

Actions define the type of activity permitted by the policy. The specifics of the activity are dependent on the capabilities of the enforcement points; while many actions will be related to network access, it's also likely that some Zero Trust systems will provide the

---

[3]This can be thought of as a score-based approach in which the score must be 100%, if you prefer.

ability to enforce other types of actions, such as application or data-centric actions. This distinction corresponds to the different types of PEPs, which may operate at the network or application layers. From a network perspective, actions should specify the permitted set of network ports and protocols. From an application or data perspective, actions could be tied to roles, attributes, application services, or data classification (more on this topic shortly). We believe that it simplifies things to think about actions as being defined independently of the targets upon which they will be performed, although in practice, some implementations may combine these together.

Here are some examples of actions:

- Access resource via HTTPS (TCP on port 443 with TLS)

- Access resource via TCP on port 3389 (RDP)

- Access resource via UDP on port 53 (DNS), and accept a response

- Access resource via TCP port 445 (Windows SMB)

- Access to web app at URL /app1 on the target

- Access to web app at URL /app1/adminUI on the target

- Perform a Linux *kill* command via SSH

- Access data tagged as "unclassified", with read/write permissions

- Access data tagged as "customer PII" with read-only permissions

You'll notice that our examples include TCP and UDP access (to be enforced by a network-level PEP), as well as a few examples that rely on application-level concepts (and application-level PEP enforcement). These latter ones are interesting, and are definitely more of a "leading edge" capability. Application level actions (application functions) are generally not in scope for Zero Trust policies today. This is because applications typically have an opaque, internal authorization model, which is not suitable to be controlled by an external system. However, with the advent of modern web applications accessed over HTTP, we're now seeing a more frequent correlation between application functions and URLs, which opens the door to these types of PEP-enforced actions in ways that were not previously possible.

For example, we may have an important internal banking web application located at `https://fundmgmt.internal.example.com/main/`, which is used by hundreds of employees. This app has an administrative UI, accessed at `https://fundmgmt.internal.example.com/adminUI/` by only the few authorized system admins. While regular users cannot perform any administrative function, because their account role doesn't permit it, they *can* navigate to the admin URL, and attempt to attack it. Given that this is a financially rewarding target for criminals, we can easily imagine that some remotely directly malware on a regular user's workstation would want to attempt this. By creating a policy that requires admin directory group membership in order to access the admin URL, we're achieving our principle of least privilege while keeping our users fully productive.

This is possible because there's a visible aspect of the application—the URL—which is used to distinguish different functions. If the application used an opaque network protocol, or a different URL scheme, this wouldn't be possible. There are a few well-known application protocols for which this type of Zero Trust policy enforcement is possible, in addition to HTTP. For example, there's no reason that systems which are proxying well-known application protocols such as SSH couldn't do the same. After all, PAM vendors already do a good job of enforcing controls around specific SSH commands, so it's not a stretch to envision a Zero Trust system (perhaps from a PAM vendor) providing something similar.

The data examples, as well as potential actions on other applications are a bit different, and are more forward-looking concepts. The idea is that a Zero Trust system would use an open security framework that enables the PEP and the application to exchange information that enhances their ability to enforce policies. We can envision, for example, an application that works in conjunction with a PEP, either via a plug-in or via configuration, and associates application protocol components with application actions, so that the PEP can enforce controls, or even perform some form of Just-In-Time application role provisioning for the subject. Or, in the other direction, a structured way for the PEP to send additional identity or contextual information to the application, so that the application can enforce the Zero Trust controls. You may recall that this latter approach is one that Google took in their BeyondCorp initiative, which we mentioned in Chapter 4. Their Access Proxy (effectively, their PEP) injected additional contextual information in HTTP headers for user actions, and the target applications could either ignore this extra information or use it.

We think that this is an emerging area and that there will be interesting developments around this in the next few years. Ideally, we'd see an open framework with which application developers and Zero Trust systems can interact and integrate. Even without this technical integration however, recall that your organization should be running access governance processes, to ensure that users only have appropriate application roles and capabilities. This is a great example of the ways in which different types of systems, and different parts of the organization, can work together in harmony.

Target

Targets define the host, system, or component that will be acted upon. Policies may define targets statically, or dynamically (which require action by the PEP in order to fully render the target). Dynamic policies are especially powerful—one of the key principles of Zero Trust and why it's so compelling. These policies provide the ability to define and enforce access based on attributes which are unknown and unknowable until runtime.

Let's look at several examples of targets, which illustrate a useful range of different types.

Access to Host 10.6.1.34

This is a simple, static, and fully rendered target—the network PEP doesn't need to do any further work in order to enforce this. While useful, targets that specify a single IP address are typically not a good choice to include in a policy. IP addresses do change, of course, and in many cases, the logically intended access is not to the host at that IP address but to the application or service running which happens to be running on that IP address. In such cases, a hostname may be a better choice of a target, rather than an IP address. We discuss this in our next example.

One final comment—there are, of course, instances where it does make sense to specify fixed IP addresses within targets, especially if the access is being granted to IT or network administrators who need to access infrastructure elements such as networking gear. You know your environment best, and will ultimately need to decide upon the most effective approach.

Access to Host `appserver1.internal.example.com`

Targets that specify hostnames are very commonly used, and are a very effective way to define policies. Hostnames, of course, get mapped to IP addresses via DNS. Policies that specify a single hostname as a target allow you to create fine-grained access controls, and are often combined with a limited set of actions, most frequently a single network protocol and port.

Zero Trust policies must be able to leverage the behavior of an organization's internal DNS systems, teams, and processes, and work with (rather than against) its behavior. For example, consider an internal user-facing application with an IP address that changes periodically. This is perfectly reasonable, for example, for a virtualized system with a rolling set of application updates, which perhaps uses a staggered approach to production rollouts. DNS is also frequently used for load balancing purposes, for geographic distribution across a set of replicated application servers, or just as a standard best practice to give IT teams the ability to make necessary network changes independent of applications.

In all cases, it's important for the Zero Trust system to be able to resolve hosts by having the distributed PEPs use the appropriate DNS server. In a distributed Zero Trust environment running across multiple disparate networks, it's often the case that a centralized PDP would not be able to resolve all hostnames, since they are in separate domains and/or on disconnected networks.

Access to Hosts on the Subnet `10.5.1.0/24`

This example shows a static target, which corresponds to multiple hosts within the subnet—in fact, this target grants access to all hosts on that subnet. This type of broad access is not ideal, and is generally in conflict with the principle of least privilege. However, as always, there are exceptions. This target could be sensibly used in a policy if, for example, it were granted to IT administrators who had a legitimate need to access all the hosts on that network[4]. Or, if the network was segmented such that all the devices on that network were of a similar type, and therefore it made sense to grant access to all of them. Most likely, this target would be used during a transitional state, when an organization is in the midst of its journey to Zero Trust and is not yet ready to impose finer-grained restrictions on access. This could be deployed as an enclave-based model with the implicit trust zone behind the PEP.

Access to Systems Tagged as `"department=Marketing"`

This example illustrates some of the real power of a Zero Trust system, since it relies upon the PEP to actually resolve the hosts after the policy has been granted to the subject by the PDP. We'll talk about this flow a bit later in this chapter, but for now, this is an example of how the Zero Trust system uses the PEP to fully render the policy based on its ability to interrogate its environment. That is, the policy creator is relying on the organization's use of metadata within the runtime system to indicate the contents of the workload, which ultimately determines who can access it.

---

[4]In this case, we'd recommend the use of a condition, which we discuss next, so that IT admins do not have continual and ongoing access to the entire network.

The actual mechanics of how a "tag" (referred to as a *label* in some systems) is applied and resolved will be implementation-dependent, but the details are not relevant here. What matters is the concept—that organizations can use a mechanism outside of standard IT and networking to control access, which binds together business or technical processes and security, often for the first time. For example, an organization could use an attribute within their Configuration Management Database (CMDB) as the source for this information, or a metadata attribute such as a tag within an IaaS environment. In both cases, this enables IT and security teams to collaborate, using the Zero Trust consumption of this metadata as a powerful and automated integration point. Any host tagged this way would automatically be detected by the Zero Trust system, and have the appropriate set of access policies applied—meaning that the right set of users will automatically get the right level of access, simply based on the usage of this tag.

What's also interesting to note about this example is that it opens up the policy model to types of resources that are not solely host-based. Today's modern applications are, more often than not, containerized and/or microservices based, and are not directly tied to their underlying host. In these cases, the Zero Trust policy model must be able to distinguish between different services, and enforce different levels of access regardless of whether multiple services are running on the same physical or virtual host or share a common IP address.

For example, service mesh systems such as **Istio** provide a policy model that follows the approach we describe here. The service mesh consists of a distributed set of PEPs, and their authorization policies include a tag-based mechanism for selecting policy targets and a mechanism for specifying conditions.[5]

Access to Systems Tagged as "stage=test"

This is similar to our previous example, but with an important distinction—the use of a tag indicating a deployment stage. The implications of this are profound, especially in a DevOps environment, when coupled with an automated toolchain that deploys new versions of applications or services in a continuous fashion. In this example, the toolchain would use the tag to indicate the appropriate development lifecycle stage, and the Zero Trust system would automatically grant the right set of subjects (either human

---

[5]Istio's built-in conditions are more focused on services and networks rather than identities, but they do include some experimental extension features and may well expand in this direction in future versions. For more information, see https://istio.io/latest/docs/concepts/security/.

or system) access to these targets. What this means is that subjects will automatically and transparently obtain the necessary access as a byproduct of the deployment processes. As a workload or service's stage is changed, its access controls will automatically follow, derived from this changed status.

From our perspective, this nicely illustrates the power of a Zero Trust system. It leverages technical work that's already being performed (the toolchain-driven deployment), using an attribute to automatically adjust access permissions. The net effect is that workloads maintain exactly the right set of minimal access controls as they progress through their lifecycle, without requiring any manual intervention. This approach can tie very well into a DevOps organization, retaining their velocity while achieving Zero Trust security principles.

Condition

Conditions specify the circumstances under which the subject is allowed to actually perform the action on the target. Note that policy models should support checking for a very wide variety of conditions; in fact, your Zero Trust implementation should support an extensible set of conditions, so that you can add custom checks. Conditions tend to be evaluated against device, authentication, or system-level attributes, although some Zero Trust implementations may support additional types.

Let's take a look at a few examples of conditions, which must be true in order for access to be permitted.

Time of Day Is Between 08:00 and 18:00

Time of day restrictions are a convenient and focused means of access control, effective for users with well-defined roles and regular hours. This condition helps defend against stolen credentials and malware, either of which might be attempting to access resources during non-working hours. This condition is also useful for planned maintenance windows for always-on devices; imagine a set of retail devices which need to connect to an IT back end each night between 01:00 and 03:00. There's no reason to permit that network connection except during that permitted time window.

This condition gives us a clear example of why it's necessary for the PEP to be able to complete the rendering of the policy. An identity may only authenticate with the PDP once per day, but the PEP needs to be able to compare the current time with allowed time windows throughout the day.

User Has Performed a Valid MFA or Step-Up Authentication Within the Last 90 Minutes

We're big fans of the appropriate use of MFA, and this type of condition should be a mandatory (and common) ingredient in every Zero Trust deployment. Deciding when and how to require step-up authentication is, of course, a balancing act, and you need to take into consideration both the user experience and the threat model you're defending against. Certain high-risk or high-value applications may justify prompting for MFA each time a user initiates a session with them, but in many cases, it's equally effective and less intrusive to require MFA once for an entire group of resources, and have that maintain validity for a period of time. Again, this type of condition is one that must be evaluated and enforced by the PEP; step-up authentication may be triggered at an arbitrary time based on user access through the PEP, and the PDP will most likely not be involved in that flow.

Note that there are a wide variety of approaches and solutions available as second factors, including FIDO2, smartphone apps, push notifications, and biometrics. Zero Trust platforms should support any or all of these, via standardized APIs, to give you the ability to choose the ones that work best for your environment.

Device Posture Meets Requirements: Anti-malware Service Is Running

This condition is used to validate that the subject's device meets security posture requirements. Note that in this example, it's relying on information retrieved from the device itself. The check for whether the anti-malware service is currently executing may be performed by the user agent PEP or by another software component on the device, but keep in mind that any information sent from a device should be considered only partially trusted.

While many IT and security organizations perform proper security hygiene on user devices, such as by restricting administrative privileges, it is of course possible that malware on the device is returning false information. So while an indication that a device's anti-malware service is running is useful information and quite valid to enforce as a condition, it should only be considered as one component of defense-in-depth.

Device Posture Meets Requirements: Endpoint Security Scan Completed Fewer Than 48 Hours Ago

This condition uses device posture information retrieved from a security scanning tool, such as an endpoint management or vulnerability scanning solution. Because the PEP retrieves this information from a server, rather than from a device, it can be treated as more trustworthy.[6] Note that in this example, the condition happens to require that a security scan has been completed recently. Another approach could be to utilize more current information, such as by having the PEP make a call into a monitoring system such as a SIEM or UEBA, and obtain near real-time information about the risk level of the given device.

A Service Desk Ticket Is in an *Open* State for This Resource

This condition is one of the most interesting and most compelling examples of how Zero Trust systems can bind together security enforcement and business processes. Like the metadata tag example we discussed for Targets, this allows organizations to leverage their desired business processes. By making access—enforced by the network or application—a byproduct of a properly executed business process, it guarantees that users will follow the process. This can have tremendous benefits in terms of auditability, repeatability, and quality, not to mention security.

In this example, the organization wants to ensure that IT admin access to a given resource is only permitted (and only possible) if there's a Service Desk ticket in the *open* state, which matches this resource. The outcome of this policy is that stakeholders will be required to create a Service Desk ticket in order for an IT admin to access the resource and perform the necessary task. And once the ticket is closed, admin access to that resource is revoked. This eliminates the need for admins and their devices to have broad and continuous network access, while keeping them fully productive. It also ensures that all admin access is tracked for compliance purposes.

This Service Desk ticket is just one example; Zero Trust systems can be integrated with essentially any business process in a similar way, driving considerable benefits across the organization.

---

[6]Of course, no system is perfect, and the security system may have failed to detect malware on the device, or may itself be compromised and returning false information.

Both the Subject and the Target Must Be Servers Tagged as Being in a "Production" State

In this example, the subject and the targets are both servers, and have a tag used to indicate their state. This condition is a way to prevent development or test apps (or developers working on non-production systems) from accidentally connecting with a production service. Of course, there should be additional layers of controls via authentication—for example, application credentials or a certificate may be needed, depending on the service-to-service authentication model. But, especially in environments with manual testing or release steps, it's too easy for developers to make a mistake; oftentimes, this work is done via the command line where it's easy to make a simple copy-and-paste or typographical error that can have a significant impact.

This type of control—using both subject and target service metadata—could be extended to further scope restrictions, for example, by application or project name. While it's unlikely that an application service that's part of project *oriole* would mistakenly attempt to connect to a service within project *bluejay*, it is certainly possible that a malicious user, or malware with access to that application's host, could attempt to perform network reconnaissance or lateral movement. Our principle of least privilege should drive us to having these types of policies in place, once our Zero Trust infrastructure and security maturity are ready for it.

Subject Criteria vs. Conditions

As we've gone through these examples, it's likely you've noticed that there are some checks that could fit into either subject criteria or conditions. That's okay—there are not necessarily any fixed rules about this, and you'll need to make some judgment calls about this based on the particulars of your organization and your chosen platform. As you gain experience, it should become apparent to you which approach will work best.

In general, consider that some types of checks will be more appropriate to do in the PDP at time of initial session establishment (such as during identity authentication), even if the PEP is technically capable of performing them. These checks are typically related to attributes that are slow to change, and therefore likely to remain fixed for the duration of a user session. Of course, it depends on how the specific Zero Trust platform is implemented, but, for example, OS version and geolocation are unlikely to change while maintaining an active session. We'll be examining attributes and where they should be evaluated later in this chapter.

Example Policies

Now that we've looked at how policies are constructed, and reviewed some samples of their components, let's put them together in a few example policies which will illustrate some of the ways in which these components can be woven together.

Our first example policy is the one we introduced in Chapter 3, when we first explained the policy model, shown in Table 17-2.

Table 17-2. *Sample Policy—User Access to Billing Application*

Policy: Users in the Billing department must be able to use the Billing web application	
Subject Criteria	Users who are members of the group `Dept_Billing` in the Identity Provider.
Action	Users must be able to access the Web UI on port 443 over HTTPS.
Target	The billing application with the FQDN `billing.internal.company.com`.
Condition	Users may be on-premises or remote. Remote users must be prompted for MFA prior to access (at time of authentication) or once in each 4-hour window. Users must be accessing this application from a company-managed device with endpoint security software running.

In this case, the subject criteria will assign this policy to users who are members of the specified identity provider group, `Dept_Billing`. Note that in this organization, only employees are stored in their identity provider, so there's no reason to have an additional check for that role within the criteria, since it's implied. Note also that in this example, they chose not to include a check for whether the user actually has an active account in the billing application. This could have been useful in case *some* but not *all* members of the Billing department are active users of this application. This is an interesting point, and illustrates a fairly common occurrence—where an organization doesn't have an identity group that perfectly maps to the set of users who should receive a given action.

The ideal scenario for Zero Trust policies, of course, is to enforce the principle of least privilege, and only grant access to precisely the right set of users. However, even an imperfect Zero Trust implementation is better than none, and we believe it's better to move forward with a policy which grants access to a few extra users, rather than being held up having to wait for changes to an identity management program and process to achieve a "perfect" group mapping. Recall that we touched on this in Chapter 5—this is a great example of how a Zero Trust project can and should move forward and deliver value even while the identity team progresses on a separate parallel track.

Back to our example, the action in this case is simple—just the ability to access the web UI over HTTPS—and the target is a simple fully qualified domain name. However, the conditions, which are used to enforce a few controls, are more interesting. First, remote users need to enter an MFA prompt when they access this application, and again 4 hours later. Users working on the (more) trusted internal company network are not required to enter MFA, since their physical presence in the building can be considered as an additional factor. The conditions also require that the device be company managed (validated by the presence of a valid certificate issued by the company CA) and that the company's endpoint security solution be running on that device.

This is a reasonable and balanced set of conditions in our estimation, allowing remote users to be productive while only imposing a minimal level of annoyance and enforcing access only from valid company-managed devices. Let's take a look at another example, which in some ways is even simpler, based on some constraints in their environment.

Table 17-3. *Sample Policy—Admin Access to Production Subnet*

Policy: Sysadmin access to production subnet	
Subject Criteria	Users who are members of the group Sysadmins in the identity provider.
Action	Users can access TCP ports 22, 3389, and 443 and use ICMP ping.
Target	Any host on subnet 10.0.0.0/8.
Condition	There must be a service desk ticket in an "open" state, and which specifies the hostname or IP address being accessed.

In the example in Table 17-3, the organization is using the policy to control sysadmin access to production servers. Their sysadmins need remote access (SSH, SFTP, Web, and RDP) to servers or network devices in their large production subnet, which contains thousands of hosts. Every working day, these sysadmins need to connect to a few of those systems to update, reconfigure, or troubleshoot. The organization doesn't want their admins to have wide-open and permanent access to this network, but they also need their admins to be able to do their jobs, which means that they need access to an arbitrary and unpredictable set of hosts every day.

This example policy solves this problem for them, by tying access control to a business process—the use of their service desk (ticketing) system. With this policy, the organization keeps their admins productive while ensuring that all access to these production systems is logged.

Note that our example organization, like many real-world enterprises, is more mature in some areas and less mature in others. In this example, their use of the service desk as a reliable and regular process for directing sysadmin tasks shows a considerable level of maturity. On the other hand, the granting of both SSH and RDP access for each server indicates that they don't have an accurate asset management system on which they can rely to map hosts to OS types. This example policy also doesn't have any MFA associated with it. Perhaps in this fictional organization, they have a cultural resistance to using it, or perhaps the organization is using some sort of compensating control, such as a credential vault.

Table 17-4. *Sample Policy—Developer Access*

Policy: Developers accessing project "Everest" resources

Subject Criteria	The subject must be a member of the `Project_Everest` directory group.
Action	All TCP, UDP, and ICMP actions.
Target	Any resource in the IaaS development environment tagged as "`project=Everest.`"
Condition	None (access is always permitted).

The sample policy shown in Table 17-4 illustrates the use of a dynamically rendered target, where the PEP evaluates the metadata for targets in an IaaS environment. While the actions are wide open, this is appropriate given that this is a development environment. This policy gives the developers the full ability to work within their IaaS environment while ensuring they cannot access other projects' resources.

Table 17-5. *Sample Policy—Server-to-Server Access*

Policy: Web server in DMZ accessing database server

Subject Criteria	The subject must have hostname ws1.company.com or ws2.company.com.
Action	Access TCP port 3306.
Target	Host app1database.internal.company.com.
Condition	None (access is always permitted).

Our final example policy, in Table 17-5, illustrates a server-to-server scenario, showing how an enterprise might define a policy permitting a web server running in the DMZ to access its associated database server on the private internal network. We can easily envision this web application providing the front end for an e-commerce site, with a myriad set of back-end services interfacing with the core database (for instance, updating inventory, or processing orders). In this example, there are multiple instances of the web server for load balancing and HA purposes, and their internal IP addresses regularly change due to the underlying virtual infrastructure, with new versions being frequently deployed. This simple policy helps the organization automatically adjust access even atop their changing infrastructure while retaining tight security.

Policies, Applied

This policy model should provide you with a structure with which to think about and create access rules, in a way that is meaningful to both technical and non-technical stakeholders. It should also be helpful as you analyze potential Zero Trust products, to give you a sense for the types of capabilities you need.

Of course, those policies don't exist in a vacuum—they require attributes (contextual inputs) in order to be evaluated, they need to be constructed to meet specific scenarios, and they have a flow associated with them in terms of when and why they are evaluated. In this section, we'll explore each of these aspects of policies, starting with attributes.

Attributes

Zero Trust policies are built around the attributes associated with identities, devices, targets, and the overall enterprise system. As illustrated in the policy model, these attributes are referenced in subject criteria, in targets, and in conditions. Attributes are key to achieving the context sensitivity of policies, and obtaining the scale and dynamism needed for Zero Trust, and fall into three categories.

Identity attributes are typically retrieved from the identity provider which authenticates the identity, although of course they may be augmented with attributes from other sources. Identity attributes include directory group memberships, as well as directly assigned attributes such as roles. Every organization will likely create custom groups, as well as assign custom attributes to their identities, and Zero Trust systems' use of these attributes in policies is a core, must-have capability.

Device attributes may be retrieved directly from the device (typically via a local agent), or from an external system such as a CMDB or endpoint management system. Some device attributes, in particular ones that are obtained from a local process running on the device, may change fairly frequently. The relative permanence of attributes is something we discuss in the following text, and should definitely be a factor as you decide where, when, and how to evaluate them.

There is another set of attributes to consider, which we term *system attributes.* This category is a bit of a catchall, and refers to those attributes associated with the broader enterprise network and ecosystem. This can include things such as the overall network threat or risk level (perhaps obtained from a SIEM), system or network load, or even attributes associated with business processes or IT functions, such as whether this is an approved maintenance window or if there is an emergency IT "breakglass" situation.

Finally, *target attributes* are used to determine targets for actions, as we discussed previously. These may be retrieved by having the PEP interrogate its local environment, or perhaps from a centralized and authoritative source such as a CMDB.

Note that in our discussion of attributes, we've approached this from the point of view of having the Zero Trust system retrieve attributes from external sources. While this will definitely be a common scenario, it's not the only possibility. It's entirely reasonable to have the Zero Trust system itself be a repository of attributes. In this case, of course, there needs to be a set of mechanisms to populate and update the attributes—recall that we covered this in Chapter 11 where we discussed security orchestration.

Given all that, let's take a look at the rate of change of different types of attributes. The table of attribute permanence is shown in Table 17-6, along with examples of attributes and their general frequency of change. Don't consider these as firm rules, but rather as a set of guidelines. Even "permanent" biometric attributes could, in fact, change, for example, due to injury or transplant. And your organization may have some guidelines around asset management, for example, which could impact the relative permanence of certain device attributes.

Overall, we believe this table will be useful because it can help you understand the types of attributes that exist, and decide where and how frequently to consider evaluating them (e.g., at authentication time vs. at access time).

Table 17-6. Attribute Permanence

Attribute Permanence	Identity Attributes (Users)	Device Attributes	System Attributes	Target Attributes
Permanent (never change)	Biometrics (e.g., fingerprints, iris scan)	Operating System	*None*	Operating System
Semipermanent (fewer than one change per year)	Citizenship Country of Residence Certifications Security Clearances	Hostname	Domain	Identifier Hostname URL
Infrequent (monthly or yearly changes)	Group memberships Roles Project Assignments	OS version or patch level Component patch level (e.g., AV signature file)	DNS Server Settings	IP Address Certificate info Network info (e.g., TLS parameters) Resource Version
Regular (weekly changes)	*None*	Device posture check Registry key values	*None*	Target posture check
Frequent (hourly or daily changes)	Geolocation Network attributes	Process Status Device IP address	Network risk level Network load Breakglass Situation	Resource Load Resource Availability

In practice, it makes sense to validate frequently changing attributes in the PEPs, likely as part of a condition. This is because these attributes may change within an active session, and the PEPs are the mechanism for doing this kind of access-time enforcement. Longer-lived attributes may make sense to evaluate as part of the subject criteria in the PDP. Of course, treat these as guidelines, as your chosen Zero Trust platform may approach things differently.

Policy Scenarios

Now that we've examined the structure of policies, and the set of attributes used as input into them, it's time for us to look at the most common set of scenarios. By this, we mean the patterns and access methods by which subjects access targets. But first, let's make sure we have a solid understanding of our guidelines and assumptions.

First (with the exception of IoT systems that we discussed in Chapter 16), there must always be at least one subject in any Zero Trust action being performed, where subjects are authenticated identities. That is, unauthenticated identities cannot be subjects, although they can certainly be targets. Second, there will likely be some level of communications occurring on a network outside the control of the Zero Trust system, within the implicit trust zone. You must think about and explicitly make decisions about the boundaries of your implicit trust zone, and it should shrink over time as you make progress on your Zero Trust journey. During your journey, there will often be a mixed set of communications to Zero Trust resources, where some communication occurs through PEPs (and is subject to Zero Trust policies), while there will be some communication, even to the same resources, which will bypass the Zero Trust PEP.

Finally, note that resources which are accessible by unauthorized users (such as public web servers) are outside the scope of Zero Trust policy models. These systems deliberately grant a level of trust to *any* remote system, permitting it to connect with and utilize the resource. Of course, even on a publicly accessible web server, other services such as administrative access to that host can (and probably should) be within the scope of a Zero Trust system. That is, Zero Trust's requirement that all subjects be authenticated identities will help you draw clear boundaries for your system. Note that while some resources in your environment will be outside the scope of Zero Trust, they will definitely still remain within scope for your security team, and must be protected by an appropriate set of controls.

Now, let's examine several scenarios, which bring together our discussions of the policy model with the Zero Trust deployment models. Note that in all these diagrams, we have omitted the PDP for clarity.

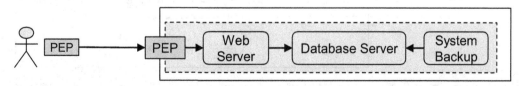

Figure 17-1. *Policy Scenario—Web Server as Target*

This first scenario, in Figure 17-1, depicts a simple deployment, using the enclave-based Zero Trust deployment model. In this example, the only policy target is the web server, controlling the user's access to it. All three servers depicted are within the Zero Trust implicit trust zone, so their access to one another isn't controlled by the PEP. That is, the PEP is only controlling access by the subject to the web server.

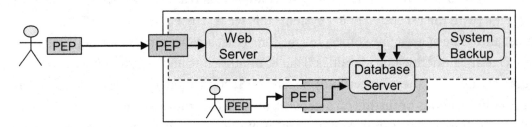

Figure 17-2. *Policy Scenario—Database Server as Target*

In the scenario shown in Figure 17-2, the database server has been placed partially behind a PEP, so it can be a target within a policy. In this example, the organization has restricted IT administrator access to the database server, so that it can only be accessed by an authenticated identity via an assigned policy. However, the web server and backup system continue to access the database server directly, since they're within the implicit trust zone. In practice, this would be achieved by firewall settings, so that admin access (via port 22) is only achievable through the PEP, while database access (e.g., port 3306) is accessible to any other server within the larger implicit trust zone.

This serves as a good real-world example of how an organization can incrementally transition to Zero Trust—by treating the different services running on the database server as distinct logical targets, they can improve their security by strictly controlling admin access without impacting their application or business operations at all. This may or may not be a temporary phase; Figure 17-3 depicts a potential next step in this journey.

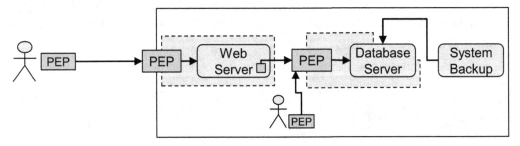

Figure 17-3. *Policy Scenario—Web Server as Subject*

Figure 17-3 shows where the organization has also placed the database server behind a PEP, so that only authenticated subjects can access this.[7] The implications of this are that the web server must now be a subject, with an identity and a means of authentication. The results are a reduced implicit trust zone (improving security) as well as improved deployment flexibility.

This latter result is an interesting and often overlooked benefit of Zero Trust. Because the web server's access to the database server is now via the Zero Trust system, the database can be moved anywhere across the enterprise's infrastructure with no impact to the web server, except perhaps for some additional latency. That is, the database server's deployment location becomes essentially irrelevant to the web server, and can be relocated to a remote or cloud-based location transparently. Without Zero Trust, the organization would not be able to achieve this without providing some sort of remote access mechanism, typically via a WAN connection. That brings with it a whole set of security and networking considerations, as well as likely additional expense. Using a PEP and a policy to provide access is far simpler, faster, and more secure.

Target-Initiated Access

Our next scenario introduces the concept of *a target-initiated* action. So far, our discussion and policy model has been approached from the perspective of an authenticated subject accessing a resource, via a PEP. That is, the subject's device will initiate the connection (if using a connection-oriented protocol such as TCP) or initiate the network traffic (if using a connectionless protocol such as UDP). The previous scenarios, showing a user accessing a web server and a web server accessing a database, are good examples of this pattern.

However, some applications and networks utilize a reverse type of communications, which means that our Zero Trust system must also support it, in order to meet our goals of securing all communications via policies. This pattern is what we term *target-initiated*: we still have an authenticated subject and access that's controlled by a PEP, but the network traffic is initiated by the policy's target, and the traffic or connection is sent to the subject. Let's explore an example that will make this concrete.

---

[7]In this example, the system backup server can still continue to access the database directly, for instance, via firewall rules and/or a distinct TCP port.

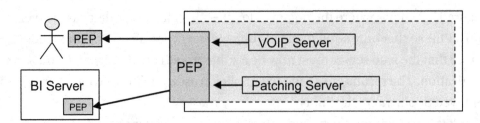

Figure 17-4.   *Policy Scenario—Target-Initiated, Enclave-Based*

In Figure 17-4, the Zero Trust system is using the enclave-based deployment model, with the PEP securing their on-premises data center network. The organization uses softphones on user devices for voice calls, and the protocol requires that calls be initiated from the VOIP server to the user's device (which is running a local user agent PEP). The organization also has a Business Intelligence (BI) analytics server running in some remote environment, which in turn is an authenticated subject with a local PEP. Their infrastructure processes require that their internal patching server periodically connect to the remote BI server to perform OS updates.

In both cases depicted in Figure 17-4, the network traffic must be routed through (and controlled by) the PEP, based on policies. From a technical perspective, this imposes certain requirements on the Zero Trust platform and its policy model. Some Zero Trust deployment models, such as the enclave-based and resource-based models, which typically utilize a direct connection between user devices and PEPs, can readily support this scenario. Solutions based on the cloud-routed deployment model typically struggle to support this. We'll look at the microsegmentation deployment model in our next scenario.

Microsegmentation

Recall that in the microsegmentation deployment model, the resources being accessed are authenticated identities, just like subjects. As a result, the access and policy models are going to be more symmetrical. This is depicted in Figure 17-5, where both the web server and the user initiate connections to the database server and all three are authenticated entities (note that we'll touch on the System Backup server shortly).

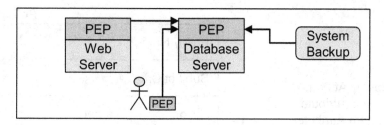

Figure 17-5. *Policy Scenario—Microsegmentation*

The implications of this are that while the concepts of *subject criteria* and *targets* will exist, the policy model will need to be slightly different in such a system. In Figure 17-5, because both the web server and database server are identities, they are both authenticated and will have similar sets of attributes. Therefore, it'll be possible to specify them using the same type of criteria, unlike our previous scenarios where subjects and targets were specified using different means.

Of course, even in the microsegmentation model, your identities must be able to interact with non-identity systems. As shown previously, the PEP must allow the backup system to access the database server. Note that we'll explore one more wrinkle around the service-to-service scenario in Chapter 18.

Now that we've seen how different types of policies can be deployed across different scenarios, let's dive into the flows associated with them.

Policy Evaluation and Enforcement Flows

Figure 17-6 depicts the logical system flow of policies through a Zero Trust system. The PDP takes as input the set of attributes for the identity, device, and system, and uses them to evaluate the set of policies in the policy store. The results of this evaluation are policies granted to this subject for the duration of this session. These results, which are transmitted to the PEPs, contain information about the subject to whom this has been granted, as well as information about the action, target, and condition. The granted policies may need further rendering by the PEP, through examination of the metadata associated with potential targets, to determine which ones match. And, the PEP is responsible for enforcing any access-time conditions in the granted policies.

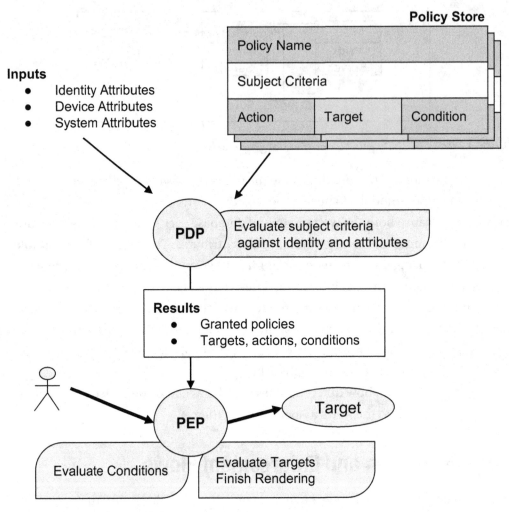

Figure 17-6. *Policy Evaluation and Enforcement*

Figure 17-6 depicts the actions that the Zero Trust system takes on policies as they flow through the PDP and PEP. While this shows *what* the system does, we also need to elaborate on the *when*. We touched on this in our earlier chapter on security orchestration, where we introduced the primary triggers that initiate actions within a Zero Trust system. Figure 17-7 shows these triggers, and what they initiate within the PDP and PEP when invoked.

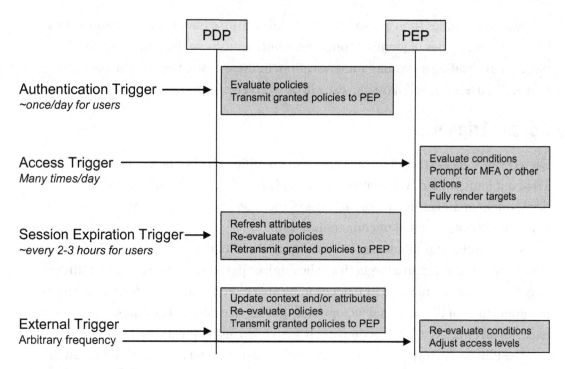

Figure 17-7. *PDP and PEP Triggers*

Authentication Trigger

Identities must of course authenticate with the PDP in order to be granted any access. Most Zero Trust systems will be integrated with an organization's identity provider (as opposed to acting as their own IdP), and the authentication trigger will result in the policy evaluation flow as shown previously in Figure 17-6. Your organization will be able to configure how frequently identities are authenticated into your Zero Trust system, and the degree to which this is transparent to end users.

There will be many factors at play in this decision, including your intended use case and authentication methods. We'll be discussing this further in Chapter 18, but, for example, you may want users' devices to authenticate immediately when they sign into their desktops at the start of their workday, if your system secures all their access and is required for them to be productive. Alternatively, some organizations may choose to start their Zero Trust journey with a VPN Replacement use case; in this scenario, users may explicitly authenticate into their systems only when they need to access specific remote resources.

System identities (non-person entities) will of course have a different authentication lifecycle. These types of identities often run continuously, so there may not be any natural flow leading to regular authentication. In these cases, the session expiration trigger discussed in the following text will be of greater importance.

Access Trigger

Each policy's access trigger is invoked when identities access a target. Different Zero Trust implementations will approach this slightly differently, depending on the deployment architecture, the capabilities of the PEP, and the type of network protocol (e.g., connection-oriented or connectionless).

Some implementations may evaluate conditions for every network packet, on every new connection to a target (if applicable), or periodically (e.g., every 5 minutes). Regardless of frequency, the PEP needs to be able to evaluate and enforce conditions, including time of day, external factors such as a service desk ticket status, and prompting users for any necessary interactions such as step-up authentication.

The PEP is also responsible for fully rendering any targets, by which we mean the PEP must interrogate its environment and discover resources that match the associated metadata requirements such as having a specific label value.

Session Expiration Trigger

Throughout this book, we haven't formally defined a *session*, which was deliberate. Different Zero Trust deployment models and platforms can have very different concepts of sessions, and this variability makes it difficult to use this term precisely. What matters is that your Zero Trust system needs to have a logical concept of a session, which is a period of time after an identity has authenticated, and during which it can actively access protected resources.

Sessions must have a limited lifespan, and at the end of the session lifespan, the system must perform a refresh, whereby it obtains updated attributes, re-evaluates policies, and communicates any changed access to the PEPs. This refresh may or may not be visible to users; this should be configurable as part of your platform's policy model. Recall that different types of attributes have different rates of change, so there will be some that will more naturally fit with being refreshed when the session is renewed.

Session durations are something that you should think about and set based on factors such as risk level, use case, and identity population. For users, a session duration of about 2–3 hours seems right to us, depending on how dynamic the environment and user population is. That's also about the maximum frequency that users will accept for being prompted for MFA, although in some environments, once per day might be more appropriate. For non-person entities, season durations are highly dependent on the use case and the degree to which your services and environment changes. In some situations, a session duration of 24 hours may well be appropriate, while in more dynamic system environments, something in the 2–3-hour range would be better. Keep in mind that a lot will depend on the capabilities of your Zero Trust platform and the overhead associated with a session refresh. Also keep in mind that the most dynamic attributes are best evaluated as conditions, which the PEPs should be able to refresh multiple times (even nearly continuously) within an active session.

External Trigger

In our experience, one of the key factors that drive the success of a Zero Trust program is the degree to which the underlying technology platform enables and supports integrations. We talked about this in the security orchestration chapter, but it's worth repeating here. In particular, Zero Trust platforms must provide some sort of API, so that external systems can initiate a refresh. The scope of the refresh will be implementation-dependent, but what's important is that the refresh must include the attributes that are relevant to the external system that's initiating the refresh. Recall that we explored an example of this in depth in Chapter 11.

Summary

In this chapter, we began by examining the logical components of Zero Trust policies—*subject criteria, actions, targets, and conditions*. We also looked at attributes, and explored their role in policies. Then we looked at things from a deployment and flow perspective, examining several policy scenarios, as well as the lifecycle of policy evaluation and triggers.

It should be clear that the picture we're painting is one of a truly dynamic and responsive system, which relies on cooperative run-time integration between IT and security components. This may be a cultural or technical change for enterprises, and it's important to acknowledge this as part of your Zero Trust journey. It's also important to understand that while the concepts and recommendations we've discussed in this chapter are broadly applicable across Zero Trust platforms and architectures, there will be a wide variety of capabilities across different Zero Trust platforms in practice. In particular, there are many different types of PEPs with different capabilities for enforcement across networks, applications, and user agents. Given that, when you choose a specific Zero Trust platform, make sure you have a deep understanding of its architecture and capabilities, so that you can design your policies and their lifecycle and flows to best align with the capabilities (and strengths and weaknesses) of your chosen platform.

Ultimately, you want a Zero Trust platform which is able to use both internal and external attributes seamlessly, with internal and external mechanisms to obtain updated contextual information with which to make access decisions based on meaningful and descriptive policies.

CHAPTER 18

Zero Trust Scenarios

Throughout this book, we've examined many different aspects of enterprise security and IT infrastructure. We've looked at things from a technical and architectural perspective, and have mentioned various use cases throughout. In this chapter, we'll be examining seven different scenarios, and discussing how you can evaluate and approach them for inclusion in your Zero Trust program. This is not an exhaustive set of use cases, but does cover most of the major scenarios.

Our goals for this chapter are to arm you with an understanding of how and when these different scenarios would be applicable in your environment, and to provide you with relevant recommendations for how to approach them. Of course, these scenarios also need to be looked at from a deployment and operational perspective, which will be part of our discussion in Chapter 19. Finally, for the sake of brevity, we're not going to be spending very much time here justifying these scenarios—hopefully, if you've made it all the way to Chapter 18, we've already convinced you of that. Let's dive in, starting with one of the most common Zero Trust use cases, which is replacing a VPN.

VPN Replacement/VPN Alternative

We talked about VPNs, their weaknesses, and the comparative benefits that Zero Trust provides previously, in Chapter 9. In this section, we'll briefly reiterate this use case in order to frame up a discussion about how you should approach a Zero Trust project focused on an enterprise VPN (remote user access) use case. Note that we're examining two related scenarios:

- Replacing an existing, in-use VPN with a Zero Trust solution
- Deploying Zero Trust for a new remote access scenario

While these two scenarios have similar technical considerations, they should clearly be approached from different perspectives in terms of justification and decision-making. New projects often represent simpler and easier decisions, as there won't be as many constraints

239

© Jason Garbis and Jerry W. Chapman 2021
J. Garbis and J. W. Chapman, *Zero Trust Security*, https://doi.org/10.1007/978-1-4842-6702-8_18

or dependencies in place. This contrasts with a VPN replacement scenario, where there'll need to be a justification for replacing an in-place and operational VPN solution. This is not to say that this is a significant barrier—we've seen many, many VPN replacement projects—just that security leaders need to be prepared to discuss and justify the decision and project from potentially several perspectives, including security, technical, operational, and financial. Note that we do strongly recommend that organizations replace their VPNs with a Zero Trust approach; there are many good reasons to do so.

Let's briefly review the architectural differences between traditional VPNs and a Zero Trust model, introduced in Chapter 9, and consolidated in Figure 18-1. Note that this scenario is only focused on providing remote users with secure access to services.

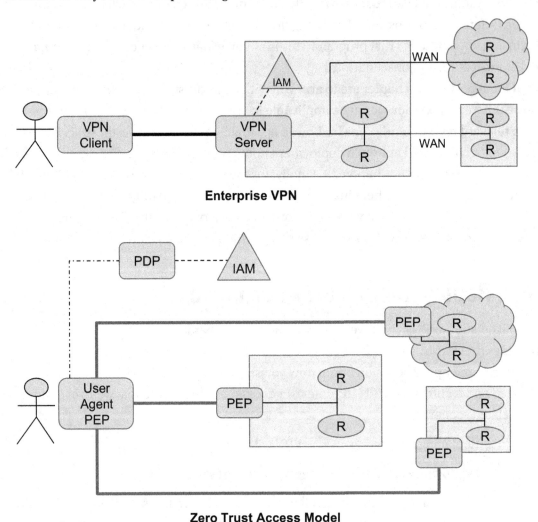

Figure 18-1. *Enterprise VPN and Zero Trust Architectures*

Traditional VPNs can only establish a single secure network tunnel from the user's device to a VPN server, which terminates the secure tunnel, and permits network traffic to proceed into the private network area. VPNs perpetuate a perimeter-based network model, requiring that any distributed resources be connected to the enterprise's core network over a WAN. Alternatively, they will require users to manually switch VPN connections when they need to access resources in different locations. In contrast, Zero Trust systems will establish multiple secure connections to distributed PEPs, so that users can access them transparently. (Note that this is true for the cloud-routed and enclave-based models. It may not necessarily be true for the microsegmentation or resource-based models, depending the specifics of the implementation.)

Considerations

In this section, we'll look at a few different angles, to help you identify candidate VPN projects for Zero Trust.

Resources

Look at the number, type, location, and value of the resources under consideration. How business critical are they? If this is a replacement, how are they being accessed today, and what headaches or pain points are associated with the current VPN?

Generally, Zero Trust solutions provide better performance than VPNs, especially for distributed resources. They also can often be deployed to protect resources in locations or environments where the enterprise cannot deploy a VPN entry point, for example, on a third-party network. If you have a highly distributed or highly dynamic set of resources, these will likely be good candidates for a Zero Trust approach—recall the dynamic target rendering from our policy model chapter.

Users and User Experience

Who are the users currently utilizing the VPN, or who need to access these new resources? Are the users all remote? Was this remote user access solution deployed rapidly (and potentially with some known issues or compromises), for example, in response to the COVID-19 work-from-home shift? Are on-premises users accessing these resources through a separate security model—for example, via firewall ACLs?

In these cases, there are often good reasons to adopt Zero Trust, for example, to overcome security or operational issues caused by a rapidly deployed VPN. If there are resources that were deployed recently, it may be the case that only remote VPN users have a secure access pathway and that your organization needs a solution for on-premises users. And finally, Zero Trust solutions, designed to secure access for all users to all resources, can eliminate siloed solutions, such as separate rules and access mechanisms for remote vs. on-premises users.

Zero Trust can be applied incrementally, group by group, or application by application, although end-user experience should definitely be a consideration. That is, be aware of the different access tools that your initial sets of users utilize, to avoid imposing unnecessary friction. For example, you likely shouldn't require that a set of end users switch back and forth between their current VPN and your Zero Trust solution throughout their workday. It'd be far better to have a group of users switch over to your Zero Trust solution for *all* their access needs, combining their current broad VPN-level access with more precise Zero Trust policies for specific resources. This way, they begin to obtain improved security while also obtaining an improved user experience. We'll be discussing this further in Chapter 19.

Identity Providers

Some VPN implementations are not integrated with enterprise identity providers; in these cases, a Zero Trust deployment can quickly deliver considerable value. By tying remote access user authentication to their enterprise identity provider, security teams eliminate an identity silo that existed within their VPN. This eliminates any work necessary to keep that silo in sync with their primary provider, for example, to respond to identity lifecycle events of Join, Move, and Leave. Even if a VPN uses an enterprise IdP, a Zero Trust solution will improve on it, by enforcing fine-grained and context-sensitive access policies. Many Zero Trust solutions also support multiple identity providers of different types, so that different user groups can authenticate against different IdPs, or so that legacy systems can be protected by modern authentication protocols.

Networking

It's critical that you obtain a clear understanding of your enterprise's network topology, data flows, and where the protected resources are housed. This knowledge will enable you to make well-informed decisions and recommendations about transitioning access from VPN to Zero Trust. Start by asking where VPN concentrators (entry points) are located, which networks they grant access to, and how distributed resources are accessed from a network perspective.

As we mentioned in the introductory part of this chapter, determine whether users are just accessing resources via a single entry point into an enterprise network. Even in this simple case, Zero Trust can add value, such as improved performance and stability, better integration with identity providers and MFA, and, of course, fine-grained access controls.

Teams or projects that require access to distributed resources typically struggle with VPNs, and is a situation where Zero Trust shines (as long as your chosen implementation and deployment model supports multiple concurrent connections to distributed PEPs). View this as an opportunity to ask "what if" questions of the networking or application teams. "What if users could access both these resources simultaneously?" "What would it mean if we could tie access to a business process, such as a service desk ticket?" "What if we could perform deeper device posture checks before users are permitted access?" These are excellent questions to spark conversations with those teams and get them onboard as supporters of your Zero Trust project.

There are other questions to ask your networking team as well, which will help you better plan for and advocate for your Zero Trust implementation. For example, find out what types of remote access policies (ACLs) your current VPN implements. How broad or narrow are they? If they grant very broad network access, which is quite common, your Zero Trust project can deliver improved security and reduced risk by greatly reducing network access without sacrificing user productivity. Determine whether there are any outstanding compliance issues or audit findings that your project can address.

If your VPN does impose restrictive network access, find out how well that works from an operational and user productivity perspective. It's likely that this causes operational effort as well as user friction in all but the most static environments. Your Zero Trust solution should be able to impose equally tight (if not tighter) access control restrictions via automated policies, relieving your IT and operational teams of manual effort.

Finally, learn how your organization is utilizing any wide area networks. These typically impose considerable costs on organizations, and Zero Trust solutions can reduce (and, in some situations, eliminate) WAN usage.

Recommendations

VPN replacement and VPN alternative are a common first Zero Trust project, and are often a good one to get started with. The benefits are clear, and the functionality of a traditional VPN is generally quite easy for a Zero Trust solution to replace. We do recommend an incremental deployment, with consideration for those user groups who may need to retain both Zero Trust and VPN access for a period of time. These solutions generally can co-exist in harmony on an end-user device, but they generally *cannot* be running at the same time, as they'll conflict at the networking level. This may be a concern if you have an "always on" VPN, for example, or want to deploy Zero Trust in a similar type of model.

One final recommendation for the VPN replacement scenario is to look carefully at the set of tools and processes that have been built around the scope and functionality of the VPN tool. Some organizations, especially those with older VPNs and older infrastructure, may have built a "web" of interdependent tools. This can pose a complex impediment to an incremental Zero Trust rollout. For example, one enterprise we worked with had a traditional VPN, which logged certain events into the user's Windows event log. They'd built a set of "glue" tools which watched the Windows event log and responded to those events by performing some network configuration tasks. Modifying these tools was an additional task, and imposed a delay on the project, as that component was maintained and managed by another team within the organization. So, be cognizant of how your enterprise IT environment operates, and ask a lot of questions up and down the IT stack, and across your IT and business process ecosystem. You may be surprised at areas and ways in which the organization has built dependencies on specific tools or workflows. Some of these may be barriers to Zero Trust adoption, but some may be current pain points that your project can eliminate. There is often a considerable set of headaches around VPNs, which again is why they often represent a sound first Zero Trust project.

Third-Party Access

Third-Party access is also a good candidate scenario for Zero Trust, since it's typically a source of headaches and risk for enterprises, and there's a clear distinction and benefit from taking a Zero Trust approach vs. traditional third-party remote access. Let's begin with a definition—for our discussion here, a third party is a non-employee individual with whom the enterprise has a legal relationship and who needs legitimate access to the enterprise's network and private resources. Specifically

- The individuals can be identified.

- The resources they need access to are known and identifiable.

- They require access to private company resources (if all they need is internet access, they could just use the guest network when on-premises).

Note that we're excluding full-time contract (non-employee) workers from this scenario; in our experience, these folks are treated much more like regular, full-time employees from an IT perspective. That is, a contract programmer on a 6-month assignment may not be a company employee, but will typically be issued a company-managed device, and be part of the enterprise's identity management system. From a security perspective, they should be managed in the same way as employees, albeit with much more restricted network access.

Let's look at a few examples of the type of third parties that are relevant to this scenario. These are often tied to outside firms with specialized expertise in a specific area, which doesn't make sense to have internal to the enterprise. For example, one classic third-party access risk is a firm responsible for the monitoring, maintenance, and servicing of building HVAC systems. These systems are typically on the enterprise network, and HVAC vendors require periodic access to those systems to keep them running efficiently. Another example is a firm that has outside financial auditors who need access to an on-premises financial management system.

These types of third-party users are exactly the ones who require additional security controls. As the NIST Zero Trust document states, "An organization cannot impose internal policies on external actors (e.g., customers or general internet users) but may be able to implement some Zero Trust-based policies on nonenterprise users who have a special relationship with the organization".

Our Zero Trust principles require that these users be authenticated and their network access be restricted to the minimum possible. Traditionally, organizations have used VPNs to provide remote access for third parties, and of course, VPNs exhibit all their weaknesses for third-party access. In addition, these third-party users are not employees, so by definition, they're not using devices that are managed by that enterprise. This means that the enterprise cannot mandate or rely on the security posture of that device, which makes it even more important to impose security controls around the network access for that device.

One final constraint is that security teams cannot in general require the installation of any specific software on those devices. This is a little less absolute than it used to be, especially with the growing prevalence of Bring Your Own Device (BYOD) and the acceptance of using personal mobile phones or tablets for work activities. For example, a third-party user may be unable to install remote access software on an enterprise-managed laptop, even if that access is a required part of their job. But it's becoming more acceptable to install remote access software on a personal tablet or a BYOD-device and use that for those work tasks.

Even if the third-party user can install remote access software on their device, it's very unlikely that they'll abide by the installation of more invasive endpoint management or security software, and it's not realistic to include these third-party devices in your enterprise's security or IT management system. Organizations simply need to accept that these systems and devices may not meet their security standards and use Zero Trust to enforce the principle of least privilege, as well as MFA. We'll talk more about this shortly, in the "Recommendations" section.

Considerations

Third-party access in general is a good candidate for a Zero Trust project, and can sometimes serve as a useful first such project. These users tend to be very well-defined, and their access is typically limited to a small and static set of resources. They also typically represent an area of risk, since these users are accessing enterprise-managed resources from devices not managed by the enterprise.

Architecture

Third-party access network architecture is likely going to be similar to your VPN; in fact, it's quite likely that these people will use your existing enterprise VPN. What's important to understand is, like in the VPN use case, how and where these people are getting onto the network, and how their network traffic traverses the enterprise to reach their target resources. The type and location of these resources should affect the placement of your PEPs, and allow you to avoid having third-party user traffic transit very much of your network. As always, the principle of least privilege applies here, and your PEPs should prevent all unnecessary network access for these users.

Users and User Experience

User experience can be a less important consideration for third-party users, compared with employees. This is especially true if this access is only required intermittently rather than daily or on an all-day basis. For example, transparent (always-on) access to Zero Trust–protected resources may be desired for employees, but not necessary for third-party users. Having said that, clearly you shouldn't deliberately make their access difficult.

Zero Trust systems often support both agent-based and agentless access, and third-party access is a use case where agentless access is often required. Depending on the type of resources being accessed, and the network protocols being used, agentless access may be a viable option. Typically, web-based applications are easily reachable with an agentless model, while non-web (non-HTTP) applications can pose some challenges. If a Zero Trust agent is technically required on user devices, but the third party refuses to install them, there are some alternatives, albeit at an additional cost. For example, the enterprise could host a virtual desktop for third-party users, into which they'd install the Zero Trust agent. Or, the enterprise could provision a managed device to be used by the third parties exclusively for access into the Zero Trust-protected environment.

Recommendations

From a user authentication and identity management perspective, we recommend having your Zero Trust system use the third party's enterprise identity management system for authentication, if possible, but only if you have a sufficient level of confidence in their maturity and identity lifecycle processes. If not, have them utilize an IdP under your control—either your primary enterprise IdP or a smaller and simpler one dedicated to third parties. Any Zero Trust solution should be able to support authenticating different user populations against different IdPs.

We also recommend that you enforce MFA for these users, each time they attempt to access your resources. This form of step-up authentication should be implemented using an MFA provider under your control, and integrated with your Zero Trust system. This ensures that you can enforce your security policies regarding the frequency and type of authentication, and eliminate the potential for credential sharing by third-party users (which is a common occurrence).

You should definitely have your Zero Trust system enforce contextual access controls, such as geolocation, and configure fine-grained access policies that restrict user access to the bare minimum. These policies should be straightforward to define, since third-party access is typically only granted for a fixed and well-defined set of targets. We also recommend that you consider tying your third-party access policies to a business process when possible, in order to further restrict (and document) this access. For example, many Zero Trust systems permit the creation of policies in which access is controlled by the existence and state of a service desk ticket. This approach will work well in scenarios where third parties only need periodic access, ensuring that all access is requested, approved, and granted only for a limited period of time.

Finally, note that if an enterprise has already made the transition to Zero Trust, and has a "café-style" network, that even on-premises third-party users must access resources from within the Zero Trust model. That is, any third-party users who are physically present in an enterprise facility will automatically only obtain the same limited access they receive as when remote. This is an important benefit of Zero Trust— occasional in-person network access by third parties no longer puts the full enterprise network at risk.

Cloud Migration

Migrating applications and functions to cloud platforms is without a doubt a huge part of today's enterprise IT and application development, and encompasses a wide variety of scenarios. The power of these platforms and the ubiquity and reliability of network connectivity make this a basically unstoppable trend, which is why it's important that Zero Trust projects and leaders embrace this and educate their colleagues on the business and application development side about this new approach. Ideally, security teams will have in place a Zero Trust platform and a structured menu of approaches and approved components, which will enable application owners to quickly embrace the cloud.

Migration Categories

Of course, "cloud migration" isn't one thing, it's many different types of things, depending on many factors. But, in general, we believe these migration projects fall into four categories.

Forklift Migration

In this scenario, the application is moved from an on-premises physical or virtual environment to an IaaS environment "as is." That is, there are no changes to application logic, topology, or technology. The end result is that the same application is running in a different place. Because this maintains the application's structure and interdependencies, this migration can be faster and simpler, but delivers more limited benefits. This migration doesn't require any development changes to the application; it should only require reconfiguration, and is well suited to COTS applications that the enterprise has licensed and therefore cannot modify.

Refactor the Application

In this scenario, the application is migrated to an IaaS environment, but it includes some technical or structural changes, ideally to take advantage of its new cloud platform. For example, the application may be modified to use a cloud-native database, or a cloud-based identity provider. Or, some of the deployment or operations infrastructure within the applications (such as the web server, or a logging server) may be rehosted on a cloud-based variant. This migration requires technical or development changes to the application, and can typically return moderate improvements. Some COTS applications will support this migration in some minor ways, for example, by supporting the use of a cloud-based database.

Rewrite the Application

This approach is the most technically difficult, but potentially provides a tremendous amount of value. In this model, application developers have the opportunity to completely rethink the application architecture, including taking a "radical" approach to embrace modern components such as containers, PaaS, microservices, or NoSQL databases, among others. Depending on the current application architecture, developers may be able to reuse elements of the application logic and data model to help accelerate things. This approach is not applicable to COTS applications.

Adopt SaaS

With this approach, organizations are making the shift from on-prem applications (either custom or COTS) to a cloud-based SaaS application. This, of course, represents a wholesale shift in application topology and access controls. It may be possible to reuse some of the on-premises application logic, especially if the enterprise is adopting the SaaS version of their on-premises application. Enterprises should be able to import some of their application data, in order to jumpstart their SaaS application's value.

In general, many (if not most) cloud migration projects are prime candidates for Zero Trust, because they encompass changes to security, network, and architecture, and therefore present an opportunity to embrace a modern and cloud-friendly security platform. In particular, Zero Trust systems, by their nature of being dynamic and context sensitive, can take advantage of the rich set of APIs presented by cloud platforms.

Considerations

These four migration scenarios each represent different opportunities to apply Zero Trust, which can definitely bring value and improve security for these in-motion applications. Let's look at these from an architectural perspective.

Architecture

As we look at these scenarios, reflect back on the discussions in our chapters on IaaS and PaaS, and SaaS, where we talked about the network access controls and architectures associated with those models. Look at your organization's planned or in-progress cloud migration architecture and approach, and influence them to ensure that they'll work most effectively with your chosen Zero Trust network topology and access policies. And pose the following questions to yourself and your organization, based on your chosen cloud migration approach.

Forklift

Is the application self-contained, and are all parts being forklifted up to the cloud? Most applications are not 100% self-contained, so if this is the case, how are data flows in and out going to be managed? How can your Zero Trust PEPs facilitate this? Are all the (non-user) components of the application going to reside within an implicit trust zone? If so, is that risk acceptable with your new security model? If not, how will they be authenticated and obtain access across via a PEP?

Refactor the Application

In addition to the preceding Forklift questions, what is the current and intended network topology? What is changing about the component interactions? In what ways can you influence the changes to the application design?

Rewrite the Application

To what degree is the application team going to be "starting from scratch," as they create a new application architecture? How will existing application components (either functional or data) be carried forward? Can the new architecture be aligned with your Zero Trust platform? Will the old and new versions need to coexist for a period of time? If so, will they need to exchange data? How will that be secured? Finally, can the application be written in a forward-thinking fashion to consume Zero Trust policies from the PDP and become an application PEP?

Adopt SaaS

This is clearly a different approach than the previous three, since the new platform is not under control of your enterprise. This may be simpler migration from a security and network perspective, since the destination is fixed. But definitely examine the SaaS platform from a security perspective and, using the guidelines we introduced in our earlier chapter, determine whether it makes sense to apply Zero Trust security to this SaaS environment.

Users and User Experience

In most cases, these newly migrated applications will have different network access models as a result of their migration to the cloud. This can disrupt or challenge the end-user experience. Your Zero Trust solution can often eliminate this friction, giving users transparent and secure access to these cloud-based applications while also enforcing dynamic and context-sensitive access policies.

Recommendations

We wholeheartedly recommend that as these applications migrate into a cloud environment, you collaborate with the application owners and include Zero Trust as part of the migration and deployment plan. The only exception to this may be adoption of SaaS applications, which may not need Zero Trust in every environment.

Finally, be proactive and collaborate with your application owner colleagues. Exposing them to your Zero Trust platform architecture and roadmap can in fact be a catalyst for accelerating cloud migration projects.

Service-to-Service Access

Service-to-service access control is definitely a legitimate, valuable, and important Zero Trust use case. Still, many enterprise Zero Trust implementations start with and focus on user-to-service access, for good reasons. Users and servers live in very different worlds, and have very different risk profiles.

Users

- Are untrusted and unpredictable

- Run their devices on untrusted, unmanaged networks

- Are mobile—access from different and changing locations

- Tend to lose their devices

- Often reuse passwords, or choose poor passwords

- Visit essentially random Internet destinations, and cannot operate with a whitelist of Internet destinations without impacting user productivity

- Receive email with phishing links, and occasionally click them

- Install arbitrary and unmanaged software on devices

That is, users are unpredictable, creative, and error-prone human beings.

On the other hand, servers (and the services that run within them) are, or at least should be, the polar opposite:

- Run on enterprise-managed networks.

- Are more trusted—100% of the services running on any given server should be known, managed, and controlled by IT.

- Don't visit random Internet destinations—in theory, the set of internal and external network destinations can be known and whitelisted.

- Don't receive email with phishing links.

- Don't lose themselves in bars or restaurants.

In fact, servers are trusted enough that many Zero Trust architectures include a segment of the network, behind a PEP, where servers communicate outside the control of the Zero Trust environment—the implicit trust zone, which we've discussed throughout the book.

Now, to be clear, we're not attempting to dissuade you from applying Zero Trust to a service-to-service use case; we're just highlighting that user-to-service often represents a higher risk. Nevertheless, service-to-service access controls should be part of every Zero Trust initiative, and may even make sense as one of the initial use cases. Let's review the value and benefits that Zero Trust can bring to this scenario.

Most importantly, Zero Trust enforces the principle of least privilege, which is key to reducing the attack surface and reducing the blast radius of any successful attack. This brings with it an associated reduction in risk. It also ensures that, because all communications are explicitly granted by policies, there's "top-down" visibility and control of service-to-service communications. That is, security and networking teams no longer have to rely on *detecting* communications occurring between services over a given protocol. Instead, the Zero Trust system, because it operates on a default-deny basis, ensures that all service-to-service communication occurs if and only if it's been granted by a policy, and therefore is explicitly allowed.

This has an interesting effect—it actually serves as a form of *referential integrity* for the network—because all service-to-service communications must be permitted by a granted policy, it ensures that this communication is anticipated by deployment systems and processes. Because unexpected communications pathways will be blocked, it helps improve the maturity and predictability of the development and deployment process. While this may appear to impose additional friction, it'll be more than repaid in terms of increased reliability, ability to automate, and improved security and resiliency. And, it ensures that deployed services are documented, and cataloged, eliminating the "don't touch that server, we don't know what it does" problem.

While this may well seem sufficiently valuable to justify the service-to-service use case, it also brings additional benefits. Zero Trust brings an overall reduction in risk, and an associated improvement in compliance. There are many compliance-driven controls that require better network segmentation, especially for high-value workloads. Zero Trust also ensures that network traffic is encrypted, in case applications are using unencrypted protocols. And finally, the fact that Zero Trust systems can dynamically and automatically respond to changes within the set of protected resources means that enterprises can adopt high-velocity development processes (such as DevOps, which we discuss shortly) without sacrificing security.

Considerations

Looking at Zero Trust models in the context of service-to-service, microsegmentation seems to be the obvious choice, and it may well be the best fit for environments where all servers have identities, and can be authenticated. This is a necessity, because recall that in the microsegmentation model, all servers are identities (Zero Trust subjects), and the access control mechanisms tend to reflect this service-to-service symmetry.

The enclave-based and cloud-routed models will also work for this use case, and in fact may be a better choice for environments where you're just getting started with Zero Trust. These models give you more flexibility, especially when you have an environment where some identified and authenticated services (subjects) need to access remote services which are targets that are protected by a PEP, but are not themselves Zero Trust subjects. In fact, this is likely going to be a common server-to-server scenario in many deployments—asymmetric service-to-service, where one service is an authenticated identity, and the other service is not, but sits behind a PEP, as shown in Figure 18-2.

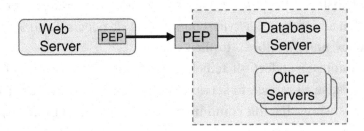

Figure 18-2. *Asymmetric Service-to-Service*

This model is a good alternative to "pure" microsegmentation that requires every service to be an identity, which may not be a good fit for some organizations or architectures. This approach is also useful for securing service-to-service access across different networks, especially for distributed application components that may occur as a result of a cloud migration. Cross-network service-to-service access control is a good use case for Zero Trust, since there's inherently a need for a security overlay that normalizes the access control model in use.

Actually, there is one additional service-to-service approach that we need to mention, which is using an IoT-style non-identity access control method. As we talked about in Chapter 16, in this model, neither of the services are authenticated identities. That is, you can decide to treat your connection-initiating services as if they were an IoT device, with access controls based on weaker forms of identification and authentication, such as MAC address, IP address, VLAN, or switch port. This is possible, but has some downsides, as we discussed in Chapter 16. For these reasons, we don't recommend this approach for service-to-service, if possible—it's far better to authenticate at least one of the identities.

Recommendations

One way to identify good candidates for the service-to-service use case is to determine where you have servers that are communicating across network or domain boundaries. This will be a natural place to deploy a PEP, because the traffic is transiting a network boundary. As a result, this can be a relatively simple problem to solve.

Targeting peer servers on a single internal LAN may be more difficult, depending on the network configuration and on how difficult or easy it is to isolate the servers behind a PEP. On the other hand, high-value or compliance-driven server isolation can be a good reason to prioritize this scenario, especially if there is a strong need from a risk or audit finding perspective. These drivers can be a catalyst for making the necessary network and access changes.

As you consider this use case, look at your environment and try to identify services that would be a good fit—in particular, services that are high value, well understood and well controlled, and perhaps highly dynamic and difficult to secure with current solutions. Automated Zero Trust policies can be a big help here, adapting access to mirror changes in your server environment, without requiring manual effort.

Also recall that many servers host multiple services, and you can choose to place only some of the services behind a PEP, leaving the others unchanged. For example, you can deploy a PEP to control server-to-server access for a Database service running on a given host while still permitting non-Zero Trust users to directly access a web server on that same host.

Finally, take a look at any microservices environments your organization has deployed. As we discussed in Chapter 14, a microservices environment such as a service mesh may not be the best Zero Trust candidate, since it likely has its own internal and self-contained authorization model. But service-to-microservice can be a good place to start, as long as there's a clear demarcation boundary and a natural fit for a PEP. Of course, your policy model must support defining microservices as targets, with attribute- and context-based access controls, in order for this to be effective.

DevOps

DevOps—which is a mash-up of the terms *Development* and *Operations*—represents a newer way of approaching application development, centered on collaboration between formerly siloed software development and operations teams. By using automated toolsets and rapid cycle times, this approach—which does require cultural and process changes—has been proven to help organizations dramatically increase their deployment velocity, release quality, and business value.

Ultimately, DevOps is about getting code quickly and continuously into production. Quite frequently, DevOps teams adopt Continuous Integration (CI) and Continuous Delivery (CD) approaches, which utilize a high degree of automation throughout the build, test, release, and deploy phases of DevOps. This automation is tied into the "infrastructure as code" approach, in which not only is the software application automatically built and deployed, but so is the virtual infrastructure upon which it's running—and both of which are described by configuration (code) in a repository.

This may sound complex—and it is—but it's given organizations the ability to get applications to market quickly, increases team productivity, stabilizes production environments, increases customer satisfaction, and provides consistent code deployments—ultimately delivering business value.

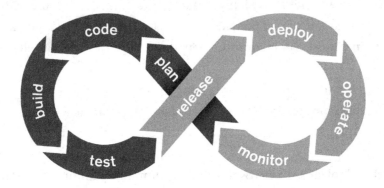

Figure 18-3. *The DevOps Cycle*

Figure 18-3 depicts the multiple phases of DevOps. This is commonly (and deliberately) portrayed using the "infinity" symbol, which represents the continuous and never-ending nature of DevOps. A natural question, of course, is where security fits into the DevOps model. The answer—the only correct answer—is "everywhere."

In fact, there's a term and a set of practices devoted to applying security throughout DevOps, termed *DevSecOps*. This approach ensures that multiple aspects of security are properly incorporated into the software design, development, deployment, and operations. This is important, because traditionally security was an afterthought of development, with detrimental results. In contrast, when security is designed in and thought through at the forefront, security frameworks can be effectively woven throughout the DevOps cycle.

Note that while in this section we're looking at DevOps from a narrow Zero Trust perspective, there is a much larger part of application security that sits outside the scope of Zero Trust—such as static code analysis, functional security testing, fuzzing/input validation, and library vulnerability management.

DevOps Phases

Let's now look at the DevOps phases, and see how Zero Trust applies to them.

Plan and Code

From a design perspective, this phase is where security teams should collaborate with and educate application developers on their Zero Trust architecture, capabilities, and policy model. Giving application designers this knowledge will help them decide where they can rely on the Zero Trust platform and where they need to take responsibility. For example, a high-value application won't need to implement MFA, device posture checks, or geolocation restrictions if it can rely on the Zero Trust platform to do so.

And, application designers may be able to leverage the Zero Trust platform to obtain additional user context, such as validation of roles or permissions. These could be consumed and enforced within the application, essentially making the application a policy enforcement point.

Build and Test

As application code proceeds through the build and test phases, this is a natural place for the Zero Trust system to use automated policies that grant access only to the right set of people and tools based on workload attributes. For example, a testing workload could be automatically spun up, and only be able to access in-progress application instances that are properly tagged as being in *test* mode.

Release and Deploy

These last steps of the release process will result in the application being placed into production, within a Zero Trust environment with a full set of policy enforcement. That is, all access to application services is controlled by policies, which are only granted to authenticated and authorized subjects. Depending on the degree of automation, Zero Trust policies may even control access to the production environment, for example, based on approved change windows or a valid Service Desk ticket.

Operate and Monitor

For this phase, Zero Trust will help ensure the stability of the environment, and control any administrative or troubleshooting access to production applications. It'll also provide identity-enriched logs, ensuring that all access is properly associated with authenticated identities.

Considerations

DevOps is an interesting and relevant use case for Zero Trust because there are so many ways to tie it to, and get value from, Zero Trust. Even basic integration gives security and application development teams the opportunity to balance and share access control approaches and policies. Breaking down this traditional silo helps "bake in" Zero Trust integration throughout the entire application lifecycle.

Designing an application component (or microservice) to consume and enforce PDP-defined policies can influence application security, and deepen the impact and value of Zero Trust in the enterprise. In essence, this can allow an application to become, in some ways, its own PEP (depending upon how much Zero Trust policy or context it can consume from the PDP). This can be woven throughout DevOps cycles—where the set of policies that are supplied to the application (and therefore enforced) will be altered to match its current phase.

Next, consider the use case we alluded to previously, where manual release and deployment of code may represent a security weakness. By applying Zero Trust policies throughout the release and deployment phases, organizations can ensure that this high-impact access is properly controlled, for example, by enforcing approved change windows.

Finally, managing access to your organization's software designs and source code is a core Zero Trust use case. These assets are clearly valuable and like any high-value data deserve to be properly secured, with access controlled by a PEP.

Recommendations

The purpose of DevOps is to provide a high-velocity, high-quality, high-reliability means of delivering application code into production, in marked contrast to the traditional Software Development Lifecycle (SDLC). DevOps is better suited to many of today's quickly changing environments, where getting incremental code into production quickly is what often drives business value.

Because Zero Trust systems are themselves inherently dynamic, and inherently responsive to user, service, and infrastructure context, they are a good fit for use within a DevOps environment. A Zero Trust system can be connected to an organization's DevOps platforms, and automatically adjust access as workloads flow through the full application lifecycle. Zero Trust also helps improve on and automate security around areas that may still require manual steps, for example, by automating access controls based on approved change windows.

DevOps and Zero Trust are both modern and effective approaches, and organizations should definitely look at how they can be integrated together in support of each other.

Mergers and Acquisitions

From a security and technical perspective, Mergers and Acquisitions (M&A) represent complex and often lengthy projects which must attempt to reconcile two previously independent enterprises. These enterprises' IT and security infrastructures were built and evolved completely separately, utilizing technologies and architectures in ways that may be incompatible (or at least difficult to reconcile). These two organizations will almost certainly have duplicate solutions in many areas, and will likely have overlapping network IP address ranges that are bound to cause problems—a too-common occurrence in our IP v4-centric world.

Recall that Zero Trust platforms, in addition to providing security, also provide a unifying or normalizing layer on top of heterogeneous resources and networks. This has many benefits within a single enterprise, as we've discussed throughout this book, and it also helps to quickly enable network access in an M&A scenario.

Specifically and tactically, a Zero Trust system can provide near-immediate IT access across domains, in order to quickly enable joint administration. Likewise, it can enable precise and secure user access to specific business-critical applications, for example, financial management systems. Given this value, let's take a look at the next level of detail.

Considerations

If one of the two enterprises already has a Zero Trust deployment in place, an M&A activity should be an obvious catalyst to expand its usage, especially if it's the acquiring company (which tends to be larger, and more able to impose its IT and security infrastructure). However, even if the acquired company is the one with Zero Trust, the merged enterprise can still use that platform to at least accelerate the integration activities. The value of this should be apparent—no other security or remote access solution can as rapidly, reliably, or precisely bring together two disparate (and often conflicting) enterprises.

A Zero Trust approach may also represent an opportunity to avoid significant costs and efforts that are typically needed to ultimately merge, normalize, or de-conflict the networks. For example, it may not be necessary to deploy a WAN to link the enterprise networks, if all users and servers get the access they need through a Zero Trust system. And, the enterprises may not need to de-conflict overlapping IP addresses on the networks if the Zero Trust system supports access mechanisms that can compensate for this.

As you approach this use case, think about which resources people need immediate access to, where they are located, and how they're protected today. Of course, each enterprise will have its own identity provider, IT management, and security tools—all of which Zero Trust can help normalize nearly immediately.

Recommendations

If you have a Zero Trust solution in place and are acquiring a firm, using it to accelerate the transition should be a "no-brainer." If you don't have such a solution already deployed, but the company you're acquiring does, strongly consider using that Zero Trust platform to help with your transition. At the very least, your employees will be able to use it to access resources belonging to the acquired company. And, you should be able to extend that system easily to grant acquired company users access to your firm's resources, for example, by deploying a PEP in your company's network. Ideally, in this situation, you can use this to make the case for adopting Zero Trust within your larger enterprise—the acquired firm has demonstrated success with it, and you should be able to leverage this quickly to deliver value.

Finally, don't forget about the server-to-server use case. In many cases, there are data synchronization or export/import activities that require production servers in one domain to communicate securely with production servers in another. Zero Trust systems make it possible to achieve this quickly and securely, without putting either organization at risk.

Divestiture

Divestiture, in which an enterprise spins out part of its business into a newly formed independent entity, typically represents a complex challenge for IT and security, but is also an exciting opportunity. The new company will certainly inherit part of the IT and security infrastructure, often including physical assets such as hardware, networking gear, networks, and buildings. While these assets are the definition of "brownfield" environments, IT and security teams will also typically be empowered to select new systems and tools to fill in gaps, or replace elements that must be decommissioned over time. This should give the IT and security teams the opportunity (and the budget) to deploy a Zero Trust system for this new environment.

In addition to deploying an infrastructure for a new company, there's also another aspect of a divestiture that lends itself to Zero Trust—the transition period. In nearly every divestiture, the business and legal transaction occurs before much of the technical work can even begin. Even as the firms are legally separated, they'll still be tied together by numerous technical systems, data flows, and business processes, which typically take months to unwind. Zero Trust can be used quite effectively to provide precise access control to critical resources that were "left behind" during this transitional period— keeping users and servers productive while preventing unauthorized network access. As the new company transitions off systems, one by one, access to them can be easily terminated via a simple policy change within the Zero Trust system.

Full Zero Trust Network/Network Transformation

This is a fitting use case with which to conclude the chapter, and to tee us up for the discussion about the journey of deploying Zero Trust, in Chapter 19. This scenario is in some ways a composite of the scenarios we've just covered, and in some ways is considerably different from all of them.

The most important difference is that going "full Zero Trust" involves a shift in networking philosophy, that of taking all your users "off net" and requiring use of the Zero Trust system to access *any* enterprise resource. Interestingly, the abrupt COVID-19-driven shift to a predominantly work-from-home user population in early 2020 accelerated many organizations' readiness to make this change. The biggest mind shift associated with this is the realization that the problem to be solved isn't "remote access"—it's just "access." In fact, taking a unified approach to securing *all* access is what underpins much of the value of a Zero Trust environment.

The term "full Zero Trust network" implies a large and comprehensive scope, but in practice, you define the limits and boundaries for your initiative—not every Zero Trust journey has to end with microsegmentation for every single resource. In some ways, it's advantageous to use the more ambiguous term "network transformation," rather than the term "full Zero Trust," which may lead some people to an incorrect conclusion.

So, as you go through this process, be sure to define limits and have a realistic vision for your end state in mind. In our experience, we've most commonly seen enterprises envision their Zero Trust end state to be as follows:

- All users are off the enterprise network.

- Most private services are protected by PEPs, typically using the enclave-based model.

- Some SaaS services may be protected by PEPs.

- There may be some sets of services using microsegmentation.

- There will be some implicit trust zones in which services are running.

The implications of this are, of course, the changes and benefits that we've been advocating throughout this book. The elimination of the trusted enterprise network gives the organization much more resiliency, and reduces both the attack surface and the blast radius. Users have "always-on" Zero Trust access, with dynamic and context-sensitive policies evaluated to provide them with sufficient access to be productive, while enforcing the principle of least privilege. This principle ensures that all access is explicitly granted by policies, increasing the organization's visibility of network and computing assets. And, the enterprise IT and security infrastructure is integrated at a data and process level, increasing efficiency and effectiveness. Let's take a look once again at the conceptual Zero Trust architecture diagram we introduced early in the book, in Chapter 3, shown again in Figure 18-4.

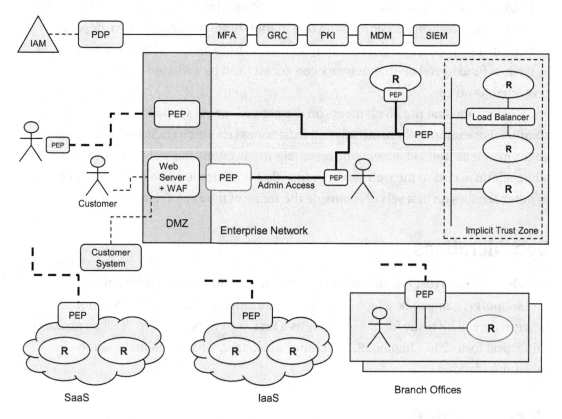

Figure 18-4. *Zero Trust Architecture*

This diagram shows the ways in which the representative enterprise from Chapter 3 has chosen to deploy their "full Zero Trust" architecture. They have incorporated most of the approaches discussed throughout the book, addressing their concerns and obtaining their desired benefits. Let's examine how they approached this.

Their PDP is connected with their enterprise identity provider (IAM), of course—this is a foundational prerequisite. And their PDP is also integrated with other IT and security infrastructure elements, such as their MFA, SIEM, GRC, endpoint management, and PKI systems. There are a set of distributed PEPs throughout their infrastructure—many of which are enforcing access into resource enclaves. The organization is also using local user agent PEPs on most users' devices, and has deployed PEPs directly onto some servers as well. Note that there's an encrypted PEP-to-PEP connection between the PEP in the DMZ and the PEP in front of the implicit trust zone—this is a configuration supported by some Zero Trust platforms.

Their Zero Trust system secures access to both SaaS and IaaS resources, and the PEPs in their IaaS environment use dynamic attributes (metadata) on the workloads to make access control decisions. Note that in their branch offices, they've deployed the PEP in a way that manages resources and users from an IoT-style perspective. That is, devices (and users) on that network can access (and be accessed by) Zero Trust-protected resources.

Finally, note that not *all* elements on the network are in scope for the Zero Trust solution. For example, there are implicit trust zones (resource enclaves) in the IaaS environment as well as between the resources in the enterprise network. Also, note that while admin access to the web server in the DMZ is controlled by a PEP, customer access to other services on that server is outside the scope of the Zero Trust solution.

Considerations

Clearly, full Zero Trust is a big initiative and even with top-down endorsement and support is going to be a technical and organizational challenge. In fact, not all enterprises will be ready for it, especially as a first Zero Trust motion. We'll be exploring this aspect further in Chapter 19, but before we do that, we want to make some recommendations.

Recommendations

While a large-scale network transformation project may not be possible initially, we do want to reinforce that reducing users' network privileges is an important goal; in fact, it's one of the most important things you can do as part of your Zero Trust initiative. It can be achieved incrementally, so even if you accomplish this subnet by subnet (or VPC by VPC, or application by application), it provides value.

We acknowledge that enterprise networks are complex and that there are many in-place elements that may appear to act as constraints or barriers. But this doesn't necessarily have to be the case. For example, consider an office with printers that users get implicit access to when they're on premises. This access can easily be provided by a Zero Trust policy, and this requirement shouldn't be an impediment to adopting Zero Trust. In fact, in some cases, in-place components can be leveraged to enable Zero Trust. One of our enterprise clients had a NAC solution that was already deployed across 50+ branch offices. As they rolled out their Zero Trust agent to users' devices, group by group, they configured the NAC to assign users in the relevant groups to the *guest* VLAN instead of the *employee* VLAN, effectively taking them off net. The beauty of this change is that end users didn't even notice—they remained fully productive and able to access all their applications.

In some ways, each of the previous six use cases is a microcosm of the ideas, approaches, and challenges of the full Zero Trust network scenario. This is what makes this such an interesting set of problems, and is also yet another good reason to begin with a more focused use case rather than full-bore Zero Trust. By starting with a smaller scenario and user population, you don't have to strategically solve every problem "at scale," and yet you'll be learning and creating things (policies, teams, processes, etc.) along the way, which will make it much easier for you to achieve this larger use case over time.

Summary

To recap, in this chapter, we analyzed seven different scenarios for applying Zero Trust in the enterprise. We've mentioned most of these use cases throughout the book, but this chapter gave us the opportunity to examine each of them in depth and to do so with the benefit of building on the knowledge and context we've learned in the preceding 17 chapters. As we surface from the details of these use cases, take a breath and a step back—in Chapter 19, we'll be looking at how your organization should approach Zero Trust from a program and initiative perspective, in order to ensure success.

Making Zero Trust Successful

In the first 18 chapters of this book, we've covered a wide variety of security and technical topics—including Zero Trust principles and architectural approaches, an exploration of a broad set of IT and security elements, and a discussion of Zero Trust policies and use cases. Those architectural principles and technical topics are the core part of any conversation about Zero Trust. However, there's still one remaining aspect, expressed in the most frequent Zero Trust question we hear: "How do I get started?" That's a valid question, but the *question behind the question* is what we believe is the missing topic: "How can I make sure my Zero Trust project is successful?" This chapter aims to answer that question.

Our best one-sentence answer is a recommendation to take a focused and incremental approach while still keeping sight of (and planning for) your larger Zero Trust initiative, and consciously taking the time to build bridges and lines of communication with your peers across the organization. This isn't to say you can't have a purely tactical Zero Trust project that's disconnected from a larger initiative—you can—but Zero Trust by its very nature requires integration with other IT or security components, which will be owned or managed by other teams. This necessitates communication and integration with those teams, which will be a major factor in determining the degree of success you'll experience with your Zero Trust projects.

In this chapter, we'll be exploring this topic, providing you with guidance about how to get started, and discussing how to make sure your project and larger Zero Trust *program* is successful. Keep in mind that, like any broad enterprise security or IT project, Zero Trust can pose nontechnical challenges as well as technical ones. In fact, sometimes, the softer aspects of program design, communication, and understanding organizational culture are harder than technology, especially for technically oriented people like the authors of this book.

© Jason Garbis and Jerry W. Chapman 2021
J. Garbis and J. W. Chapman, *Zero Trust Security*, https://doi.org/10.1007/978-1-4842-6702-8_19

We'll be looking at Zero Trust initiatives from two perspectives—top-down and bottom-up.[1] This is a convenient and useful way for us to separate and talk about things, but in reality, it's an artificial distinction. Every Zero Trust project and initiative will combine elements of both of these perspectives, so don't view them as mutually exclusive—this is just a useful way of organizing the discussion in this chapter. Specifically, even if your organization has a strategic, top-down vision and mission for Zero Trust, you'll still have tactical projects and decisions to make. Likewise, even a tactical "under the radar" Zero Trust project aimed at solving a focused problem will require coordination and integration with other tools and teams, and will therefore contain at least some elements of a strategic initiative. In fact, deliberately including strategic aspects within a tactical first Zero Trust project is an excellent way to set yourself up for approved and supported second and third projects. Having said all that, let's dive in, starting with the strategic perspective.

Zero Trust: A Strategic Approach (Top-Down)

A strategic approach to Zero Trust (by definition) requires a champion at the executive level in the organization, ideally a C-level executive. As Zero Trust is not an IT-only initiative, cross business-leader alignment is very important for full endorsement and adoption of a Zero Trust strategy within the enterprise. While security teams may understand that Zero Trust represents the state of the art in security best practices, that may not be sufficiently motivating to spark the organization to embark on a strategic Zero Trust journey. In many cases, it may require a distinct catalyst, such as new security or executive leadership, a data breach, M&A, or even a byproduct of pandemic-driven access and security changes. Other catalysts could include changing regulatory requirements, or audit findings within the organization.

Because this will be a cross-organizational initiative, security teams need to be aware there will be business objectives that need to be met, and that this strategic initiative will necessarily involve business and oversight processes. These shouldn't be perceived as roadblocks, but rather as necessary diligence in executing an initiative of strategic importance to the business. With that in mind, we'll now discuss some organizational structures that may play a role in a Zero Trust strategy. Keep in mind, not every organization has or needs all of these—we are to some degree depicting the "maximal

---

[1]We've heard rumors about a third approach—"middle-out"—from practitioners in Silicon Valley.

set," which may only exist in larger and more formal organizations. Having said that, as you begin building your Zero Trust strategy, take stock of which of the following organizational structures are in place or perhaps should be established: Governance Board, Architecture Review Board, and Change Management Board. Let's examine each in turn.

Governance Board

Typically, Governance boards create policies that provide direction for the organization and support the overall (financial and people) health of the organization. Governance boards are often used to help an organization achieve its Governance, Risk, and Compliance (GRC) objectives, and may functionally be part of a GRC group. They should be inclusive of the following elements of the organization, as they will be relevant to Zero Trust:

- Risk

- Audit

- Operations

- Security

- Identity

The teams responsible for each of these areas should have some input into crafting guidelines for the Zero Trust initiative, and their input and support will be critical to its success. Specifically, this board often has veto power as technologies are reviewed and considered for inclusion in new initiatives. At a higher business level, understanding the organization's risk threshold, and management of that threshold, will be a key element that determines the level of support for the Zero Trust initiative.

Architecture Review Board

An Architecture Review board (sometimes referred to as an Enterprise Architecture board) is responsible for reviewing current and planned technology in the enterprise, and will be quite involved with and relevant to a Zero Trust Strategy. The board also usually defines the enterprise's architecture standards, which are an important part of any Zero Trust initiative. The technical requirements for Zero Trust can be quite complex (as noted throughout this book), but can quickly be integrated with existing technology as long as architectural standards are both utilized and enforced. This type of consistency and enterprise-wide visibility is one reason that organizations have enterprise architecture boards. Finally, the members of this board will be able to provide collective wisdom about the impact of making changes to the environment, which is clearly relevant to any Zero Trust initiative.

Change Management Board

Finally, a Change Management board should be included in any initiative, as it will be ultimately responsible for the timing and scheduling of promoting new solutions into a production environment. As Zero Trust becomes a larger and more operational part of the organization, application and infrastructure integration with Zero Trust systems will become imperative. This may actually accelerate change management processes, since with Zero Trust, integration and deployment can become more policy based and automated.

Recall, not every organization needs this level of formality, but if you already have these teams and their associated processes in place, they will enhance your Zero Trust strategy, and accelerate your ability to integrate Zero Trust elements with your environment.

Value Drivers

While the implementation of Zero Trust is usually technology focused, business goals will ultimately be the impetus behind these projects. Let's shift gears and discuss the business-level value drivers that a Zero Trust initiative can deliver: Security, Audit and Compliance, Agility/New Business Initiatives, Customer/Partner Integrations, and Technology Modernization.

Security

Security is an obvious value driver, given that it's the focus of Zero Trust. As such, it's usually one of the driving forces behind any Zero Trust initiative. Note that in any given project, the security benefit could be as simple as incorporating MFA into the user experience or as complex as deploying an enterprise-wide Zero Trust network. Also, note that in some cases, security may not be the primary focus for every project within a Zero

Trust initiative. For example, you may have a project which uses an already-deployed Zero Trust platform to enable customers' systems to integrate with yours. This may not actually improve security, but instead satisfy the Customer/Partner Integration driver, which we discuss later.

Audit and Compliance

Audit and Compliance improvements may not be as obvious or technical a value add, but with the enhanced logging associated with an identity-centric approach, you'll get improved audit results and better compliance attainment. Visibility into which identities are exercising which business processes and accessing which technology assets is core to meeting enterprise audits requirements. And, Zero Trust projects often reduce audit costs and cycle times, due to providing easily accessible and easily understandable access logs. Get an understanding of the types of audit log reports your Zero Trust system provides, and how they map to the types of reports your internal and external auditors are looking for. This can deliver real value to your organization.

Agility/New Business Initiatives

Zero Trust is often used to securely enable application agility or new business initiatives, which can be of huge value to an organization. For example, many organizations are taking a "Cloud First" approach, and Zero Trust can be used to provide guardrails and direction. In general, Zero Trust's automated and context-based security model is very well suited to enable rapidly moving and innovative business initiatives based on secure, precise access controls.

Customer/Partner Integrations

One of the core tenets of Zero Trust is enabling and benefitting from secure integration across normally siloed technologies. This is true both within the enterprise and externally. As a result, enterprises can use Zero Trust platforms to enable new types of system, data, and process integrations with customers and partners. This could be as simple as enabling secure customer access to a normally private web application or as complex as real-time data exchange across enterprises. Both can drive significant business value and innovation.

Technology Modernization

Finally, the value driver of Technology Modernization is somewhat broad; it can represent a wide variety of benefits including upgrades of outdated security or IT infrastructure, decommissioning of now-ineffective systems, and transitions to modern replacements. Much of this modernization will be applied to the IT and security systems that we discussed throughout Part II of this book, although there will be others as well.

We've found that these five general categories are a useful way to measure and categorize the impact that each Zero Trust project will have, as a component of the enterprise's broader Zero Trust initiative. That is, it helps to roughly quantify and visually depict the answer to the question "*What is the business trying to achieve with this investment of time and money?*" These value drivers will apply equally well to tactical and strategic projects (although the magnitude of benefit may differ). Representing these in a visual *radar diagram* is an effective way of communicating this, and we'll be walking through a sample scenario later in this chapter. These comparisons can help you and your team more objectively evaluate, compare, and prioritize candidate projects through the life of your initiative.

Now that we've explored how organizations should approach Zero Trust from a strategic perspective, let's look at it from a tactical point of view.

Zero Trust: A Tactical Approach (Bottom-Up)

We define a tactical Zero Trust project as one which is focused in scope and duration, and is aimed at solving a specific set of problems. Most importantly, the solution is approached in a way that embraces the principles of Zero Trust security, and may be using security tools and platforms in ways that are new and different for the organization. While a first Zero Trust project will introduce new concepts and new platforms into an organization (and will therefore introduce change), it must be done in a way that's in harmony with the organization's overall security, risk, and architectural approaches.

These types of standalone projects can be initiated from a variety of sources. For example, they may be driven by application teams with a specific access need. In this situation, the security team can help educate the application owners about why Zero Trust is the best approach. In fact, having a business or application group as a sponsor is an excellent way to start with Zero Trust, since they'll be supportive of the project, and can help knock down any political or technical barriers you may encounter.

In many cases, though, the security team itself will be the one pushing for a first Zero Trust project, in order to solve a specific security or risk problem with an eye toward using this to begin their Zero Trust journey. These projects can definitely be successful, but do carry the risk of appearing to be a "solution in search of a problem," and can run into pushback from networking or business teams who don't see the value of making a change. Don't ignore this risk or just hope that you don't encounter it—this can be a real and significant impediment, since most Zero Trust deployments require changes to IT elements outside the security team's scope, such as end-user experience, or network configuration. The key here is to identify a pilot Zero Trust project that solves some current pain points, ideally which are a headache for teams beyond just security, and which will spark their interest and support for the project. Review the six focused use cases from Chapter 18—these could be good candidates for first projects. Also, keep your ears open for new business initiatives underway in your organization; if Zero Trust can more easily and securely enable them, those may be a fit as well.

Keep in mind also that strategic Zero Trust initiatives need to start somewhere, and even within this context, we recommend beginning with a smaller and more focused project, for a variety of reasons. It gives you a vehicle with which to perform vendor or platform research, and do a smaller-scale proof of concept (POC). It also gives you the chance to try things out, make mistakes, and learn from them in a lower-stakes situation. Zero Trust is a journey, and because every enterprise's IT and security landscape is unique, every enterprise's journey will be unique. Embrace this, and learn by doing iteratively. There will be many unknowns when you begin, and you won't get everything right on the first try. The most important thing is to show at least partial success, and build momentum and support for Zero Trust within your organization.

At a minimum, even the most tactical Zero Trust project teams will need to include people from identity management and networking, and will need to involve people responsible for the enterprise architecture. Our next section, where we introduce a sample bottom-up project, should help make this clear.

Sample Zero Trust Deployments

The goal of this section is to show two sample Zero Trust deployments from a project and milestone perspective. These should give you an idea about how and why these two fictional project teams chose to approach things. Keep in mind that these are just representative samples, and are intended to help you make informed decisions for your real-world projects.

Scenario 1: A Tactical Zero Trust Project

In our first scenario, this transportation services organization has outsourced operations of their financial management systems to a third party, which provides them with this critical business service across a pool of about 30 part-time financial analysts. Although the third-party users are remote (and in fact are located in two different countries), the organization's finance systems remain housed at headquarters, deployed onto traditional hardware-based servers. This architecture is necessary, since the financial systems are integrated with many other on-premises systems which are essential to the business' operations.

Currently, the third-party users access the financial system via a traditional VPN, but due to a change in IT auditors, the organization now has several security findings which they must remediate. Specifically, they must now enforce MFA for third-party users, and must also tie into those organizations' identity lifecycle events to ensure that departed users' access is properly disabled.

While the security team could solve these problems by applying a standalone MFA solution, and by establishing a business process to ensure user offboarding, they have been researching and learning about Zero Trust, and are excited to have found a focused initial project. A high-level view of the project timeline and flow is shown in Figure 19-1, with the steps separated between those taken by the project team, and those which involve the enterprise architecture team. Note that in this example, the third-party users already have access using the VPN solution, and the auditors are not requiring changes for 6 months, so there is not a high degree of pressure or urgency for an immediate change. This benefits the project team, as they can be more deliberate about researching and evaluating Zero Trust platforms. With all that context, let's examine each step of the project in turn.

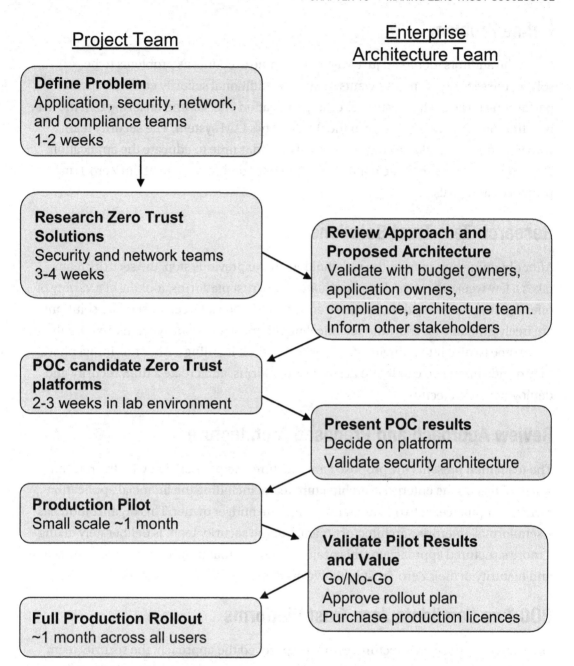

Figure 19-1. *Sample Tactical Zero Trust Project Timeline*

Define Problem

While the auditors identified just MFA and zombie accounts as problems to be solved, the security team also wants to impose additional security controls, such as performing basic device posture checks, geolocation checks, and ensuring that the user is in the correct directory group in the third-party's IAM system. The security team, who is leading this, takes a couple weeks of calendar time to educate the application, networking, and compliance teams about the intended scope and about Zero Trust principles and goals.

Research Zero Trust Solutions

After obtaining buy-in from the stakeholders in the previous step, the security team takes a few weeks to research and evaluate Zero Trust platforms, looking at a variety of offerings from large vendors, smaller vendors, and open source. Most of the solutions are freely available for trial, and technical members of the security team each use their spare time to dive into a single offering, sharing their learnings. After this initial phase, they decide upon two candidate Zero Trust platforms, and create a draft security and deployment architecture.

Review Approach and Proposed Architecture

The team then presents the proposed architecture and project plan with the relevant stakeholders on the enterprise architecture team, including the financial application owner, compliance, network, operations, and the budget owner. This organization has a semiformal enterprise architecture team, but the security team is deliberately taking a more structured approach for this project, knowing that they intend to grow the scope and maturity of their Zero Trust initiative over time.

POC Two Candidate Zero Trust Platforms

Once the enterprise architecture team has approved the approach, the security team brings in their two candidate Zero Trust platforms, and performs a Proof of Concept in their non-production lab environment. This lets them evaluate these solutions in a quantifiable way against the defined criteria. Because this is a well-scoped and not too complex scenario, this only takes them 2–3 weeks of part-time effort to complete and choose a platform.

Present POC Results

Once that's completed, the security team reassembles the enterprise architecture team to present their findings, demonstrate the higher-scoring solution, and make a recommendation about the chosen platform and security architecture. This presentation covers integrations, user experience, and operational implications, as well as core security functions.

Production Pilot

All the stakeholders in the enterprise architecture team approve the plan, so the security team deploys a pilot instance of the Zero Trust platform. They use this phase to coordinate with the third party's identity management team for integration and to roll out the Zero Trust (and integrated MFA) software to 10 end users across the two locations. These users retain their existing VPN access from their devices, so that if they encounter an issue with the Zero Trust approach, they can immediately switch back without impacting their productivity. The security team takes about 1.5 weeks to roll out the new system, and has end users run it in production for another 2.5 weeks. There are a few minor hiccups and some user education issues, but the pilot is largely a success.

Validate Pilot Results and Value

Because the pilot was a success, the final formal meeting with the enterprise architecture team is easy to have. The security team presents the results, and makes a strong "go" recommendation, which is approved. The team also approves their plan for rolling this out to production (and, very importantly, decommissioning the current VPN solution). The team also purchases production licenses from their selected vendor.

Full Production Rollout

The security team deploys the Zero Trust solution for the remaining third-party users, and decommissions their VPN access solution. Also, they use this time to hand off production operations of the Zero Trust solution to their network operations team. This team has been involved throughout the process, so this isn't a surprise. Finally, while this happens to have been the first Zero Trust project, it won't be the last. The security team makes sure to promote the success of this project, and its remediation of the open audit issues, in order to generate momentum and support for future projects that will build on their Zero Trust platform.

Of course, a real-world project may be more complex than this, and can involve a lot more interaction between the various teams. We're also using the *enterprise architecture team* here as a bit of a placeholder; your organization may have a team with a different name that performs a similar function. And also note that different organizations approach things differently. For example, in some organizations, the enterprise architecture team may only meet to be informed by the security team, while in others, they may have decision-making authority (and, therefore, veto power over the project).

Let's now take a look at a very different scenario, approaching Zero Trust from a strategic perspective.

Scenario 2: A Strategic Zero Trust Initiative

This scenario begins with a lucky break. The security team at this pharmaceutical company had recently hired a junior security engineer, and one of their first tasks was to work on consolidating, reconciling, normalizing, and overall just trying to help the SOC make sense of the large volume of noisy and messy event logs emanating from their thousands of Windows devices. This is exactly the kind of unglamorous work that often gets deferred due to more urgent tasks. In this case, the engineer discovered some intermittent anomalous activity, and raised this as "Hey, can someone help me understand what's going on? This doesn't look right to me." It turns out that there was malware present on their network, which appeared to be performing low-and-slow reconnaissance. They quickly brought in an outside Incident Response team, who successfully remediated.

It was during the post-event analysis that the organization realized just how lucky they had been. The malware's initial entry point to the network was never fully determined, although they suspected it may have been via a targeted phishing email. But they did conclude that it was being controlled by a remote command-and-control server, and had been methodically propagating across their flat network via a combination of unpatched Windows machines and poor admin password practices. The major finding of the IR team report was that they seemed to have detected the attacker early enough to have prevented data exfiltration but that if this had been a ransomware attack, the vast majority of their network would have been taken out within a few hours.

The strategic impact of this "near miss" was swift and decisive—as a pharma company, their entire company is built on the confidentiality, integrity, and availability of their research data and manufacturing systems. The executive leadership team and Board of Directors rightfully demanded that these vulnerabilities be addressed, and the

CEO empowered the CISO to make changes. The CISO, whose security leadership team had been discussing and evaluating Zero Trust, put together a strategic plan to adopt it, with two broad phases.

Phase 1 was intended to better secure the organization's highest-value assets, by enforcing Zero Trust access by end users, developers, and system administrators. New controls to be enforced included widespread use of MFA, deep device posture checks, better network segmentation, and elimination of broad admin network access. Phase 2 was planned to further segment the network, moving all users "off net" with a Zero Trust café-style network. It also included a migration away from their complex set of on-premises directories and toward cloud-based Identity-as-a-Service, using modern and passwordless authentication. Finally, this phase was planned to incorporate and broaden the organization's nascent use of cloud-based IaaS and PaaS platforms, to enable faster and more effective collaboration with customers and partners.

Of course, each of these phases was broken down into individual projects, and the organization used the five value drivers to map out each project. The first project in this journey was focused on addressing the most immediate security weaknesses identified in the incident, and is portrayed in Figure 19-2, with the intended impact of each driver ranked on a scale of 0 (low) to 10 (high).

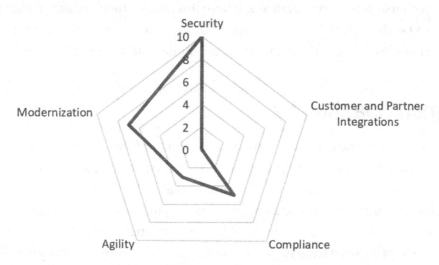

Figure 19-2. *Zero Trust Project Value—Radar Chart*

Specifically, this first project focused on improving end-user security for access to the organization's most critical production systems. The initial set of Zero Trust policies required MFA, and validated device certificate and posture checks before users were granted access. They applied these controls uniformly, regardless of whether the user's device was directly connected to the enterprise network or remote—after all, the malware that initiated this project was running locally on the network.

By design—in order to keep this first Zero Trust project focused—there was less of an impact on the other value drivers. This project did address a number of open security compliance audit findings. But it made no changes to customer or partner integrations, and only modestly improved agility by eliminating several siloed access control systems. The team did rate this project as substantially modernizing their security infrastructure, given that it represented their first production Zero Trust deployment.

In conjunction with the initial project, the CISO and CIO collaborated to establish more formal structures and processes around their existing Architecture and Change Management boards, to ensure that there was sufficient cross-team communications and collaboration. They decided not to establish a formal Governance board, since the Architecture board had already been including risk and compliance as part of their decision-making process. However, the CISO chose to add an experienced outside consultant to the team, to ensure objectivity and broaden their perspective.

Overall, this example illustrates how an organization might choose to execute the first part of a strategic Zero Trust initiative, given a strong catalyst and enthusiastic CEO backing. Of course, not every initiative will have this much "juice" to unlock budget, knock down barriers, and (if necessary) knock heads. Our next section addresses some common obstacles that security leaders may encounter during their Zero Trust journeys.

Common Roadblocks

This chapter wouldn't be complete without a discussion of real-world challenges that we've seen associated with Zero Trust projects and initiatives. Enterprise IT and security is hard and complex, and some Zero Trust projects will fail. This is unfortunate, but true. The good news is that most will be a success, and the guidance and recommendation we've provided throughout this book should set you on a pathway to succeed. And keep in mind that there will *always* be technical glitches and some shortcomings or rough parts of any complex system, Zero Trust included. Perfection is an unattainable goal, but dramatic improvements in security and efficiency are attainable and realistic. Having said that, let's look at commonly encountered roadblocks, and ways to avoid or overcome them.

Identity Management Immaturity

Zero Trust is closely tied to identity management, and Zero Trust projects run the risk of being delayed by a perceived or actual lack of IAM maturity. This immaturity can manifest itself in different ways, such as the too-common "our directory is a mess" anecdote, the proliferation of groups (sometimes tens of thousands), or an in-motion project to consolidate or reconcile identity providers. This is the reality for many IAM teams, but nonetheless shouldn't be a barrier to Zero Trust adoption.

Zero Trust systems will leverage an identity provider for user authentication, and you can decide to what degree you choose to use IAM attributes and groups within your Zero Trust policies. Note that, because Zero Trust systems automate the usage of these identity attributes, they can actually be a catalyst for improved maturity and data integrity in your IAM system, even if it's just for a narrow slice. Recall that we discussed this previously, in the Chapter 5 section "Zero Trust as Catalyst for Improving IAM."

Political Resistance

Unfortunately, security leaders in some organizations will face politically driven resistance to change. We define this as people who impose barriers to change, despite the clear benefits to the organization. This may be driven by culture, technical bias, or an emotional stake in current security tools or architectures. There are several ways to counter this. First and foremost is education. Some people may resist out of ignorance, so work to educate them on the concrete benefits of Zero Trust, and convince them that it's not just a marketing buzzword. Second, if your program has a strong and energetic executive sponsor, they should be able to break down this barrier. Third, you can also build a champion for your project from within the line of business—projects that result in increased revenues or lower costs are especially powerful at breaking down barriers. Finally, sometimes you can find someone within the opposing organization who is willing to work with you. Because Zero Trust systems are inherently integratable, there may be some creative ways to tie into and augment the existing infrastructure, avoiding the perception that you're going to be "ripping and replacing" their environment.

Regulatory or Compliance Constraints

Many enterprises are regulated, or at least have some set of data or systems that are subject to regulatory compliance requirements. Typically, government and industry-issued regulations lag behind technology by a few years, and can make it more difficult for organizations to adopt newer approaches to meeting these requirements. In many cases, your third-party/external auditor will be the key decider, so it's important to be proactive about engaging with them. Don't hesitate to work with them early in your Zero Trust project, and collaborate with them and educate them, to ensure that they understand your trajectory. This will help ensure a positive outcome.

Discovery and Visibility of Resources

Obtaining an accurate picture of all resources in a complex enterprise IT environment can definitely be a challenge. This can be especially true for those environments that have grown without a great deal of oversight, or are fast-moving. This is often expressed through anecdotal comments such as "I don't know who is accessing what, how can I control them?"

The case studies from Chapter 4 illustrate two different approaches. Both BeyondCorp and PagerDuty deployed their Zero Trust platforms broadly across complex production networks, defining fine-grained access control policies. They took an observational approach, collecting and analyzing network data to ensure that their system wouldn't interrupt user productivity. This was effective, but did require time and effort. In contrast, the Software-Defined Perimeter case study took an incremental approach, onboarding users and groups incrementally. They also started with some coarser-grained access controls, and incrementally tightened them up over time.

Both these approaches are valid. It's important to recognize that *you* get to decide where and how to deploy your Zero Trust platform, and how fine-grained the access controls are. So don't fall into the trap of assuming that you need perfect visibility of every connection and every data flow before you can begin. Work with the information you have, or use one of the many open source or commercial tools to provide network discovery and resource visibility.

Analysis Paralysis

The goal of attempting to fully understand, identify risks, and scope out any new technology or approach is laudable, but has a too-common downside of indefinitely delaying any decision or action. This "paralysis through analysis" is frustrating for all involved. It can be cultural within an organization, or it may be somewhat self-imposed by a security team that's attempting to drive change through consensus, which is never an easy needle to thread.

We've seen organizations struggle with this as they embark on Zero Trust, and have their projects stretch out over multiple years without achieving more than a few dozen users in production. This is easy to see in retrospect (and in the abstract), but is often difficult to recognize in the moment. This is because most of us, and most teams, want to do a proper, thorough job of planning, researching, and validating.

This type of paralysis can arise when organizations are proceeding on a strategic Zero Trust journey, and have to obtain approval from a wide variety of stakeholders before deploying anything into production. This can be problematic. This is especially true if these other teams require that the new systems meet the same level of operational maturity, automation, and integration as other systems which have been in production for years. This can lead to a "chicken and egg" problem, especially if the project and architecture is such that the organization needs to deploy a large and complex infrastructure before even the first group of production users can be deployed.

We're not advocating that project teams or security architects take shortcuts or avoid doing proper research and validation—far from it. But we are advocating that teams collaborate with all relevant stakeholders, and approach their initiative from the perspective of how they can get Zero Trust into pilot or production as quickly as possible, even if it's initially limited in scope. While operations teams are understandably rigorous and conservative about change, most will be willing to collaborate with you. For example, you can propose running Zero Trust access in parallel with existing access methods until the team has a high degree of confidence in the new system. Only then would you decommission the older access method.

Closing out this section on common roadblocks, we definitely don't want to end on a negative note. Like all enterprise IT and security projects, Zero Trust projects involve some degree of risk and unknowns. But the vast majority of well-run projects are successful, and deliver value to the organization, even when they hit a few speed bumps along the way. From our perspective, the most important thing is to iterate, learn, and not be afraid to make changes to your in-progress Zero Trust architecture. Ensure that every Zero Trust project is broken into consumable, achievable milestones. At the start of your journey, you'll never know all the answers, but do enough homework so that you know some of the answers, and most of the questions. Have faith in yourself and your team—you'll discover what you need along the way.

Summary

In this chapter, we described top-down and bottom-up approaches to Zero Trust. In practice, most organizations will utilize elements of each in a blended approach. We believe that in all cases, identifying a good initial candidate project is key to success. Look at the six focused use cases from Chapter 18 to get ideas for where to start. And build connections with your peers across your organization—start socializing the ideas behind Zero Trust and the benefits it can provide, and ask a lot of questions. Are there areas where the organization has some current operational, security, efficiency, or user experience headaches? Are there any audit findings that need to be addressed? What about projects that are using new environments, such as IaaS or PaaS? Are there problems that are low risk but high return?

Also consider whether you want your initial project to be high visibility or low visibility. There's no wrong answer! A lower visibility project gives you the opportunity to make mistakes (and learn from them) with fewer repercussions, although the downside is that you may have to fight harder for resources. A higher visibility project can break down these barriers, but may increase scrutiny and have a lower tolerance for mistakes.

Our perspective is that the best indication of success for Zero Trust project number 1 is that you're immediately able to get enthusiastic support for project numbers 2 and 3. Be attuned to the types of qualitative and quantitative measurements that your organization cares about, and be prepared to capture and present them to demonstrate value obtained. And build bridges with your peers across the organization. Both strategic and tactical Zero Trust projects involve change across the enterprise, and this can be hard to achieve without support. Zero Trust projects can be challenging, but the results are worth the effort.

CHAPTER 20

Conclusion

Although we've reached the end of this book, it's more than likely that you're still at the beginning of your Zero Trust journey. We've covered a great deal of material, spanning topics that are conceptual, technical, strategic, and organizational, and yet, despite the breadth of topics, we acknowledge that we weren't able to cover everything. Zero Trust is very broad in scope—essentially as broad as enterprise IT—and is fast-moving. New technologies, platforms, and solutions arise seemingly every day. Not to mention, each and every enterprise has assembled IT and security components in unique combinations to meet their specific needs. As such, we remain confident that there is plenty of remaining future work in this area. (In fact, we've created a companion website at `https://ZeroTrustSecurity.guide` where we're hosting content that complements the book, and lets us continue our dialogue).

Given the ever-changing nature of this space, what we've tried to impart throughout this book is more than just knowledge, but also the wisdom to know where to draw boundaries. It's neither possible nor appropriate to force-fit your Zero Trust system into every part of your environment. In fact, deliberately excluding certain components of your IT infrastructure will help with your focus, velocity, and success. You're the best person to ensure that you chose the most appropriate and effective security platform, tools, and processes for each part of your IT and security ecosystem.

As you go through this process, keep in mind our definition of Zero Trust, which we introduced in Chapter 2:

> *A Zero Trust system is an integrated security platform that uses contextual information from identity, security and IT Infrastructure, and risk and analytics tools to inform and enable the dynamic enforcement of security policies uniformly across the enterprise. Zero Trust shifts security from an ineffective perimeter-centric model to a resource and identity-centric model. As a result, organizations can continuously adapt access controls to a changing environment, obtaining improved security, reduced risk, simplified and resilient operations, and increased business agility.*

© Jason Garbis and Jerry W. Chapman 2021
J. Garbis and J. W. Chapman, *Zero Trust Security*, https://doi.org/10.1007/978-1-4842-6702-8_20

This definition should serve as baseline principles for your organization's overall Zero Trust program, and inform your decision-making and priorities throughout your journey

Ultimately, security is a means to an end for each organization, a way to enable the creative and dedicated human beings in your enterprise to reliably, efficiently, and confidentially accomplish their missions. A well-designed and well-deployed Zero Trust security system will work transparently, staying out of the way while strictly enforcing security controls for both users and services, automatically adjusting access based on context, and only interrupting users when necessary. Secure and appropriate access will be a natural byproduct of processes and actions, rather than an imposition.

Hopefully, we've armed you with sufficient knowledge, context, skills, and tools, so that you're well prepared to confidently proceed on your Zero Trust journey. Like mythical adventurers about to set forth on a grand quest, you now have armaments, magic spells, potions, and provisions. Assemble your team, build alliances, and go forth to slay monsters. Godspeed.

CHAPTER 21

Afterword

—Christopher Steffen, CISSP, CISA
Research Director, Information Security and Compliance,
Enterprise Management Associates

If you made it this far, congratulations! The nearly 300 pages before this have been very enlightening and, I hope, gave you some food for thought on your Zero Trust journey.

I use the term "journey" very specifically, because implementing Zero Trust is not a "one and done" solution. Rarely (if ever) are any of you going to have a clean slate/greenfield to implement. It *is* a journey, and one that will be very worth the effort for you and your organization. The security advantages for your organization are obvious, but the ease of management and administration for the operations and security staff are a huge benefit as well.

As you take the knowledge from this book and prepare for your Zero Trust journey, I want to share several things with you, most of which have already been covered, so consider this a summary.

Plan, Plan, Then Plan Some More

So many Zero Trust implementations fail because of incomplete planning. Understand that this is different than a lack of planning, since most organizations have some kind of game plan going into the project. This book provides a great foundation for understanding Zero Trust architectures and implementations, and there are plenty of resources to help you build upon this. Since you are likely starting with some infrastructure/security solutions in place, examine how you can evolve them based on the principles discussed throughout the book.

J. Garbis and J. W. Chapman, *Zero Trust Security*, https://doi.org/10.1007/978-1-4842-6702-8_21

Zero Trust Is (Unfortunately) Political

Because of the scope of most Zero Trust projects, it has a lot of stakeholders. Getting all of those stakeholders to agree on anything can be a massive challenge and can derail the project before it starts. You'll have to put your best political maneuvering cap on to get the project completed, and willing support (and funding and resources) from your key stakeholders is critical to your success. Executive support and sponsorship set the tone from the top and clear a lot of roadblocks—but don't discount the line of business support, either. Their recommendations up their specific ladder will carry a lot of weight.

Dream Big, Start Small

Zero Trust does not have to be implemented all at once. In fact, it should *not* be. Better to start with a specific test group and team, potentially already using infrastructure and solutions readily available. Once you establish a proof of concept and the value of Zero Trust, the political problems decrease and support increases.

Show Me the Money

Unless you are the security/network administrator with seemingly unlimited budget and resources (what a dream that would be), there's a pretty decent chance that you will have to plan your Zero Trust project over the years and with help. There are significant benefits to Zero Trust (again, outlined in this book) for many of the divisions of your company, especially operations, DevOps, and compliance. Make certain to align your goals with theirs, and maybe—just maybe—you can get some of the valuable budget dollars from those departments.

Digital Transformation Is Your Friend

So many organizations are going through a digital transformation by updating policies and procedures to take advantage of the latest technologies, such as cloud and microservices. Incorporate your Zero Trust framework as part of the digital transformation process for your organization. You were going to have to update the security controls for those digital transformation projects anyway, so take the opportunity to align them with your Zero Trust vision.

Zero Trust is not just the buzzword bingo center square: it is the way that we will look at enterprise security for the next decade. You have taken the first steps on your Zero Trust journey, and I wish you nothing but success!

Further Reading: An Annotated List

Industry Standards and Specifications

Standards and specifications serve an incredibly important role in our industry; the interoperability that they have unlocked has delivered tremendous value. Thank you to all who have contributed to them.

OAuth2 – RFC 6749: The OAuth2 Authorization Framework: `https://tools.ietf.org/html/rfc6749`

OAuth2 – RFC 6750: The OAuth 2.0 Authorization Framework: Bearer Token Usage `https://tools.ietf.org/html/rfc6750`

JSON Web Token (JWT) – RFC 7519: `https://tools.ietf.org/html/rfc7519`

JWT is an open standard framework for securely representing claims to be transferred between two parties.

SCIM – RFC 7652: The System for Cross-domain Identity Management: `https://tools.ietf.org/wg/scim/` and `http://www.simplecloud.info/`

LDAP: RFC 4150: LDAP overview ("roadmap") specification `https://tools.ietf.org/html/rfc4510`

HTOP: RFC 4226: HOTP: An HMAC-Based One-Time Password Algorithm `https://tools.ietf.org/html/rfc4226`

DNS over TLS: RFC 7858 `https://tools.ietf.org/html/rfc7858`

DNS over HTTPs: RFC 8484 `https://tools.ietf.org/html/rfc8484`

These two RFCs outline the proposed standards for two different ways to improve the security of DNS requests:

FIPS 199, Standards for Security Categorization of Federal Information and Information Systems, US National Institute of Standards and Technology, 2004 `https://csrc.nist.gov/publications/detail/fips/199/final`

J. Garbis and J. W. Chapman, *Zero Trust Security*, https://doi.org/10.1007/978-1-4842-6702-8

The Software-Defined Perimeter Specification 1.0, Cloud Security Alliance, 2014 `https://cloudsecurityalliance.org/artifacts/sdp-specification-v1-0/`

This is the initial definition of Software-Defined Perimeter architecture.

Software-Defined Perimeter Architecture Guide, Cloud Security Alliance, 2019 `https://cloudsecurityalliance.org/artifacts/sdp-architecture-guide-v2/`

This document explores the SDP architecture in more detail, including deployment models.

Single-Packet Authorization (SPA): `https://www.cipherdyne.org/blog/2012/09/single-packet-authorization-the-fwknop-approach.html`

This document explains the concepts and provides an open source implementation of Single-Packet Authorization.

The FIDO Alliance: Moving the World Beyond Passwords using WebAuthn & CTAP: `https://fidoalliance.org/` and `https://fidoalliance.org/specifications/`

The CTAP Standards define the application layer protocol for communications between roaming and client applications including passwordless solutions.

XACML: eXtensible Access Control Markup Language `https://www.oasis-open.org/committees/tc_home.php?wg_abbrev=xacml`

NAC: The Extensible Authentication Protocol (EAP): RFP 3748 `https://tools.ietf.org/html/rfc3748` and 802.1x: `https://1.ieee802.org/security/802-1x/`

STIX: The Structured Threat Intelligence eXchange and TAXII: the Trusted Automated eXchange of Intelligence Information: `https://oasis-open.github.io/cti-documentation/`

Books

Zero Trust Networks by Evan Gilman and Doug Barth (O'Reilly, 2017)

This book provides an excellent analysis and foundation for Zero Trust from a networking perspective, and explores the PagerDuty case study in depth.

Cyber Warfare – Truth, Tactics, and Strategies by Dr. Chase Cunningham (Packt, 2020)

This highly readable book looks at information security from a warfighter's perspective, weaving in the drivers and concepts of Zero Trust.

Defensive Security Handbook: Best Practices for Securing Infrastructure by Lee Brotherston and Amanda Berlin (O'Reilly, 2017)

This book serves as a self-described "Security 101 Handbook," aiming at helping people create (or understand) a broad security program in their enterprise.

Research Documents and Publications

NIST Documents

NIST Special Publication 800.207 – Zero Trust Architecture, August 2020 `https://csrc.nist.gov/publications/detail/sp/800-207/final`

We highly recommend you read this document, as it's a strong complement to (and in many ways a foundation for) our work in this book.

This is NIST's associated Zero Trust proof of concept project: `https://www.nccoe.nist.gov/projects/building-blocks/zero-trust-architecture`

NIST Special Publication 800-162: Guide to Attribute Based Access Control (ABAC) Definition and Considerations, 2014 `https://csrc.nist.gov/publications/detail/sp/800-162/final`

Google's BeyondCorp Whitepapers

Available under `https://research.google/pubs/` (search for "BeyondCorp")

Overview: `https://security.googleblog.com/2019/06/how-google-adopted-beyondcorp.html`

BeyondCorp: A New Approach to Enterprise Security, ;login: December 2014, Vol. 39, No. 6.

BeyondCorp: Design to Deployment at Google, :login; Spring 2016 Vol. 41, No. 1

BeyondCorp: The Access Proxy, ;login: Winter 2016, Vol. 41, No. 4

Migrating to BeyondCorp: Maintaining Productivity While Improving Security, ;login: Summer 2017, Vol. 42, No. 2

BeyondCorp: The User Experience: ;login: Fall 2017, Vol. 42, No. 3

BeyondCorp: Building a Healthy Fleet, ;login: Fall 2018, Vol. 43, No. 3

Other Documents

IETF Impact of TLS 1.3 to Operational Network Security Practices: `https://datatracker.ietf.org/doc/draft-ietf-opsec-ns-impact/`

This very readable document does an excellent job explaining how the shift to TLS 1.3 impacts various network security use cases.

The Threatened Net: How the Web Became a Perilous Place. eBook from *The Washington Post* journalist Craig Timberg, 2015: `http://www.washingtonpost.com/sf/business/2015/05/30/net-of-insecurity-part-1/`

No More Chewy Centers: Introducing the Zero Trust Model Of Information Security, Forrester Research, Inc. September 2010 `https://www.forrester.com/report/No+More+Chewy+Centers+The+Zero+Trust+Model+Of+Information+Security/-/E-RES56682`

The Zero Trust eXtended Ecosystem: Data, Forrester Research, Inc., August 2020 `https://www.forrester.com/report/The+Zero+Trust+eXtended+Ecosystem+Data/-/E-RES161356`

For some counterpoints on encrypted DNS, examining the trade-offs, see the January 2021 publication "Adopting Encrypted DNS in Enterprise Environments" from the National Security Agency, `https://media.defense.gov/2021/Jan/14/2002564889/-1/-1/0/CSI_ADOPTING_ENCRYPTED_DNS_U_OO_102904_21.PDF` as well as `https://www.zdnet.com/article/dns-overhttps-causes-more-problems-than-it-solves-experts-say/`

`https://go.forrester.com/blogs/smackdown-enterprise-monitoring-vs-tls-1-3-and-dns-over-https/`

Service Meshes

Istio Service Mesh: `https://istio.io/`

Linkerd Service Mesh: `https://linkerd.io/`

Index

A

Access control levels, 83
Access control methods, 176
Access gateway, 176
Access management
    authentication
        certificate-based authentication, 81
        FIDO2, 82
        LDAP, 79
        mobile and biometrics, 82
        OAuth2, 80
        OIDC, 81
        RADIUS, 79
        SAML, 80
    authorization, 82–84
Access trigger, 236
Actions, 213–215
Agility/new business initiatives, 271
API gateways, 101
Application delivery controllers
    (ADCs), 101
Architecture
    conceptual
        PEPs (*see* Policy Enforcement
        Points (PEPs))
        policy components, 33, 34
    NIST zero trust model, 29, 30
Architecture review board, 269
Assertions, 80

Asymmetric service-to-service, 254
Attribute-based access control
    (ABAC), 34, 84
Attribute Permanence, 228
Audit and compliance, 271
Authentication trigger, 148, 235, 236
Authorization, 82–84
Automation, 15
Automation and orchestration, 12
Availability, 101

B

BeyondCorp, 53
BeyondCorp access proxy, 56
Bring Your Own Device (BYOD), 113, 246

C

Certificate-based authentication, 81
Change management board, 270
Cloud access control, 176, 178
Cloud access security brokers (CASB), 28,
    186, 188
Cloud migration
    categories
        adopt SaaS, 249
        Forklift migration, 249
        refactor application, 249
        rewrite application, 249

© Jason Garbis and Jerry W. Chapman 2021
J. Garbis and J. W. Chapman, *Zero Trust Security*, https://doi.org/10.1007/978-1-4842-6702-8

Printed in the United States
By Bookmasters